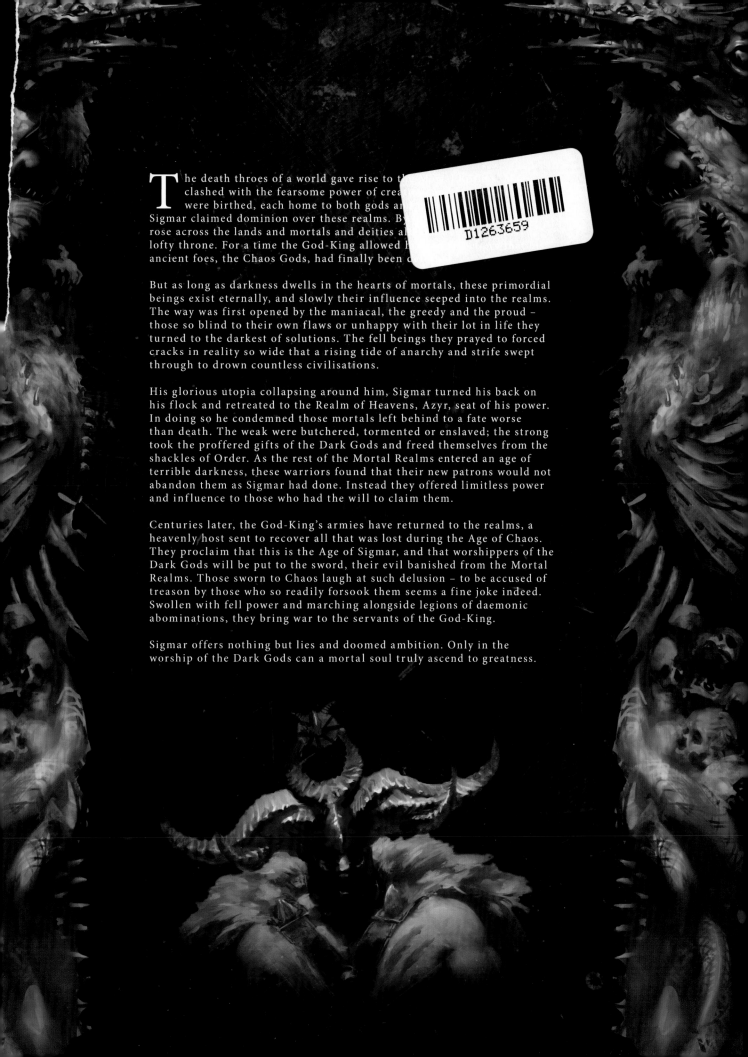

The death throes of a world gave rise to t[...] clashed with the fearsome power of crea[...] were birthed, each home to both gods a[...] Sigmar claimed dominion over these realms. By[...] rose across the lands and mortals and deities a[...] lofty throne. For a time the God-King allowed h[...] ancient foes, the Chaos Gods, had finally been c[...]

But as long as darkness dwells in the hearts of mortals, these primordial beings exist eternally, and slowly their influence seeped into the realms. The way was first opened by the maniacal, the greedy and the proud – those so blind to their own flaws or unhappy with their lot in life they turned to the darkest of solutions. The fell beings they prayed to forced cracks in reality so wide that a rising tide of anarchy and strife swept through to drown countless civilisations.

His glorious utopia collapsing around him, Sigmar turned his back on his flock and retreated to the Realm of Heavens, Azyr, seat of his power. In doing so he condemned those mortals left behind to a fate worse than death. The weak were butchered, tormented or enslaved; the strong took the proffered gifts of the Dark Gods and freed themselves from the shackles of Order. As the rest of the Mortal Realms entered an age of terrible darkness, these warriors found that their new patrons would not abandon them as Sigmar had done. Instead they offered limitless power and influence to those who had the will to claim them.

Centuries later, the God-King's armies have returned to the realms, a heavenly host sent to recover all that was lost during the Age of Chaos. They proclaim that this is the Age of Sigmar, and that worshippers of the Dark Gods will be put to the sword, their evil banished from the Mortal Realms. Those sworn to Chaos laugh at such delusion – to be accused of treason by those who so readily forsook them seems a fine joke indeed. Swollen with fell power and marching alongside legions of daemonic abominations, they bring war to the servants of the God-King.

Sigmar offers nothing but lies and doomed ambition. Only in the worship of the Dark Gods can a mortal soul truly ascend to greatness.

GLORY OR DEATH

The call of the Everchosen echoes out across the Mortal Realms, and the greatest champions of the Dark Gods stand ready to answer. Warbands from far and wide make the deadly pilgrimage to the Eightpoints, the domain of Archaon, Exalted Grand Marshal of the Apocalypse. There they must brave a gauntlet of rival gangs, ravenous beasts and a bleak and unforgiving wilderness if they are to reach the gates of the Varanspire and claim their rightful place at the Everchosen's side.

Welcome to the Bloodwind Spoil, a Chaos-twisted wasteland that stretches out before the Varanspire's fortified walls like an open wound. There is no law here beyond that of the drawn blade, and not an ounce of honour or mercy to be found. There is only a brutal struggle for existence, in which the mightiest flourish and ravening predators grow fat upon the corpses of the weak. The very land itself seeks to prey upon the lost souls who venture here; bubbling swamps of malformed flesh swallow unwary travellers, vampiric choke-vines drag them screaming into darkness, and floating polyps of crystal drain both soul and blood away in an agonising

moment. Amidst these deadly environments, bands of killers duel, fighting an endless, desperate battle to prove their superiority and power to mighty Archaon by butchering their rivals and raising their foul totems across the land. Only the most ferocious amongst them will triumph, and perhaps be honoured with a place in the Everchosen's iron legions, to fight in his ceaseless crusades against the Mortal Realms.

Warcry is a game of bloody skirmish combat, in which you control a warband of vicious killers as they reave their way across the Bloodwind Spoil. Time-worn ruins and blasted

Sheer, unrelenting hatred marks the conflict between the Iron Golems and the Untamed Beasts. These two wildly different cultures both worship the power of Chaos, but this shared belief will not prevent them tearing one another apart in a quest for power and influence.

wastes play host to furious lightning-swift engagements, blade-wielding fiends howl and leap from the shadows to fall upon their prey, armoured giants wade into battle swinging warhammers with bone-breaking force, and eerily silent assassins open throats and bellies with casual precision. The nature of these engagements can be as varied as the warbands who fight them. Perhaps your warriors seek to cut the head from a rival tribe by slaying their leader, or maybe they require new and deadlier weapons, which they plan to strip from the corpses of their foes. In these running battles, cunning, cruelty and bold action will win the day, though one can never trust the deadly and mercurial landscapes of the Eightpoints. The rules of Warcry allow you to simulate the hostile conditions of this island domain, from scalding storms of boiling blood to freezing blizzards and stampedes of vicious predators.

No matter which warband you choose to command, each of your warriors will earn experience and prestige for each foe they cut down, equipping themselves with looted weapons and wargear, and learning special skills that will make them all the more formidable in combat. As a warband's power grows, so to does their territory and their infamous reputation. In time, perhaps, word of their deeds might reach the ear of Archaon the Everchosen himself.

Within this book you will read of several of the deadliest and most feared warbands to haunt the wilds of the Eightpoints. Each of these cultures is devoted to Chaos and the Dark Gods, but each expresses their worship in a unique manner shaped by the dreadful lands from which they hail. Featured within are unique narrative campaigns that exemplify their culture and way of war. These campaigns detail your warband's rise from minor players to powerful warlords, and each offers a unique reward to grant to your fiercest champion or favoured cut-throat. It is not solely those devoted to the Ruinous Powers who find themselves battling across the Eightpoints; included within are campaigns for several other factions from each Grand Alliance, including hard-bitten Stormcast Eternals, belligerent Ironjawz and many more. Choose your allegiance, and dominate the Bloodwind Spoil in the name of the gods!

YOUR JOURNEY CONTINUES...

The jaw-dropping expanse of the Eight Realms is all but limitless, and so are the opportunities for exciting games of Warhammer Age of Sigmar.

The Warhammer Age of Sigmar Core Book is your in-depth guide to this fantastical setting. As well as a full and detailed history of the Mortal Realms, from the legendary tales of the Age of Myth to the triumphant crusades of the Stormcast Eternals, you will find a detailed overview of several of the most heavily contested realms. Included within are introductions to each of the Grand Alliances battling across these magical lands, from the tireless legions of Death to the rampaging, howling hordes of Destruction.

Exciting narrative sections, breathtaking world-building and detailed timelines – along with a showcase section presenting beautifully painted Citadel Miniatures in all their glory – will offer plenty of inspiration for your own hobby collection.

Of course, within the pages of the Core Book you will also find the full core rules for the Warhammer Age of Sigmar tabletop game, laying out each stage of a battle in intuitive and easy-to-follow stages. Whether you wish to take on your friends in a balanced competitive match, or prefer to simulate a mythic encounter between fantastical armies in the form of a narrative campaign, this weighty tome provides everything you need to lead your mighty army into battle!

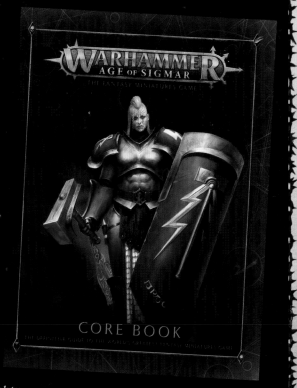

For most mortals, the only method of travel between the Mortal Realms is via the ancient, arcane passages known as Realmgates. These doorways can take almost any form – one might manifest as a gigantic, shimmering lake, while another could be a whirling constellation of dancing lights that appears as if at random to snatch up bewildered townsfolk and deposit them in a far distant land. Though some Realmgates are connected to multiple realms, the majority link only two points in space and time, offering passage along a single route. There is only one location that is tied to every one of the Eight Realms. It is known as the Eightpoints, and it is home to the stronghold of Archaon the Everchosen, Exalted Grand Marshal of the Apocalypse. This strange island was not always a haven for tyranny and evil. During the Age of Myth it was called the Allpoints, and it was a nexus of trade and travel populated

by aelves, duardin and men. Grand cities were raised beneath the giant arcways that led to each of the Eight Realms, and the Allpoints prospered greatly as the God-King Sigmar began to reunite his scattered people and forge a new civilisation. Then came the horrors of the Age of Chaos, as the forces of the Dark Gods swept into reality. Daemonic legions and hordes of savage warriors laid siege to the kingdom at the centre of all things. Though the Allpoints resisted fiercely, it could not stand in the face of such fury. One by one its defending armies were slaughtered, and Archaon built the Varanspire, his great fortress, at the centre of the inter-realm island. It would be a capital stronghold and staging ground for the mortal armies of Chaos, and a proving ground for his vaunted Varanguard, mightiest champions of ruin. In the years since, the power of the Eightpoints has only grown greater.

The call of the Everchosen echoes out across the Eight Realms, and the disparate nations of Chaos-worshipping mortals answer. Some hear tell of the Exalted Grand Marshal of the Apocalypse and the power invested in him by the Dark Gods, and know they must join in his unholy war. Others are drawn by omens and auguries read in the butchered organs of slain foes, or spelled out in swirling storm-clouds that vomit boiling blood. Once the call is heard it cannot be denied, and these scattered tribes and kingdoms send forth their mightiest champions to answer it. These warriors must make the long and hazardous journey to the Varanspire, seat of Archaon's power, and there petition the Everchosen for the right to take part in his apocalyptic crusades. To reach this dread fortress, a warband must first pass through the Realmgate that connects their own realm to the Eightpoints. This is no small feat, for

these locations are fiercely contested by rival armies, and any who attempt to traverse them run the risk of being caught up in a storm of bloodshed. Only by entering the Eightpoints unnoticed, weaving between waves of clashing warriors and bypassing the most formidable defences, can the warband have any hope of reaching their destination. The same is true once they are in the island realm itself. An enormous militarised highway extends from the Varanspire to each of the arcways. A warband travelling up one of these roads would be crushed beneath the ceaseless march of Archaon's legions. They instead must traverse the lethal wastes that lie between each of these highways, the vast and ever-changing lands that encircle the Varanspire. Archaon desires only the fiercest and most ruthless warriors for his cause, and there is no more fitting test of worth than this unforgiving gauntlet.

The Eightpoints is a vast and endlessly varied land, thoroughly suffused with the transmutational power of Chaos. Within its shifting borders can be found all manner of deadly environments – gheist-haunted ruins dating back to the Age of Myth, forests of sentient, blood-drinking trees, spires of cursed crystal that drain the mind and petrify the flesh, and a thousand-thousand other twisted landmarks. Scattered amidst this wild, untameable place are encampments and frontier settlements, ruled over by merciless warlords and home to some of the most wretched killers and deviants in the realms. The region known as the Bloodwind Spoil is a heavily populated stretch of the Eightpoints. Two of the Varanspire's fortified highways pass through its hostile lands, leading to the arcways that provide passage to the Realms of Metal and Beasts. These routes are thick with marching armies and overlooked

by winding outcrops of jagged rock, offering a pathway to the heartlands of the Eightpoints to cunning warbands willing to brave their many dangers. Beyond this spear of mountainous terrain lie open plains, constantly wracked by the boiling gales of gore that give the region its name. Rising out of this harsh land is Carngrad, one of the largest settlements outside of the Varanspire itself – an anarchic, disordered shanty town whose streets run with blood and whose shadowy alleys are filled with the most savage cut-throats and butchers in the realms. Those warbands who make the long pilgrimage to the Eightpoints establish makeshift war camps amidst the wilds of the Spoil, and from these outposts plot the death of their rivals and their ascension to the ranks of the Everchosen's armies. They will

The Bloodwind Spoil is home to all manner of unspeakable horrors and long-forgotten secrets. It is a stark and darkly imposing land, dominated by towering mountain ranges and great plains. What few scattered settlements stand amidst the sorcerous wilds are populated by merciless killers sworn to the Dark Gods. Dotted across this deadly expanse are relics of the past, ancient ruins from the Age of Myth long since fallen to the depredations of Chaos.

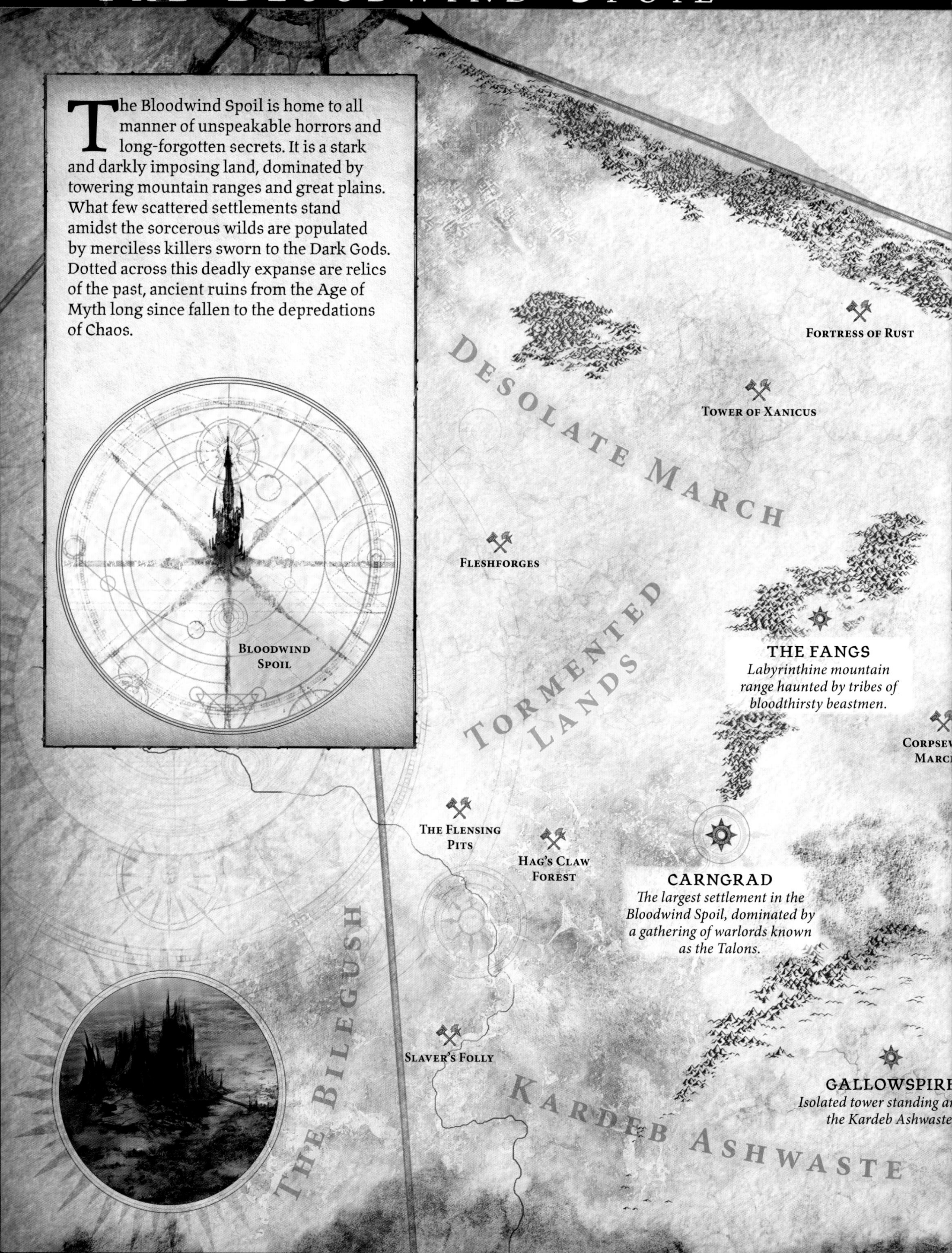

BLOODWIND SPOIL

DESOLATE MARCH

FORTRESS OF RUST

TOWER OF XANICUS

FLESHFORGES

TORMENTED LANDS

THE FANGS
Labyrinthine mountain range haunted by tribes of bloodthirsty beastmen.

CORPSEW MARC

THE FLENSING PITS

HAG'S CLAW FOREST

CARNGRAD
The largest settlement in the Bloodwind Spoil, dominated by a gathering of warlords known as the Talons.

SLAVER'S FOLLY

THE BILEGUSH

KARDEB ASHWASTE

GALLOWSPIRE
Isolated tower standing a the Kardeb Ashwaste

THE SCREAMING COIL
Ancient soul-engine corrupted by the worshippers of the Dark Prince.

FORLORN HOPE
The largest mountain peak in the Skullpikes, Forlorn Hope is haloed by deadly thunderstorms.

SKULLPIKE MOUNTAINS

VARANTHAX'S MAW
Enormous, volcanic forge-complex built into the skeleton of a drake.

BLOOD LAKE BASIN

LOST VELORUM
Buried ruins of a city of Order that was sacked during the Age of Chaos.

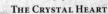
THE CRYSTAL HEART

BLOOD LAKE BASIN
An enormous expanse of water stained red by the blood of slain beasts.

UNGRY
RSH

SOULFLAYER DESERT

ROTMIRE

IRON
GOLEM

Hailing from the Ferrium Mountains in Chamon, the Iron Golems lord over a Dreadhold built atop an active volcano. It is said that their forebears enslaved a Sun Dragon within the mountain, and that they harness the raging magma-flows it spits forth to forge their weapons and armour. They believe themselves chosen by Archaon to provide arms for his endless hordes. The Iron Golems know that flesh is impermanent, whereas metal is eternal, able to be shaped and reshaped through the forging fires. It is these flames that they see as the true embodiment of Chaos, and upon defeating their enemies they pile the corpses and discarded armaments onto burning pyres. While the bodies smoulder, the armour and weapons are melted down before being wrought into stark obelisks.

'We create war.'

UNTAMED BEASTS

The Untamed Beasts are a nomadic tribe that hunt across the Jagged Savannah in Ghur. Predatory and shamanistic, they prey solely upon other carnivores, devouring the flesh of savage meat-eating creatures in order to gain their strength and cunning. They see Chaos as the Devourer of Existence and Archaon as the Eater of Worlds, and they long to join in his hunt. Each member of the Untamed Beasts carries pelts and fetishes of the predators they have consumed, and through profane oaths they bind the spirits of these creatures to their own being, allowing them preternatural bursts of animal ferocity. These primal warriors despise those who display any sign of civilisation, such as establishing permanent settlements or wearing forge-crafted armour. To them, such behaviour is merely deluded weakness, for nothing of mortal make can survive the wrath of the Devourer, and to pretend otherwise is a grand blasphemy. The skins of those they have slain are strung from trees along with crude banners, while the butchered and bloody carcasses are left to rot.

'Hunt the hunter.'

CORVUS CABAL

The Corvus Cabal are murderers and shadow-stalkers that dwell atop the mesas of Carrion Reach in Ulgu. They worship an aspect of Chaos they call the Great Gatherer, a patron of cut-throats and thieves typically depicted as an immense, black-feathered prey-bird hunched atop a nest of bleached bones, a pile of stolen treasure glittering beneath its talons. No Corvus warrior can end a hunt without a fitting trophy to offer the Gatherer – those that fail to do so are cast from the highest peaks of the Reach. The Corvus Cabal believe that Archaon is an avatar of the Gatherer, and that his endless wars of conquest will satiate their deity's bottomless avarice, and so they send their most lethal killers to earn the Everchosen's favour. The Corvus raise their shrines across the wastes of the Varanspire – stringing razor-thorned trees with the corpses of their victims, alongside offerings of trophies and looted wargear.

'*Pick clean the corpse.*'

CYPHER
LORDS

From the outside, the ziggurat-city of
Nochseed appears a place of culture and
reason, as enlightened as any of the other
great strongholds of Hysh. In fact, this
facade of civility hides a terrible truth. The
masked Cypher Lords of Nochseed have
sworn their souls to Chaos, worshipping
it as a formless entity of infinite aspects,
a pure, protean essence of trickery
and madness. The Cypher Lords seek
not simply to defeat their foes, but to
drive them to insanity with sorcerous
illusions and alchemical bombs that spew
hallucinatory poisons. The ultimate goal
of these mysterious cultists is to earn
a place as Archaon's spymasters and
assassins, the better to spread the insanity
of Chaos across the realms. Eyes wrought
of silver and gold can be found across the
Varanspire, seeing all and relaying their
secrets back to the Cypher Lords.

*'Let madness
reign.'*

THE UNMADE

Hailing from the island of Tzlid, close to the Shyish Nadir, the Unmade are a tribe of cannibal killers obsessed with pain and bodily mutilation. To these sadistic creatures, true worship of Chaos can be achieved only through the giving and receiving of agony. When a member of the tribe comes of age, their face is ritually flayed from their skull, cured and attached to their armour. With each fresh atrocity, the Unmade sacrifice yet more of their flesh, replacing limbs with barbed weapons and cruel impaling blades. In this way they better fashion themselves into instruments of torment, removing the last vestiges of their humanity and devoting themselves utterly to the Dark Gods. The tortured remains of their victims are left in gibbets and cages for all to see, for the Unmade delight in spreading terror almost as much as they do in inflicting pain.

'Agony is our gift.'

THE SPLINTERED FANG

Unlike many warrior cults, the Splintered Fang see no dishonour in the use of poison as a weapon. Indeed, it is perhaps their most vital asset. There is a ritualistic component to the brewing of their most lethal toxins, overseen by shamans of the Coiling Ones – daemonic entities worshipped by the tribe as embodiments of cunning and strength. These mystics are regarded with awe by the warriors of the Splintered Fang, for they can command serpents with a thought, setting them upon their enemies in a slithering mass. Their blood rituals channel the power of Chaos, bolstering the already formidable toxins of their serpent familiars with daemonic power. In battle, the Splintered Fang favour impaling blades and barbed, serrated weapons, the better to deliver their deadly gifts into the bloodstreams of their foes. They strike swiftly and score telling blows, then step back and circle their prey, allowing the poisons to do their terrible work. Victims die in agony, their flesh swelling and expanding, and their blood clotting like spoiled milk. Some are stricken by unnatural mutations, as fangs and jagged scales burst from their bones and their flesh peels away like a shed skin.

'One cut, one kill.'

'The flame within.'

SCIONS
OF THE
FLAME

The Scions of the Flame are zealots and firebrands all, warrior-priests who seek to engulf the realms in a cleansing inferno. They worship Chaos in the form of the Ever-Raging Flame – a malevolent embodiment of the Realm of Fire – believing that both flesh and spirit are hardened and made greater in the searing crucible of its fury. To wit, they embrace the passionate rage of Aqshian magic, to the point of consuming the flesh of elemental beasts in order to channel its power. Scions of the Flame hunt and kill magmavores and ash salamanders, eating the blazing hearts of these creatures in strange pre-battle rituals. Those found unworthy are incinerated from within, unable to absorb such fearsome heat. Others become living torches, their weapons radiating intense flame as they carve their foes apart in the throes of religious ecstasy. The Scions believe that the fires ignited by the Everchosen's realm-spanning wars will grow to swallow all living things, and so they seek to pledge themselves to Archaon's cause and earn a place in the fiery apocalypse to come.

SPIRE
TYRANTS

The Spire Tyrants are the champions of the Varanspire's infamous fighting pits, the most ferocious gladiators to have survived these gauntlets of bloody violence. Their lives are dominated by ceaseless killing, for only the most unrelenting souls have a chance of escaping the arenas. Those few that ascend to the heights of infamy are merciless, brutal killers. Having mastered the arena, they now seek to earngreater glory at the Everchosen's side.

Though they are by their very nature arrogant and egotistical, the Spire Tyrants form mutually beneficial partnerships in order to survive the harsh wastes of the Varanspire. These allegiances are bound by a pack mentality forged in the arena – the greatest warrior amongst their number takes charge, ruling through intimidation and brute force. These pit champions can never let down their guard, for those they command will seize upon the briefest moment of weakness to secure their own ascension. Despite the fragile hierarchy that binds them together, the Spire Tyrants fight with expert cohesion and cunning, relying upon an instinctive knowledge of warfare honed over decades of killing.

'We are His chosen.'

UNTOLD DANGERS

There are few deadlier places in all the realms than the wilds of the Eightpoints. Here, the fell power of Chaos suffuses reality, twisting the land and warping living flesh. One must not only avoid the crushing boots of the armoured legions that pour forth from the gates of the Varanspire in untold numbers, but must also be wary of the region's countless predatory beasts. Twisted monsters and flesh-warped abominations filled with a ravenous hunger stalk the land. The very ground beneath one's feet is treacherous – patches of ashen grass might hide a slavering pool of disembodied, fang-filled mouths, while creeping vines of crystal impale those who stray close, draining their blood dry in a matter of moments. Yet with sufficient fortune and cunning, the dangers of the Eightpoints can be turned against one's enemies. Many of the Chaos-twisted monsters that haunt this island can – with a sufficient offering of flesh or plunder – be swayed to a common cause, lured and loosed upon rival warriors. Yet one must never make the mistake of believing these beasts tamed, nor underestimate their cruel savagery and insatiable desire to feed.

'I thought I knew true savagery until I came to this cursed place.'

RAPTORYX

Raptoryx are a threat that anyone crossing the great plains of the Eightpoints would be foolish not to take into account. A consequence of the taint of Chaos infesting the native wildlife of the inter-realm island over the course of centuries, Raptoryx are an unnatural amalgamation of lizard and prey-bird. Though not capable of true flight, a Raptoryx can leap and glide with surprising grace, twisting in mid-air to avoid arrows and sling-bullets. These predators possess a vicious cunning and are impressively ferocious, willing to attack and capable of slaying creatures many times their size. Reptilian frills flushed with blood, they tear at the eyes and throat with their razor-sharp beaks, while raking the unfortunate victim with bladed hind limbs. Worse still, their high-pitched cries echo far across the wilderness – kill one Raptoryx and more will soon come racing on, drawn by their kin's death cries and the sweet scent of spilled blood. Those willing to trust to fate might attempt to harness the fierceness of these carnivorous beasts. They can never truly be tamed, such is their ferocity, but they will follow a warband, feasting upon the scraps of mutilated flesh left in its wake, and even driving the warriors' prey out into the open like hunting hounds.

CHAOS FURIES

The spiteful, vicious creatures known as Chaos Furies are minor daemons that hunt not out of predatory hunger, but from a desire to kill and maim. Though small and spindly, they possess a wiry strength and are more than capable of cutting down mortal warriors foolish enough to underestimate them. In packs they can prove especially deadly – those who have spent time in the wilds of the Eightpoints know well to seek cover when they spot a bat-winged flock on the horizon and hear the shrieking cries of the daemons as they converse in garbled Dark Tongue. Chaos Furies can be found in vast numbers across the Varanspire, perched upon the heights of shattered ruins like miniature gargoyles, peering out across the wasteland in search of prey. Though they are treacherous by nature, if bribed or cajoled into service these daemons can be extremely useful; their quick fingers, razor-sharp daggers and ability to fly make them reliable scouts and raiders, able to steal away precious items before a rival can lay claim to them.

The wilds of the Varanspire are suffused with Chaos energy. The mutative power of this unnatural magic gives birth to all manner of horrors, from the bladed saskarid to the venom-spewing blight serpent and dreaded corpsegorger.

'Devious little wretches, Furies. I've seen them slay warlords and slaves alike.'

RAIDERS OF THE SPOIL

Only the unthinkably brave or foolish would stray into the Eightpoints, for it is the centre of Archaon the Everchosen's power and utterly saturated with Chaos magic. Enemies of the Dark Gods find no haven here, only a brief and brutal struggle for survival. Most are hunted down and butchered, their tortured carcasses staked high as a warning to trespassers in the Everchosen's domain. Yet a rare few elite warriors risk a terrible end in the name of duty, slipping past the militarised roads and their thousands of cruel warriors. Hidden amidst the wilds of the Eightpoints are many secrets – rare arcane materials coveted by mages and sorcerers, ruined vaults dating from the Age of Myth, repositories of lost knowledge and countless other prizes worth risking life and limb to attain.

GLOOMSPITE GITZ

Like a cascade of fungal spores raining down across the realms, the Gloomspite hordes spread mildewed foulness wherever they roam. The gateways of the Eightpoints are perhaps the most fiercely guarded strongholds in all the realms, but still these devious greenskins and their allies have slipped into the heartlands of the region, spilling into the subterranean caverns that run beneath the island in search of fragments of loonstone. This meteoric substance is the stuff from which their deity, the Bad Moon, is formed, and the Gloomspite Gitz will do almost anything to lay their hands on it, including venturing deep into the forbidden lands of the Eightpoints. Though they are constantly hunted and preyed upon by both Chaos warbands and voracious predators, it seems all but impossible to entirely scour the Gloomspite infestation. No sooner is one of their cavern lurklairs purged than another emerges, and packs of whooping, bounding loons spill forth to raid and pillage.

NIGHTHAUNT

In the aftermath of the Shyish necroquake, tormented souls have arisen in all corners of the Mortal Realms, and not even the Eightpoints has been spared the curse of undeath. Shrieking gheists and blade-limbed revenants have emerged across the wilds of the Varanspire, preying upon Chaos-worshipping tribes and pilgrims. At first, these incursions seemed little more than the after-tremors of a great earthquake, ripples of random, vicious violence with no greater purpose than to spread fear and devastation as far as possible. However, several of Archaon's seers have noticed a sinister pattern to the assaults of the Nighthaunt. They strike always at areas of great magical might and concentrations of soul energy – corrupted shrines, subterranean ruins dating from the Age of Myth, and other places of power. Nagash – ever a cold and calculating being – is clearly directing his spectral servants in the completion of some great task, though none but the dead are privy to his aims.

STORMCAST ETERNALS

A Stormcast Eternal venturing into the Eightpoints risks an agonising death, for no beings are despised by the servants of Chaos so much as the God-King's champions. The mere sight of a gleaming, sigmarite-armoured warrior abroad in the wastes beyond the Varanspire would drive the populace into a murderous frenzy. Yet there are secrets buried deep beneath the surface of this Chaos-controlled region that the God-King is desperate to recover, ancient relics that have lain hidden for generations, but since the necroquake have once more begun to resonate with tremendous power. Thus, Sigmar turns to his Vanguard Auxiliary Chambers, experts in infiltration and guerrilla warfare. Guided by their astral compasses and skilled in the arts of evasion and lightning strikes, these warriors elude hunting packs and ravening warbands as they slip into the hidden places of the Eightpoints in search of the God-King's secrets. Each warrior in their number knows well enough that this quest might demand a painful, perhaps final sacrifice, but still these heroes do not shy away from their holy mission.

SEEKERS OF POWER

The murderous warbands that stalk the wilds of the Eightpoints hail from across the Mortal Realms. They are as visually distinct from one another as they are culturally unique, each clad in their own characteristic battle-dress and wielding a variety of brutal weaponry. All share an aspiration to rise to the heights of glory, and will slaughter without mercy any who stand in their way.

'From far and wide they come, malice in their hearts and murder in their eyes.'

IRON GOLEM

Ogor Breacher *Signifer* *Dominar* *Armator*

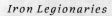

Iron Legionaries *Drillmaster*

Not even the spectral Nighthaunts can stand before the brutish might of an Ogor Breacher.

UNTAMED BEASTS

Heart-eater

Preytaker

Plains-runner

Preytaker

First Fang

Plains-runner

Rocktusk Prowler

Beastspeaker

The Untamed Beasts prize Rocktusk Prowlers, whose fearsome jaws can crush the finest armour.

CYPHER LORDS

Thrallmaster   *Mirrorblade*   *Luminate*   *Mirrorblade*

Mirrorblade   *Mindbound*

Wherever they roam, the Cypher Lords leave madness and devastation in their wake.

CORVUS CABAL

Shrike Talon

Cabalist

Shadow Piercer

Cabalist

Cabalist with Familiar

Spire Stalker

Cabalist

Spire Stalker

Striking from above with terrible swiftness, a Shrike Talon seeks a bloody trophy for the Gatherer.

SPLINTERED FANG

Trueblood

Clearbloods

Serpent Caller

Clearblood

Pureblood

Venombloods

The Splintered Fang care nothing for honour, only that the enemy is routed utterly.

THE UNMADE

Blissful One

Ascended Ones

Awakened Ones

Joyous One

The blade-limbed horror known as a Blissful One leaps and twirls madly through the fray.

PLAYING WARCRY

To step foot in the Eightpoints is to enter a world of glorious battle and thrilling danger. This section of the book will act as your guide, providing rules that allow you to adventure across these dark lands.

Over the following pages you'll find all the rules needed to play games of Warcry. The core rules are quick to learn and will allow you to get stuck into the action right away. After you've mastered the basics, you'll find a whole host of different game modes in the latter sections of this book.

One of Warcry's great strengths is that it offers flexibility and depth in how you approach the game, allowing you to tailor it to best suit your tastes. For example, you may wish to take part in large multiplayer battles, delve into a campaign to see your warriors grow in strength and renown, or challenge an opponent to an evenly matched, competitive battle. The rules in this book are adaptable enough to cater to all types of player, and are arranged in easy-to-navigate sections.

CORE RULES

The core rules section contains everything you need to know to start playing games of Warcry. It details the rules for setting up a battle between two rival warbands, including how to set up the fighters and battlefield, and the victory conditions that are in play. It also explains how fighters can move, jump, attack and unleash powerful abilities to achieve victory.

THREE WAYS TO PLAY

Once you've read the core rules, and played a few games of Warcry, the later sections of this book offer three different ways to approach your games: open play, narrative play and matched play.

Open play is intended for casual gaming, and makes it quick and easy to set up a game of Warcry. The open play section (pg 52-61) contains rules for playing multiplayer team battles and frantic free-for-alls.

Narrative play places the stories of the different factions in Warcry at its centre. The narrative play section (pg 62-71) details rules for running campaigns. In a campaign, your warband grows in power and fame from battle to battle as they strive to achieve their ultimate goal.

Matched play centres around tightly balanced and competitive games of Warcry. The matched play section (pg 72-79) includes 12 Pitched Battle battleplans, as well as advice for running a Warcry tournament.

CAMPAIGN SECTION

The final section of this book (pg 80-151) goes hand in hand with the narrative play section. It contains campaign quests tailored to the different factions of Warcry, including their bespoke artefacts and command traits. Here you will also find tables to generate the background of your warband, as well as names for your fighters.

CORE RULES

The following rules explain how to play a game of Warcry, taking you through every step of fighting a brutal battle within the blood-soaked lands of the Eightpoints.

Warcry is a miniatures skirmish game played between two or more players. Each game of Warcry is referred to as a **battle**, and in a battle each player controls a group of Citadel Miniatures that are pitched against their opponent's. Each Citadel Miniature is referred to as a **fighter**, and collectively all the Citadel Miniatures one player controls are referred to as a **warband**. Most Citadel Miniatures are mounted upon a base. A miniature's base is treated as part of the fighter. A battle takes place on a flat surface referred to as the **battlefield**, which may be populated with one or more **terrain features**. Each of these terms is explained in full across the following pages.

In each Warcry battle, the goal will be different. Sometimes you will need to take down your opponent's fighters; other times you might need to hold a key location on the battlefield or secure a valuable artefact.

TOOLS OF WAR

In order to fight a battle you will require a ruler or tape measure (to measure distances) and some dice. Warcry uses regular six-sided dice (sometimes abbreviated to D6). Some rules refer to 2D6, 3D6 and so on – in such cases, roll that many dice and add the results together. If a rule requires you to roll a D3, roll a regular six-sided dice and halve the total, rounding up. If a rule requires a dice roll of, for example, 3 or more, this is often abbreviated to 3+.

Tokens

Warcry comes with a set of tokens and markers to help keep track of the battle. Tokens can be placed on the battlefield or on a fighter card. Some of them, like the damage tokens, have a pointed edge to indicate which fighter they refer to if placed next to multiple fighters. Most tokens do not interact with the battle in any way beyond helping the players to remember information, and if they interfere with the movement of a fighter they should be placed out of the way (the exceptions to this are objective markers and treasure tokens – see page 37).

The 10 special tokens included do not relate to any specific rule, but the number on each can be used to help the players to remember any rule that may come into play (such as a lasting bonus to a friendly fighter). Lastly, the initiative token can be used to remind players whose turn it is.

1. Activation token
2. Wait token
3. Objective marker
4. Damage token
5. Treasure tokens
6. Special tokens
7. Initiative token

33

FIGHTER AND ABILITY CARDS

Each fighter in a warband has a corresponding **fighter card** which details that fighter's characteristics (their **Move**, **Toughness** and **Wounds**), the weapons they are armed with, and the **runemarks** that fighter has. Each warband also has an **ability card** that details unique attacks and manoeuvres they can use during the battle.

On the back of each ability card is a list of the different types of fighters that can be included in that warband. Sometimes there will be multiple different Citadel Miniatures that are the same type of fighter (for example, the Plains-runners for the Untamed Beasts). In such cases, there will be 1 fighter card that is shared by each of these fighters.

Lastly, each set of fighter cards comes with **divider cards**. These can be placed under a fighter card shared by multiple fighters to keep track of any tokens that apply to individual fighters.

Ability Cards
1. Faction runemark
2. Faction name
3. Runemarks required to use ability
4. Ability
5. Fighter types (reverse of card)

Fighter Cards
1. Image of a fighter
2. Faction runemark
3. Move characteristic
4. Toughness characteristic
5. Wounds characteristic
6. Points value
7. Fighter's first weapon
8. Range characteristics
9. Attacks characteristics
10. Strength characteristics
11. Damage characteristics
12. Fighter's second weapon
13. Runemarks
14. Divider card

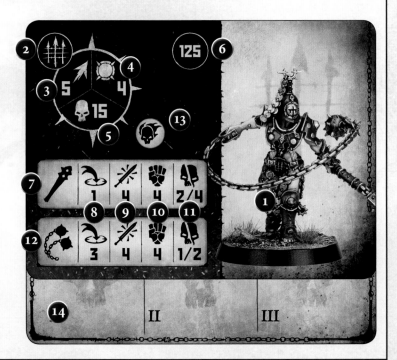

GENERAL RULES

RE-ROLLS

Some rules allow you to re-roll a dice roll (for example when making a **hit roll**), which means you get to roll some or all of the dice again. The rule that allows the re-roll will specify exactly how many of the dice can be re-rolled. A dice roll can never be re-rolled more than once.

ROLL-OFFS

Sometimes a rule may require the players to make a roll-off. When this is the case, each of the players rolls a dice, and whoever rolls highest wins the roll-off. If there is a tie for the highest roll, make the roll-off again.

MEASURING DISTANCES

Distances in Warcry are measured in inches ("), between the closest points of the bases of the fighters you're measuring to and from. If a rule requires something to be within a certain range of something else, they are considered to be **within** if the distance between them is equal to or less than the specified distance. If a rule requires a fighter to be **wholly within**, every part of that fighter's base must be within range.

Usually, measuring distances will take into account both the vertical and horizontal distance between two models, but in some cases a rule might specify to measure the horizontal distance, or the vertical distance, only. You can measure distances whenever you wish.

VISIBILITY

Many rules in Warcry require one fighter (usually the target of an attack action or ability) to be **visible** to another fighter (usually the fighter making the attack action or using the ability).

One fighter is said to be visible to another fighter if a direct line could be drawn between the two fighters without passing through a terrain feature or another fighter.

If you are unsure whether a fighter is visible, stoop down behind the fighter making the attack action or using the ability to see if any part of the target fighter is visible from any part of the fighter making the attack action.

When checking to see if two fighters are visible to each other, do not include either of the bases each fighter is mounted upon.

FRIENDLY AND ENEMY FIGHTERS

A player considers all fighters in their warband to be friendly fighters and all fighters in other warbands to be enemy fighters. Likewise, a fighter considers all other fighters in their warband to be friendly fighters, and all fighters in other warbands to be enemy fighters.

If a rule for an action or ability performed by a fighter refers to 'other friendly fighters', it means fighters from that fighter's warband, excluding itself.

RUNEMARKS

In Warcry, many rules interact with the runemarks on each fighter card. For example a fighter's faction is determined by their **faction runemark**. Certain abilities require a fighter to have certain runemarks for that fighter to be able to use them, and other runemarks give fighters access to special rules, such as being able to fly.

You can find a list of the different runemarks on pages 50-51.

LEADERS

In every warband there will be one fighter with the **Leader** runemark (☀). If a rule refers to the leader of a warband, it is referring to the fighter with that runemark.

SEQUENCING

In most cases rules will be resolved one at a time. However, from time to time, rules may appear to come into play at the same time and it may be unclear as to which is resolved first. If this occurs in the combat phase, the player whose turn it is to activate a fighter chooses the order in which the rules are resolved; in any other phase, the player with the initiative chooses. In any other case, the players roll off and the winner chooses.

These two fighters are 5" apart. The First Fang is 3" vertically above the battlefield floor, and the horizontal distance between the two fighters is 4".

4"

3"

5"

SETTING UP A BATTLE

Blades glint in the sun and war cries split the air as two rival bands of killers face off. Only one can emerge victorious – for the defeated there is only ignominy and death.

This section explains how to set up a battle between two warbands. There are rules later on in this book that detail battles with more than two players (pg 52-61), and rules that detail a special kind of battle known as a **convergence** (pg 65). For most games of Warcry, however, you will use the rules in this section.

THE BATTLEFIELD

Warcry battles are fought upon a battlefield. This can be any flat surface upon which the fighters can stand. Warcry battlefield mats are 22" in width and 30" in length, and the battleplan cards are designed to work especially well with these battlefield mats, but any flat surface roughly 22" by 30" will be suitable.

If a rule refers to the **battlefield floor**, this includes only the flat surface the battle is played upon and not any of the terrain features. For example, if a rule requires an objective to be placed on the battlefield floor, it cannot be placed on a terrain feature. If a rule refers to the **battlefield**, this includes both the battlefield floor and terrain features.

THE WARBANDS

Each player in a Warcry battle controls a warband of fighters. When first setting up the battle, the players each muster a warband by adhering to the following rules:

1. The warband must include at least 3 and no more than 15 fighters.

2. The combined points value of all the fighters in a player's warband cannot exceed 1000.

3. All fighters in a player's warband must share the same faction runemark.

4. There can be only 1 fighter in the warband with the **Leader** runemark (☀).

Once both players have mustered their warbands, they reveal their warbands to each other.

THE PRIORITY ROLL

The players now roll off. This is an important roll-off as it will determine who takes priority when setting up the battle. This roll-off is referred to as the **priority roll**.

BATTLE GROUPS

Starting with the player who lost the priority roll, each player splits their warband into three groups: the **Dagger**, the **Shield** and the **Hammer**. Each of these groups is referred to as a **battle group**. Each battle group must have at least 1 fighter and cannot have more than half the total fighters in the warband. In addition, at least a third of the fighters in the warband (rounding up) must be in the Shield.

THE BATTLEPLAN

Warcry battles use randomly drawn **battleplan cards** to decide how the terrain and warbands are set up, what the victory condition of the battle is, and if there are any twists in play. Once both warbands have been separated into their battle groups, the players organise the battleplan cards into the following four decks and give each deck a shuffle:

- ✸ **TERRAIN DECK**
- ◉ **DEPLOYMENT DECK**
- ⚔ **VICTORY DECK**
- ✕ **TWIST DECK**

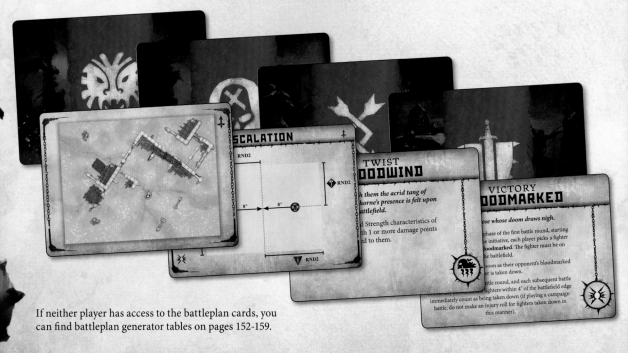

If neither player has access to the battleplan cards, you can find battleplan generator tables on pages 152-159.

The player that won the priority roll deals out a card from each deck, placing it face up so that all players can see the card. The upwards arrow on the terrain cards corresponds to the upwards arrow on the deployment cards, so players know which way they are orientated.

Once all battleplan cards have been drawn, the rest can be packed away as they will have no further effect upon the battle. The players next resolve the cards in the following order:

1. TERRAIN CARD
Every terrain card has a unique layout of terrain features. Set up the terrain features shown on the terrain card in the locations shown for them.

> The terrain cards in Warcry allow players to set up a range of battlefields using the terrain features in the core set. However, Warcry is the perfect game for players to really embrace the narrative and create thematic battlefields with unique terrain features. If all players agree, you can substitute one or more of the terrain features with different terrain features from your collection.

2. DEPLOYMENT CARD
On every deployment card there are two sets of these three symbols: ⚔ (Dagger), ⛨ (Shield) and ⚒ (Hammer). One set is in red; the other is in blue. These are referred to as **deployment points**, and each corresponds to one of the battle groups in a player's warband.

The player that won the priority roll chooses which player uses the red deployment points and which player uses the blue deployment points for the battle. The locations of each player's deployment points are shown on the deployment card.

The player that won the priority roll then sets up their Dagger, followed by their opponent. Then the players set up their Shields in the same order, and finally their Hammers in the same order. Each time a battle group is set up, all fighters from that battle group must be set up wholly within 3" horizontally, but any distance vertically, of the corresponding deployment point on the battlefield floor or a platform (pg 46).

> ### Reserve Battle Groups
> If a deployment point for a battle group is labelled 'RND2' or 'RND3', this indicates that the battle group is currently in reserve and will arrive mid-battle. Do not set up reserve battle groups on the battlefield before the battle begins; instead, place them to one side.

3. VICTORY CARD
The card drawn from the victory deck determines how the winner of the battle is chosen, and how long the battle will last. If the victory card instructs the players to determine who is the attacker and who is the defender, to place any objective markers or treasure tokens, or to do anything else before the battle begins, this is done in this step.

TIED GAMES
When the battle ends, if neither player has achieved the victory conditions on the victory card, the battle continues for another battle round before ending. Check the victory conditions once more to see if one of the players is declared the winner. If neither player has achieved the victory conditions, keep playing further battle rounds until all the fighters left on the battlefield are from one player's warband – that player is declared the winner.

4. TWIST CARD
The card drawn from the twist deck has a special rule that applies to that battle.

THE BATTLE BEGINS
With the battlefield and warbands set up, and the battleplan decided, the players are now ready to begin the battle.

Objectives and Treasure
Sometimes the victory deck will require the players to place objectives or treasure on the battlefield. To do so, place an objective marker or treasure token at the indicated location.

When measuring distances to objectives and treasure, always measure to and from the centre of the marker or token.

Controlling Objectives
A player gains control of an objective if, at the end of a battle round, they have more friendly fighters within 3" of it than there are enemy fighters within 3" of it. Once a player gains control of an objective, it remains under their control until another player gains control of it.

Carrying Treasure
If, at any point when making a move action, a fighter moves within 1" of a treasure token, the player can choose for that fighter to pick up that treasure. Remove the token from the battlefield. That fighter is now said to be carrying that treasure. A fighter cannot pick up treasure if they are already carrying treasure.

A fighter carrying treasure can use an action to drop the treasure (see page 39 for rules on actions). If a fighter carrying treasure is taken down (pg 44), they automatically drop the treasure before the fighter's model is removed from play. In both cases, the player controlling that fighter picks a point on a platform or the battlefield floor that is within 1" horizontally of the fighter and either vertically level or any distance vertically lower, and places the treasure token there.

THE BATTLE ROUND

Blood flows in gushing rivers as the combatants meet in battle, hacking and tearing at one another with single-minded ferocity.

A Warcry battle is fought in a series of rounds referred to as **battle rounds**, each of which is split into three phases: the **hero phase**, the **reserve phase** and the **combat phase**. Once all phases have finished, a new battle round begins. The victory card will dictate after which battle round the battle ends.

BATTLE ROUND SEQUENCE

1. HERO PHASE
Players determine who has the initiative during that battle round, and then decide how to use their wild dice.

2. RESERVE PHASE
In battle rounds after the first, reserve fighters may arrive on the battlefield.

3. COMBAT PHASE
Players take it in turns to activate the fighters in their warband.

HERO PHASE

At the start of the hero phase, each player rolls 6 dice. These dice are referred to as **initiative dice**. After rolling the initiative dice, each player counts any **singles**. A single is a dice that does not have a matching score on any other dice in that player's roll. The player with the most singles has the initiative. In the case of a tie, the players roll off and the winner has the initiative.

The remaining dice are referred to as **ability dice**, and can be used to perform abilities in the combat phase (see opposite). If 2 of your ability dice have the same score, it is referred to as a [double]. If 3 of your ability dice have the same score, it is referred to as a [triple]. Finally, if 4 or more of your ability dice have the same score, it is referred to as a [quad].

At the start of each battle round, any remaining singles and ability dice from the previous battle round are discarded.

EXAMPLE HERO PHASE

It is the start of the second battle round. Both players begin the hero phase by rolling their 6 initiative dice. Player A rolls as follows:

Player A has two singles, a [double] with a value of 3, and a [double] with a value of 5.

Player B rolls as follows:

Player B has one single, a [double] with a value of 4, and a [triple] with a value of 6.

Player A has the initiative, and so now chooses how to use their wild dice. They currently have one wild dice, and choose to spend it to turn their [double] 5 into a [triple] 5. Player A places the wild dice next to their two 5's, with the matching value face-up (shown by the red dice).

Now it's Player B's turn. In the last battle round, they chose not to spend their wild dice, and so now have two wild dice. They spend their first wild dice to turn their [triple] 6 into a [quad] 6 – the best score possible! They spend their second wild dice to add another single.

Player A and Player B now have an equal number of singles, so there is a chance that Player B will seize the initiative. The players roll off and Player B's gambit pays off – they win the initiative and choose to take the first turn in the combat phase.

WILD DICE

After the initiative has been determined, each player receives 1 **wild dice**. A wild dice is an extra dice that can be used during the hero phase to add to either a player's singles or ability dice.

The player with the initiative first declares how they will use any of their wild dice, followed by the player who does not have the initiative. Wild dice can be used in the following ways:

- A wild dice can be used to add 1 to the number of singles the player has. In this case, it does not matter what the value of the wild dice is. Any number of wild dice can be used in this way.

- A wild dice can be used to turn 1 of your singles into a [double], to improve a [double] to a [triple], or to improve a [triple] to a [quad]. In this case, the value of the wild dice is set to match the value of the single or ability dice it is paired with. You cannot add multiple wild dice to the same single or same ability dice (e.g. to turn a [double] into a [quad]).

Each wild dice can only be used once per battle. Wild dice that are not used in a battle round can be used in a subsequent battle round instead.

Seizing the Initiative

Once both players have declared any wild dice they will use this battle round, count the number of singles each player has once more. If the player without the initiative now has more singles than the player with the initiative, they now have the initiative instead. If the number of singles each player has is now tied (and was not previously), the players roll off and the winner has the initiative.

RESERVE PHASE

The reserve phase comes into play in battle rounds after the first. During the reserve phase, reserve battle groups (pg 37) may be set up on the battlefield. The deployment card will indicate in which battle round any reserve battle groups come into play: 'RND2' indicates that battle group will arrive in the reserve phase of the second battle round, and 'RND3' indicates it will arrive in the reserve phase of the third battle round.

Starting with the player with the initiative, players set up the fighters from any battle groups coming into play in that battle round wholly within 3" horizontally, but any distance vertically, of their deployment point.

Some deployment cards have reserve deployment points that are situated off the battlefield map. In these cases, there will be a **deployment line** next to that deployment point. Deployment lines are either the length of half a battlefield edge or the length of a whole battlefield edge. If the deployment point is next to a deployment line, the battle group coming into play in that battle round must be set up wholly within 3" horizontally of that deployment line.

If it is ever impossible to set up all the fighters from a reserve battle group (for example, due to the positions of other fighters), each fighter from that battle group must be set up one at a time, as close as possible to either their deployment point (if it is on the battlefield map) or their deployment line.

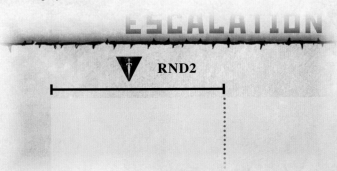

This deployment line is the length of half the battlefield edge. It indicates that the Dagger battle group for this player will arrive on the battlefield within 3" of this deployment line in the second battle round.

COMBAT PHASE

In the combat phase, the players take it in turns to activate their fighters. The player with the initiative picks which player takes the first turn.

When it is a player's turn, they can activate one fighter in their warband. This is referred to as that fighter's **activation**. The player must pick 1 fighter to activate if they can, but cannot pick a fighter that has already activated this phase. If the player cannot pick a fighter (for example, if all their fighters have already activated this phase), they must pass instead. Then their opponent can activate 1 fighter or pass. Keep on taking turns to activate fighters until both players pass one after the other.

ACTIONS

When a player activates a fighter, that fighter makes 2 actions chosen from the list below. Carry out the first action before deciding on the second. A fighter can make the same action twice in a row if you wish (for example, a move action followed by a move action).

MOVE

ATTACK

DISENGAGE

WAIT

Each of these actions is explained in detail over the following pages.

SYUGAH RAWTHROAT

Syugah Rawthroat is renowned as one of the finest trackers of the Untamed Beasts. The hunter speaks in a low, guttural growl, the result of taking an arrow in the throat during a battle against a rival tribe. It is said that Syugah's taste for hookbeak flesh has granted him the terrifying speed and endurance of those predatory avians. When the hunt is on and the quarry in sight, he is inevitably found at the head of the chase, roaring with savage delight as he readies his sawtooth axe for a killing strike.

'The prey is close. I can smell their fear upon the wind.'

ABILITIES

A fighter can also use 1 ability during its activation if the player activating that fighter has sufficient ability dice. The ability can be used either before the first action or after the first or second actions made by that fighter.

Each warband has set of unique abilities on its ability card. There are also 5 universal abilities that fighters from any warband can use (see opposite). Each ability will stipulate if it requires a [double], a [triple] or a [quad].

Once a fighter has used an ability, discard the ability dice used for that ability. You can use a [triple] for an ability that requires a [double], or a [quad] for an ability that requires a [triple] or [double], but if you do so all those ability dice are discarded.

The rule for an ability may sometimes refer to the **value** of that ability. This refers to the score shown on the ability dice used for that ability. For example, if a player has a [double] consisting of 2 ability dice with the score of '5' shown on each ability dice, the value of that ability is 5.

BONUS ACTIONS
If an ability lets a fighter make any **bonus actions**, these are actions in addition to the 2 actions they can carry out during an activation.

RUNEMARKS
Some abilities can only be used by fighters with certain runemarks. Any runemarks required will be shown to the left of the ability on the ability card. For example, the Inspiring Presence ability (see below) can only be used by fighters with the **Leader** runemark (✸). The runemarks a fighter has can be found on their fighter card (pg 34).

DESPERATE LAST STAND
When all but 1 fighter in a player's warband have been taken down (pg 44), the remaining fighter can use any number of abilities if the player activating that fighter has sufficient ability dice. This means that the fighter can use multiple abilities at each point when it would normally only be able to use 1 (for example, it can use multiple abilities before its first action, and multiple abilities again after its first or second action).

UNIVERSAL ABILITIES	
	[Double] Rush: Add 1 to the Move characteristic of this fighter until the end of their activation.
	[Double] Onslaught: Add 1 to the Attacks characteristic of attack actions made by this fighter until the end of their activation.
	[Triple] Respite: A fighter cannot use this ability if they are within 1" of any enemy fighters. Remove a number of damage points allocated to this fighter equal to the value of this ability.
✸	**[Triple] Inspiring Presence:** Pick a friendly fighter that has not activated yet this battle round and that is within 6" of this fighter. You can activate that fighter immediately after the activation of this fighter ends.
	[Quad] Rampage: This fighter makes a bonus move action. Then, they can make a bonus attack action.

MOVE ACTIONS

Agile warriors leap across jutting beams and ruined walls, plunging from on high to sink their daggers into throats and backs. Heavily armoured monsters lumber forwards relentlessly, swinging fearsome instruments of death.

A fighter can change their position on the battlefield by making a move action. Every fighter has a Move characteristic, which is shown on their fighter card. This determines the number of inches a fighter can move in total in a single move action.

When a fighter makes a move action, there are 4 types of move they can make: **normal moves**, **jumping**, **climbing** and **flying**. A fighter can use these types of move in any combination as part of a single move action, so long as the total distance in inches moved does not exceed the fighter's Move characteristic.

The distance a fighter moves is measured using the part of the fighter's base that moves furthest from its starting position (including pivoting).

There are general limitations that must be adhered to when making a move action:

- A fighter cannot move through other fighters.

- A fighter cannot move through any part of a terrain feature.

- No part of a fighter can ever move over the battlefield edge.

- If a fighter is within 1" of any enemy fighters when they start a move action, they must finish that move action at least as close (or closer) to the enemy fighter that was nearest to them at the start of the move action. If there were 2 or more enemy fighters equally near to the fighter making the move action, the fighter must finish that move action at least as close (or closer) to all of them.

NORMAL MOVES
A fighter can make a normal move if the centre of their base is on the battlefield floor or on a platform (pg 46). When a fighter moves normally, the centre of their base

must remain on the battlefield floor or a platform at all times, unless they are moving over low terrain (see below).

JUMPING
A fighter that is on the battlefield can jump. If they do so, the fighter can move in a straight line horizontally through the air, and any distance vertically downwards through the air.

Count the horizontal distance moved towards the number of inches that fighter can move in total in that move action as normal, but

do not count the distance moved vertically downwards. However, each time the fighter moves 3" or more vertically downwards when jumping, they suffer impact damage (see opposite).

If a fighter finishes their move action in the air, immediately move them vertically downwards until a part of their base is either on or touching part of a terrain feature or the battlefield floor. If the fighter moves 3" or more vertically downwards in this manner, they suffer impact damage (see opposite).

Moving Over Low Terrain
When fighters make a normal move, they can move without penalty over a part of a terrain feature that extends vertically 1" high or less off the battlefield floor or the platform upon which it is placed. This means that any vertical distance moved while moving over such a part of a terrain feature does not count against the total number of inches fighters can move in that move action.

The Plains-runner has a Move characteristic of 5, so they can move up to 5" when making a move action. The fallen pillar is less than 1" high, so it is treated as low terrain.

MACER KOLTRECH

Macer Koltrech is a pale giant of a man. Like many of his comrades, his skin has been bleached grey by the constant chemical ash-fall of the Ferrium Mountains, where the Golems' stronghold lies. As a signifer, he has the honour of bearing the metal sigil of the Iron Golems into battle. The rhythmic pounding of Koltrech's warhammer upon the graven symbol announces the arrival of these plate-clad brutes on the battlefield, and strikes a hopeless terror into the foe.

'War is upon you, vermin! Death is here!'

Falling

There are a few situations that can cause a fighter to fall. Firstly, if a fighter finishes a move action with the centre of their base not on either the battlefield floor or on a platform and that fighter is not climbing (see right), that fighter is said to have fallen. Secondly, if a fighter is climbing when that fighter's activation finishes, that fighter is said to have fallen. Lastly, fighters can fall as a result of being attacked near the edge of a platform (pg 46).

If a fighter is said to have fallen, the opposing player picks a point on a platform or the battlefield floor that is within 2" horizontally of the fighter that has fallen and is vertically lower. The fallen fighter is then placed with the centre of their base on that point. The player cannot pick a point that would cause the fallen fighter to be placed on or through another fighter or through a terrain feature. If it is impossible not to do so, and the centre of the base of the fallen fighter is on a platform, they remain where they are. If the centre of the base of the fallen fighter is not on a platform, they are immediately taken down (pg 44) instead.

If the fallen fighter is now 3" or more vertically lower than their location before they fell, that fighter suffers impact damage.

Impact Damage

If a fighter suffers impact damage, roll a dice. On a 4-5, allocate 1 damage point to that fighter (pg 44). On a 6, allocate 3 damage points to that fighter.

CLIMBING

If a fighter is touching a part of a terrain feature defined as an **obstacle** (pg 46), that fighter can begin to climb. If they do so, that fighter can move vertically up or down that terrain feature (and also horizontally once at the top). Once a fighter begins to climb, they are said to be climbing until the centre of their base is on the battlefield floor or a platform.

Fighters with the **Mount** runemark (⚒) cannot climb.

FLYING

Fighters with the **Fly** runemark (⚘) can fly as part of a move action. If they do so, the fighter can move through the air vertically and horizontally. Count the horizontal distance moved towards the number of inches that fighter can move in total in that move action as normal, but do not count the distance moved vertically. Once a fighter begins to fly, they are said to be flying until the centre of their base is on the battlefield floor or a platform. A fighter cannot end a move action flying.

Disallowed Moves

If a fighter's move causes them to break one of the limitations of move actions, it is referred to as a 'disallowed move'. For example, if a fighter jumped and the vertical distance moved downwards caused them to pass through another fighter, this is a disallowed move.

Fighters cannot make disallowed moves. If one occurs during a move action, place the fighter making the move action back at their starting position and choose a new direction for them to move. Remember – as players are allowed to pre-measure any distances, you can plan your move action ahead to make sure it is not a disallowed move.

This fighter makes a dramatic jump over an enemy fighter with their first action, ready to strike with their second.

When making the jump, only the horizontal distance is measured. However, after the jump, as the fighter has moved down 3" vertically, they first suffer impact damage.

Although the edge of this fighter's base hangs over the edge of this platform, this is an allowed move because the centre of their base has remained above the platform at all times. This allows models with larger bases to still use walkways and small platforms.

As a fighter can move, jump, climb and even fly all in the same move action, it allows players to get creative with their fighter's movement.

For the fighter's first activation, they make a normal move across the platform. Upon reaching the edge, they jump across the gap. When the fighter makes contact with the wall, they decide to start climbing. For the fighter's second action, they climb up the wall before moving onto the upper platform to finish their activation.

ATTACK ACTIONS

Some warriors fight with unrestrained ferocity, hacking at their foes until they are little more than bloody chunks of meat. Others dance through battle with preternatural grace, opening throats and piercing hearts with every strike.

On every fighter card there will be 1 or more **weapons** that the fighter can use when making an attack action. Each weapon has 4 characteristics: the **Range** characteristic, the **Attacks** characteristic, the **Strength** characteristic and the **Damage** characteristic.

Sometimes a rule will refer to a characteristic of an attack action (for example, the Attacks characteristic of an attack action). This is simply an alternative way of referring to the corresponding characteristic of the weapon being used to make that attack action, but only for the duration of that attack action.

To make an attack action with a fighter, follow these 4 steps:

1. PICK A WEAPON AND TARGET
First, you must pick a weapon from the fighter card of the fighter making the attack action, and a visible enemy fighter to be the target of the attack action.

If there are any enemy fighters within 1" of the fighter making the attack action, one of those enemy fighters must be picked to be the target, and the weapon used cannot have a minimum range (see right).

If there are no enemy fighters within 1" of the fighter making the attack action, you can pick any enemy fighter to be the target as long as they are within range of the weapon that will be used.

RANGE
The range of a weapon is a number of inches equal to its Range characteristic. For example if a weapon has a Range characteristic of 3, an enemy fighter within 3" of the fighter making the attack action can be targeted by attack actions using that weapon (see Measuring Distances, pg 35). Some weapons have a **minimum range**, which means that they cannot be used to target fighters that are within a certain range. For example, a weapon that has a Range characteristic of 6-20 can target a fighter within 20", but not if that fighter is within 6".

2. ROLL TO HIT
Roll a number of dice equal to the Attacks characteristic of the weapon being used to make the attack action. This is referred to as the **hit roll**.

Next, you will need to determine which of the dice have missed, which have scored a **hit** and which have scored a **critical hit**. To do so, compare the **Strength** characteristic of the weapon being used for that attack action with the **Toughness** characteristic of the enemy fighter targeted by the attack action and consult the table below.

3. ALLOCATE DAMAGE
The Damage characteristic of each weapon has 2 values (divided by a '/'). These dictate how many damage points are allocated to the enemy fighter targeted by that attack action. For each hit, allocate a number of damage points equal to the first value of the Damage characteristic For each critical hit, allocate a number of damage points equal to the second value of the Damage characteristic, instead of the first.

For example, if a weapon with a Damage characteristic of 1/3 scored 2 hits, 1 critical hit and 1 miss, the total number of damage points allocated to the target fighter of that attack action would be 5 (1+1+3+0).

4. REMOVE TAKEN DOWN FIGHTERS
Damage points are allocated one at a time. If the number of damage points allocated to a fighter equals its **Wounds** characteristic, that fighter is said to be **taken down**. Place a taken down fighter to one side – they are removed from the battlefield. A taken down fighter takes no further part in the battle – they cannot be activated, cannot make actions and cannot use abilities.

When a fighter is taken down any left over damage points from the attack action are discarded.

STRENGTH VS TOUGHNESS	HIT	CRITICAL HIT
Strength is greater than Toughness	3-5	6
Strength is equal to Toughness	4-5	6
Strength is lower than Toughness	5	6

DISENGAGE ACTIONS

If a fighter is within 1" of an enemy fighter, they can make a disengage action to move away. When a fighter makes a disengage action, that fighter can make a normal move (pg 41) up to 3" in any direction but must finish the action more than 1" away from any enemy fighters. If this is impossible, the fighter cannot use the disengage action and must use another action instead.

Disengage Actions vs Move Actions

Although the position of a fighter changes as part of a disengage action, it is not considered to be a move action in any way. This means any abilities or rules that interact specifically with move actions do not interact with disengage actions. In addition, a fighter cannot jump, climb or fly as part of a disengage action.

WAIT ACTIONS

A wait action can be used in two ways. If a fighter makes the wait action as their last action in their activation, their activation ends. The wait action is used in this manner simply when the fighter has nothing else to do (for example, if they are not in range to attack and do not wish to move).

Alternatively, if a fighter uses the wait action as their first action in their activation, the fighter is said to be waiting. Place a wait token by the fighter to indicate it is waiting. If a fighter makes a wait action in this manner the activation ends, but that fighter can be activated once more later in that combat phase. When that fighter is activated for the second time, they can only make 1 action in that activation.

Wait Actions and Abilities

If a fighter activates for a second time in the combat phase as a result of a wait action, they can use 1 ability in their second activation even if an ability was used the first time they activated. In addition, when activating for the second time, that 1 ability can be used by the fighter either before their action or after their action. When a rule or ability refers to 'this fighter's activation', it means the fighter's current activation.

TERRAIN

During any battle there will be 1 or more terrain features on the battlefield, as dictated by the terrain card in play. Fighters can interact with terrain features in numerous ways when making move actions (pg 41). This section introduces the other interactions fighters can have with terrain features, and also describes the unique types of terrain features.

TERRAIN FEATURES

Terrain features come in many shapes and sizes. When a rule refers to a terrain feature, it refers to the scenery model itself and any base it is mounted upon, but not any empty space around or within it.

OBSTACLES

Some terrain features, or some parts of terrain features, can be defined as an **obstacle**. An obstacle is any part of a terrain feature that prevents a fighter from moving horizontally and that extends vertically more than 1"

high from the battlefield floor or the platform upon which it is placed.

When an attack action targets an enemy fighter that is within ½" of an obstacle, the target fighter of that attack action receives the benefit of cover if the fighter making the attack action is closer to that obstacle than they are to the target fighter.

> ### Cover
> If a fighter receives the benefit of cover when targeted by an attack action, add 1 to their Toughness characteristic for that attack action.

PLATFORMS

Some terrain features, or some parts of a terrain feature, can be defined as a **platform**. A platform is a horizontally flat surface on a terrain feature with a surface area larger than 1" by 1", that is raised 1" or higher above the battlefield floor.

When an attack action targets an enemy fighter that is on a platform, the target fighter of that attack action receives the benefit of cover if the fighter making the attack action is 3" or more vertically below the target fighter.

FALLING OFF TERRAIN

When an attack action targets an enemy fighter that is within ½" of the edge of a platform that is open (i.e. an edge that is not enclosed by an obstacle, such as a wall) and scores any critical hits, the target fighter of that attack must take a falling test after the attack action has been resolved. To do so, the player controlling that fighter rolls a dice. On a 1, the fighter is said to have fallen (pg 42).

This rule does not affect fighters with the **Fly** runemark (🐦).

1. Obstacle
2. Platform
3. Stairs
4. Door
5. Archway
6. Deadly Terrain
7. Low Terrain

DEADLY TERRAIN

Some terrain features, or parts of terrain features, are said to be **deadly terrain**. If you are using the terrain that comes with Warcry, you can see which parts of those terrain features are deadly terrain on page 46.

If you are using other terrain features, you should agree with your opponent which parts of those terrain features are deadly terrain when the battlefield is first set up. Parts of terrain features that are deadly terrain can still be platforms or obstacles if they fall under the definitions of either.

If a fighter ever moves onto deadly terrain, for example, if they begin to climb deadly terrain or finish a jump upon deadly terrain, they immediately suffer impact damage (pg 42). In addition, if a fallen fighter (pg 42) is placed within 1" of deadly terrain, they immediately suffer impact damage.

Note, it is possible for a fighter to suffer impact damage more than once due to deadly terrain. For example, if a fallen fighter is placed within 1" of deadly terrain and is now 3" or more vertically lower than their location before they fell, that fighter would suffer impact damage twice (and would therefore make 2 dice rolls).

STAIRS AND LADDERS

Some terrain features, or parts of terrain features, are said to be **stairs** or **ladders**. You can see an example of stairs on page 46. Stairs and ladders are treated as obstacles, with the following exceptions:

- Fighters that finish their activation climbing stairs or a ladder are not said to have fallen and can remain part way up stairs or a ladder (if it is not possible to physically place the fighter in their current location, make a note of where they are).

- When an attack action targets an enemy fighter that has ended their activation climbing stairs or a ladder and scores any critical hits, the target fighter must take a falling test (pg 46) after the attack action has been resolved.

ARCHWAYS AND DOORS

Some terrain features, or parts of terrain features, are said to be **archways** or **doors**. If you are using the terrain that comes with Warcry, you can see which parts of those terrain features are archways or doors on page 46.

If you are using other terrain features, you should agree with your opponent which parts of those terrain features are either archways or doors when the battlefield is first set up. Archways and doors can still be platforms or obstacles if they fall under the definitions of either (usually they will be obstacles, but something like a trapdoor could be part of a platform).

As part of a move action, if a fighter is touching a part of a terrain feature defined as an archway or a door, that fighter can make a normal move through it even if the miniature or its base is too large to physically fit through (or it is blocked completely, as in the case of a closed door). This is an exception to the rule which states that a fighter cannot move through any part of a terrain feature.

To move through an archway or a door, first measure the distance in a straight line through the horizontal centre of the archway or doorway. If the fighter has sufficient movement to pass through the archway or door and be placed on the other side, they can move through it.

When fighters move through archways and doors, all other movement rules must still be followed (for example, they cannot move through another fighter).

RESTRICTIONS

Fighters with any of the following runemarks cannot move through **archways**:

- Gargantuan �
- Mount �

Fighters with any of the following runemarks cannot move through **doors**:

- Gargantuan �
- Mount �
- Beast �

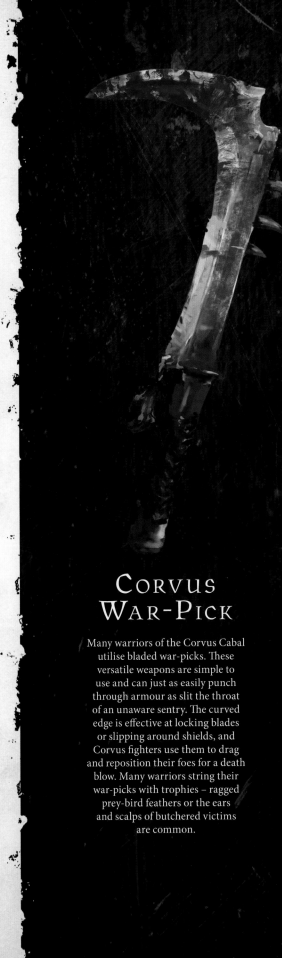

CORVUS WAR-PICK

Many warriors of the Corvus Cabal utilise bladed war-picks. These versatile weapons are simple to use and can just as easily punch through armour as slit the throat of an unaware sentry. The curved edge is effective at locking blades or slipping around shields, and Corvus fighters use them to drag and reposition their foes for a death blow. Many warriors string their war-picks with trophies – ragged prey-bird feathers or the ears and scalps of butchered victims are common.

CHAOTIC BEASTS

The corrupting power of Chaos has fully defiled the Eightpoints over the course of centuries, transforming flora and fauna alike into unnatural, mutated abominations. Many of the beasts that make their lairs in the lands around the Varanspire are little more than frenzied monsters, but others possess an unsettling cunning, and will even follow a warband into battle in return for fresh meat or some other, darker incentive.

A fighter with the ✴ faction runemark on their fighter card is referred to as a **chaotic beast**. A chaotic beast is a type of fighter that belongs to no player's warband. Chaotic beasts will come into play during a battle when twist cards with the **Wild Creatures** runemark (✴) are drawn. Like all other fighters, chaotic beasts each have a fighter card that details their characteristics and weapons, and an ability card.

Each ✴ twist card will explain if and how any chaotic beasts are set up on the battlefield. During a battle, if there are any chaotic beasts on the battlefield, use the following rules:

TERRITORIAL PREDATORS
Chaotic beasts treat all fighters as enemy fighters, except for fighters that have the same combination of runemarks as themselves, which they treat as friendly fighters. This means that a chaotic beast will treat another chaotic beast as an enemy fighter if it does not have identical runemarks (e.g. if it has a different fighter card). However, chaotic beasts will always treat thralls (see opposite) as enemy fighters even if they share identical runemarks.

BESTIAL INTELLECTS
When it is a player's turn to choose a fighter from their warband to activate, they can instead choose a chaotic beast that has not yet activated. When they do so, the player first rolls a dice. On a 3-6 they can activate that chaotic beast as normal. On a 1-2, their opponent can instead activate that chaotic beast. When this happens, it still counts as the turn of the player who chose the chaotic beast, despite their opponent being the one who gets to activate it.

If you are playing a battle with more than 2 players and a roll of a 1-2 occurs when activating a chaotic beast, the opponents of the activating player roll off and the winner can activate that chaotic beast.

If there are any chaotic beasts in play that have not yet been activated that combat phase, a player must pick 1 of those chaotic beasts to activate and cannot pass.

A chaotic beast can never use the wait action as its first action in its activation.

CHAOTIC BEASTS AND ABILITIES
When a player activates a chaotic beast, they can use any of their ability dice to use abilities with that chaotic beast. A chaotic beast can use abilities in the same manner as any other fighter. As well as the universal abilities (pg 40), chaotic beasts have their own abilities. The abilities for Furies and Raptoryx are shown below.

CHAOTIC BEASTS ABILITIES

	[Double] Cower: Until the end of the battle round, count each critical hit from attack actions that target this fighter as a hit instead.
	[Double] Crazed Flock: Until the end of this fighter's activation, for each other friendly fighter within 3" of this fighter that has the same runemarks as this fighter, add 1 to the Attacks and Strength characteristics of attack actions made by this fighter that have a Range characteristic of 3 or less.

THRALLS

Savage creatures twisted by the touch of Chaos can be found all across the Eightpoints. The warbands that seek Archaon's favour can dominate these weak-minded beasts with the enrapturing call of raised monoliths, or else bring them into servitude through dark pacts and gruesome offerings.

In certain battles, a player may be able to include special fighters in their warband known as **thralls**. This is usually in a campaign battle (pg 63) when a warband's territory rules allow them to do so, but there are also other ways of including thralls in a warband (for example, the Sinister Bargain twist card allows a player to include 1 thrall in their warband).

If a player is allowed to include any thralls in their warband, they can choose any fighter with the **Chaotic Beast** faction runemark (✻) that has the **Thrall** runemark (♟) to become their thrall, and include that fighter in their warband for that battle. Thralls are ignored for the purposes of the rule that requires fighters in a warband to all share the same faction runemark.

When a chaotic beast is chosen to become a thrall, it is no longer subject to the Territorial Predators or the Bestial Intellects rules, and is instead treated as a friendly fighter in that player's warband.

When a player activates a thrall in their warband, they can use any of their ability dice to use abilities with that thrall. A thrall can use the universal abilities (pg 40) and the abilities on their ability card.

Corvus Cabal Spire Stalker

SCYTHE-LIMB

The Unmade make no distinction between the weapons they wield and their own flesh and bone. To them, the blades and impaling hooks they attach to their bodies are merely extensions of their physical form. The Unmade's greatest warriors are as much metal as organic matter, having sacrificed their flesh in order to become more efficient instruments of torment. Armed with scythe-limbs, these zealots leap and spin across the battlefield in a terrifyingly erratic dance, sending the limbs and flesh of their foes spiralling into the air in their wake.

RUNEMARKS

Below you will find a list of the runemarks used in Warcry. These symbols appear on fighter cards, and govern which weapons and abilities each warrior can use in battle. They are also found on battleplan cards, where they denote the specific environmental and strategic context of each combat encounter.

FIGHTERS

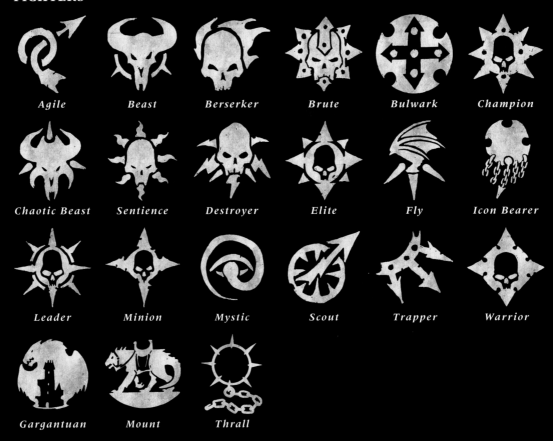

Agile   Beast   Berserker   Brute   Bulwark   Champion

Chaotic Beast   Sentience   Destroyer   Elite   Fly   Icon Bearer

Leader   Minion   Mystic   Scout   Trapper   Warrior

Gargantuan   Mount   Thrall

WEAPONS

Blast   Axe   Reach Weapon   Claws   Club   Dagger   Fangs

Ranged Weapon   Scythe   Spear   Mace   Sword   Unarmed

FACTIONS

Iron Golem   Untamed Beasts   Corvus Cabal   Cypher Lords   Scions of the Flame   Splintered Fang

The Unmade   Spire Tyrants

CHARACTERISTICS

Attacks   Damage   Move   Range   Strength   Toughness   Wounds

---

TWISTS

Climate   Environment   Fate   Magical Phenomena   Orientation   Psychology   Wild Creatures

---

TREASURE

Creature   Orrery   Realmstone   Potions   Skull   Supplies   Totem   Weapons

---

DEPLOYMENT

Dagger   Hammer   Shield

CARD DECKS

Terrain   Deployment   Victory   Twist   Symmetrical

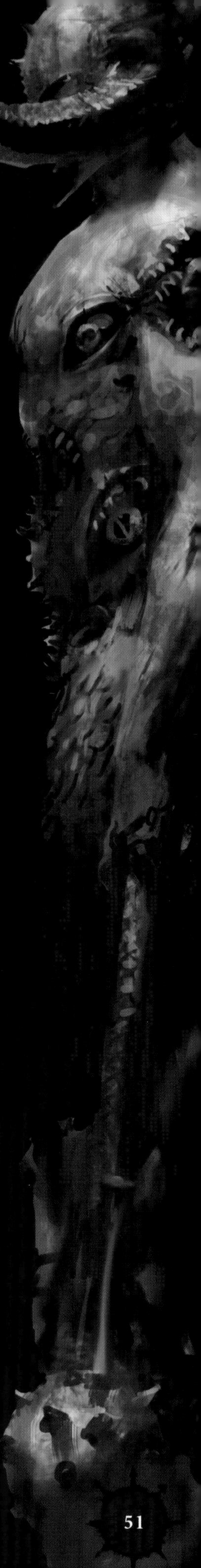

OPEN PLAY

Open play is the most flexible of the three play styles, and is ideal for casual games where the focus is on creating a fun game with ease. This section covers how to set up battles involving more than two players, be they epic team-battles or chaotic free-for-alls.

The core rules allow you to quickly set up an open play game of Warcry involving two players, but battles with multiple opponents can be a lot of fun too. In this section you will find two types of multiplayer battle:

Coalition of Death and **Triumph & Treachery** battles. The Coalition of Death rules pit two teams of players against each other, whereas in Triumph & Treachery it's every fighter for themselves. The rules in

this section are not intended for competitive play, but are great if you are looking to fight an exciting one-off battle with your friends that involves everyone.

COALITION OF DEATH

The skies darken as battle lines are drawn. Many powerful warbands have been united under two rival alliances, and now, as they face each other, the air is thick with the promise of bloodshed and violence to come.

Coalition of Death games feature two sides made up of multiple warbands. To organise a Coalition of Death battle, the players first need to divide themselves into two teams. It does not matter if one team has fewer players than the other team, as long as each team is able to field a roughly equal points' worth of fighters.

FRIENDLY AND ENEMY FIGHTERS

In a Coalition of Death battle, fighters in a warband consider only fighters in their warband to be friendly fighters, but consider all fighters in warbands on the opposing team to be enemy fighters. Fighters in different warbands on the same team consider each other to be neither friendly nor enemy fighters. In gameplay terms, this means actions or abilities used by a fighter do not affect fighters from other warbands on the same team.

THE BATTLEFIELD

The battlefield is assumed to be 2 Warcry battlefield mats placed next to one another on the long battlefield edge to form a 30" by 44" rectangle. This is a good-sized battlefield for teams that consist of 2-4 players.

THE WARBANDS

Each player musters 1 warband, adhering to the following rules:

1. The warband must include at least 3 fighters.

2. All fighters in the warband must share the same faction runemark (pg 35).

3. The warband can include any number of thralls (pg 49).

4. There can be only 1 leader (pg 35) in each warband.

Rather than having a points limit for each warband, the players agree on a total points limit for each team and then divide the points between the players' warbands as they see fit.

Once both teams have mustered all their warbands, all players reveal their warbands to each other.

THE PRIORITY ROLL

If one team has fewer players than the other, that team automatically wins the priority roll. Otherwise, one player from each team rolls off to determine which team wins the priority roll.

BATTLE GROUPS

Starting with the team who lost the priority roll, each player splits their warband into a Dagger, Shield and Hammer following the rules on page 36.

THE BATTLEPLAN

To generate a Coalition of Death battleplan, resolve the following steps in order:

1. TERRAIN

The team that lost the priority roll sets up the battlefield terrain, placing as little or as much as they like.

2. DEPLOYMENT

Roll a D3 on the table below to determine which deployment set-up (pg 54) is used during the battle.

D3	DEPLOYMENT SET-UP
1	**Disparate Forces**
2	**Battle Lines**
3	**Hammer and Anvil**

The team that won the priority roll then chooses how the deployment set-up orientates with the battlefield (the upper long edge on the deployment map can be orientated to either of the battlefield long edges) and chooses either the red or blue deployment points to be theirs.

These deployment set-ups include deployment zones. Fighters can be set up anywhere wholly within the deployment zone that corresponds to the battle group they are in (Dagger, Shield or Hammer). The team that won the priority roll first sets up their Daggers, followed by the opposing team. Then the teams set up their Shields in the same order, and finally their Hammers in the same order.

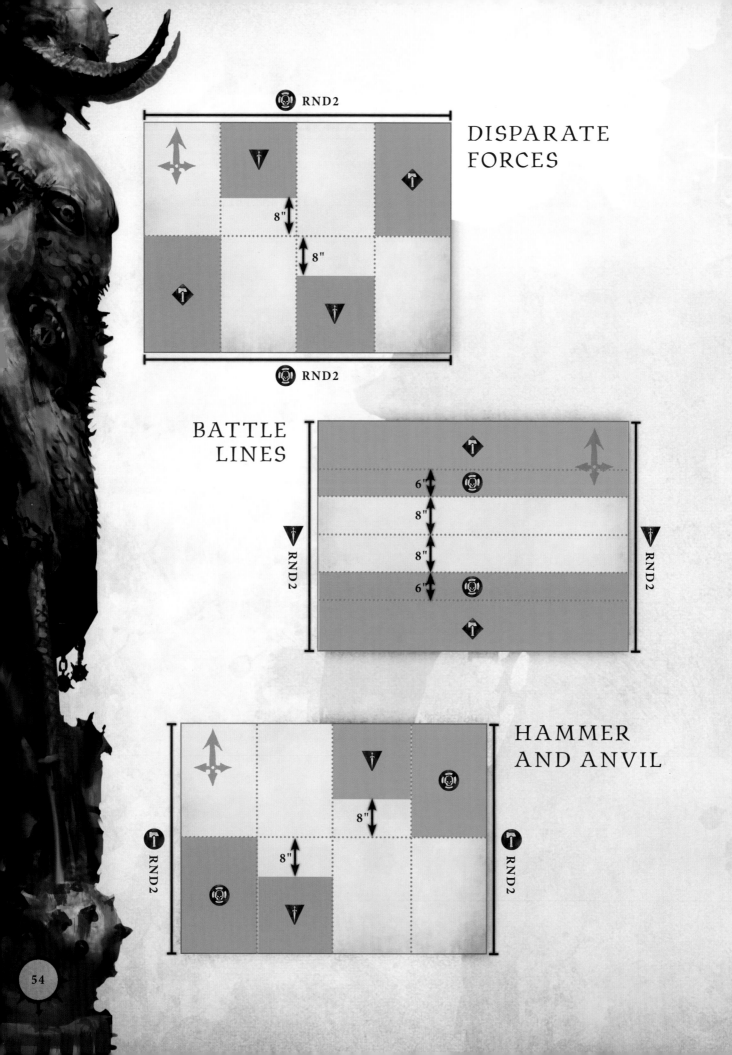

RND2

RND2

DISPARATE
FORCES

8"

8"

BATTLE
LINES

RND2

RND2

6"

8"

8"

6"

HAMMER
AND ANVIL

RND2

RND2

8"

8"

54

3. VICTORY

The battle ends after 3 battle rounds. In each battle round there are 2 victory conditions in play, and these victory conditions change from battle round to battle round. At the start of each battle round, before the hero phase, roll a dice on each of the two tables below and overleaf to determine which 2 victory conditions are in effect for that battle round. When the battle ends, the team with the most victory points wins the battle. The rules for tied games (pg 37) are still in effect.

D6	COALITION OF DEATH VICTORY CONDITION 1
1	**NO MERCY** At the end of the battle round, each team counts the number of enemy fighters that were taken down this battle round. The team with the higher result scores 1 victory point. If the result is tied, neither team scores a victory point.
2	**BLOODMARKED** At the start of the combat phase, starting with the team that has the initiative, each team picks 3 fighters from their team to be **bloodmarked**. These fighters must be on the battlefield. If there are less than 3 fighters from the team on the battlefield, each of the remaining fighters in that team must be bloodmarked. At the end of the battle round, each team counts the number of enemy bloodmarked fighters that were taken down this battle round. The team with the higher result scores 1 victory point. If the result is tied, neither team scores a victory point.
3	**THE HUNTED** At the start of the combat phase, starting with the team that has the initiative, each team can pick up to 3 enemy fighters to be **hunted**. These fighters must be on the battlefield. At the end of the battle round, each team counts the number of hunted fighters from the opposing team that were taken down this battle round. The team with the higher result scores 1 victory point. If the result is tied, neither team scores a victory point.
4	**SHOCK AND AWE** At the end of the battle round, each team counts the number of enemy Dagger fighters that were taken down this battle round. The team with the higher result scores 1 victory point. If the result is tied, neither team scores a victory point. Re-roll this result if no fighters from any Dagger battle group are currently on the battlefield.
5	**DOMINATE** At the end of the battle round, each team counts the number of enemy Shield fighters that were taken down this battle round. The team with the higher result scores 1 victory point. If the result is tied, neither team scores a victory point. Re-roll this result if no fighters from any Shield battle group are currently on the battlefield.
6	**VANQUISH** At the end of the battle round, each team counts the number of enemy Hammer fighters that were taken down this battle round. The team with the higher result scores 1 victory point. If the result is tied, neither team scores a victory point. Re-roll this result if no fighters from any Hammer battle group are currently on the battlefield.

D6	COALITION OF DEATH VICTORY CONDITION 2
1	**HIGHER GROUND** At the end of the battle round, each team counts the number of fighters from their team that are on platforms. The team that has the most scores 1 victory point. If the result is tied, neither team scores a victory point.
2	**VANTAGE POINT** At the end of the battle round, locate the fighter that is the highest vertically. The team that fighter belongs to scores 1 victory point. If multiple fighters are the highest vertically, the team that has the most fighters that are highest vertically scores 1 victory point. If the result is tied, neither team scores a victory point.
3	**HOLD GROUND** At the end of the battle round, each team counts the number of fighters from their team that are within 6" horizontally of the centre of the battlefield. The team that has the most scores 1 victory point. If the result is tied, neither team scores a victory point.
4	**INVADE** At the end of the battle round, each team counts the number of fighters from their Daggers that are wholly within a deployment zone of the opposing team. The team that has the most scores 1 victory point. If the result is tied, neither team scores a victory point. Re-roll this result if no fighters from any Dagger battle group are currently on the battlefield.
5	**CONQUER** At the end of the battle round, each team counts the number of fighters from their Shields that are wholly within a deployment zone of the opposing team. The team that has the most scores 1 victory point. If the result is tied, neither team scores a victory point. Re-roll this result if no fighters from any Shield battle group are currently on the battlefield.
6	**OCCUPY** At the end of the battle round, each team counts the number of fighters from their Hammers that are wholly within a deployment zone of the opposing team. The team that has the most scores 1 victory point. If the result is tied, neither team scores a victory point. Re-roll this result if no fighters from any Hammer battle group are currently on the battlefield.

4. TWIST
Draw a twist card as normal.

PLAYING COALITION OF DEATH
When fighting a Coalition of Death battle, follow the core rules with the following amendments:

HERO PHASE
Each player has their own 6 initiative dice. These dice cannot be swapped between players in the team. When determining initiative, total up the number of singles for each team. The team with the most singles has the initiative. In the case of a tie, the team with fewer players has the initiative. Otherwise, 1 player from each team rolls off and the winning team has the initiative.

WILD DICE
Each player receives 1 wild dice at the start of the hero phase. The team with the initiative first declares how each of their players will use their wild dice, followed by the other team. Wild dice cannot be shared between players on a team and cannot be used to turn another player's singles into a double or be added to another player's ability dice.

If one team has fewer players than the other, each player in the smaller team receives 1 additional wild dice at the start of the battle.

RESERVE PHASE
During the reserve phase, the team with the initiative first deploys any reserve battle groups that come into play, followed by the opposing team.

COMBAT PHASE
During the combat phase, each team takes it in turns activating fighters, starting with the team that has the initiative. When it is a team's turn, each player in that team activates 1 of their fighters, one player at a time. The order in which players take these activations can vary from turn to turn, but each player fully completes 1 activation with their fighter before the next player in their team activates 1 of their fighters.

In a Coalition of Death battle, if a fighter is said to have fallen (pg 42), one player on the opposing team is nominated by the opposing team to be the 'opposing player' to resolve the rule.

TRIUMPH & TREACHERY

Drawn together by fate or dark design, several warbands meet in battle amidst the wilds of the Eightpoints. Strategy is cast aside in favour of raw aggression as the conflict descends into a frenzied bloodbath.

Games of Triumph & Treachery are multiplayer battles for 3-4 players that pit every player against the others. To organise a Triumph & Treachery battle, follow these rules:

PRIORITY ORDER

When setting up a battle, the players first roll off to determine **priority order**. The winner of the roll-off is first in the priority order, the player who came second is second in the priority order, and so on through to the player who came last, who is last in the priority order. If any players were tied during the roll-off, those players roll off again to determine who is before the other in the priority order.

THE WARBANDS

Each player musters 1 warband as described in the core rules (pg 36).

Once all players have mustered all their warbands, all players reveal their warbands to each other.

BATTLE GROUPS

In reverse priority order, each player splits their warband into a Dagger, Shield and Hammer following the rules on page 36.

THE BATTLEPLAN

To generate a Triumph & Treachery battleplan, resolve the following steps in order:

1. TERRAIN

Draw a terrain card as normal.

2. DEPLOYMENT

Roll a D3 on the table below to determine which deployment set-up (pg 58) is used during the battle.

D3	DEPLOYMENT SET-UP
1	**A Storm Gathers**
2	**Vying Forces**
3	Betrayal

In priority order, each player chooses which colour deployment points they will use and then sets up their Dagger. Then the players set up their Shields in priority order, and finally their Hammers in priority order.

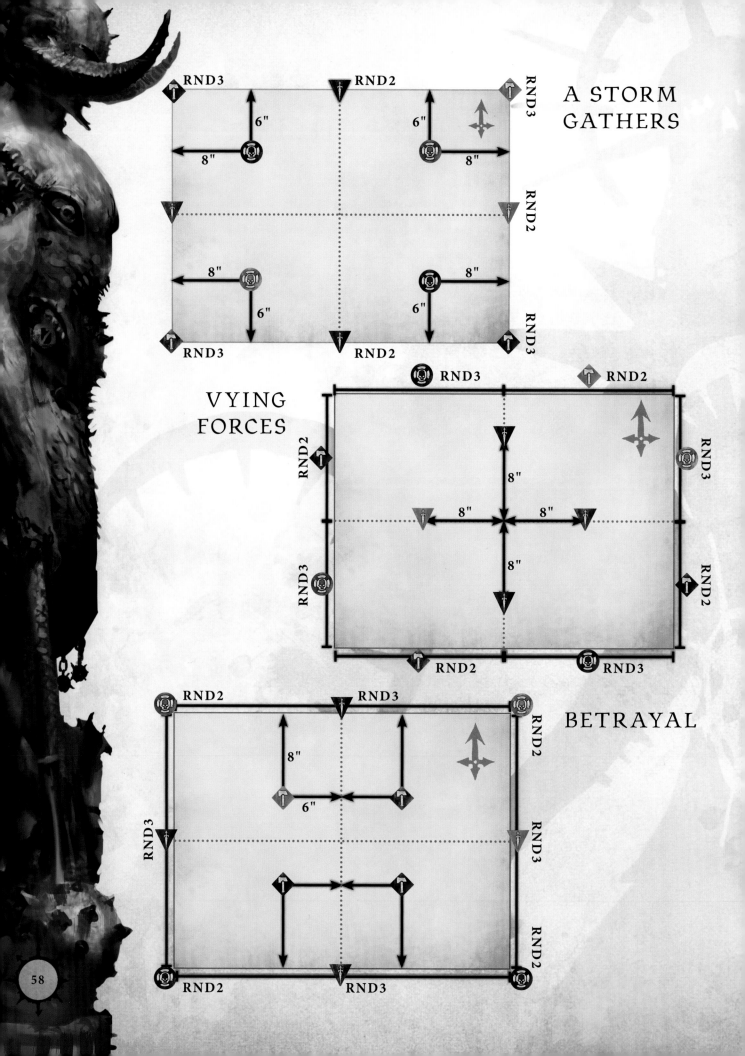

A STORM
GATHERS

RND3　RND2　RND3

6"　6"

8"　8"

RND3

RND2

8"　8"

6"　6"

RND3　RND2　RND3

VYING
FORCES

RND3　RND2

RND2

8"

RND3

8"　8"

RND3

8"

RND2

RND2　RND3

BETRAYAL

RND2　RND3　RND2

8"

RND3　RND3

6"

RND2　RND2

RND2　RND3

3. VICTORY

There are 6 potential victory conditions in Triumph & Treachery. Roll a dice on the table below to determine which victory condition is in play. The rules for tied games (pg 37) are still in effect.

D6	TRIUMPH & TREACHERY VICTORY CONDITION
1	**DRAWN AND QUARTERED** In priority order, each player places 1 objective. Objectives can be placed anywhere on the battlefield that is more than 3" horizontally from the centre of the battlefield and more than 4" from the battlefield edge and any other objectives. At the end of each battle round, the player who controls the most objectives scores 2 victory points. If more than one player controls the most objectives, each of those players scores 1 victory point instead. The battle ends after 3 battle rounds. When the battle ends, the player with the most victory points wins the battle.
2	**DIMINISHING GAINS** In priority order, each player places 1 objective. Objectives can be placed anywhere on the battlefield that is more than 3" horizontally from the centre of the battlefield and more than 4" from the battlefield edge and any other objectives. At the end of each battle round, the player who controls the most objectives scores 2 victory points. If more than one player controls the most objectives, each of those players scores 1 victory point instead. In addition, at the end of each battle round, after victory points have been scored, the player with the least victory points chooses 1 objective and removes it from play. If players are tied for the least victory points, those players roll off and the winner chooses which objective is removed. The battle ends after 3 battle rounds. When the battle ends, the player with the most victory points wins the battle.
3	**VANTAGE POINT** The players roll off and the winner places 1 objective on a platform at least 6" vertically above the battlefield floor. If there are no platforms that high, the player instead places 1 objective on a platform at least 3" vertically above the battlefield floor. The player that controls the objective at the end of each battle round scores 1 victory point. The battle ends after 3 battle rounds. When the battle ends, the player with the most victory points wins the battle.
4	**BLOODMARKED** At the start of the combat phase of each battle round, in reverse initiative order, each player chooses 1 fighter from their warband that is on the battlefield to be **bloodmarked**. A fighter is bloodmarked for that battle round only, unless they are chosen again in a subsequent battle round. At the end of that battle round, each player scores 1 victory point if their bloodmarked fighter has not been taken down. The battle ends after 3 battle rounds. When the battle ends, the player with the most victory points wins the battle.
5	**NO MERCY** During each battle round, each player counts the number of enemy fighters taken down during the activation of a friendly fighter. At the end of each battle round, the player with the highest total for that battle round scores 1 victory point. The battle ends after 3 battle rounds. When the battle ends, the player with the most victory points wins the battle.
6	**THE PRIZE** The players roll off and the winner places 1 treasure token within 6" horizontally of the centre of the battlefield. At the end of each battle round, the player whose fighter is carrying the treasure scores 1 victory point. The battle ends after 3 battle rounds. When the battle ends, the player with the most victory points wins the battle.

HIDDEN AGENDA

Once the victory condition has been determined, each player then chooses a Hidden Agenda from the table below. A Hidden Agenda is a secondary objective. Each player secretly notes down their Hidden Agenda and any other relevant details for it to be revealed at the end of the battle.

THE CHAMPION	HIDDEN ARTEFACT	HOLD THE CENTRE
At the end of the third battle round, you score 1 victory point if your leader is on the battlefield and all other leaders have been taken down.	Secretly note down one of your fighters to be the bearer of the hidden artefact. The fighter must be on the battlefield. At the start of the combat phase of the third battle round, reveal which of your fighters bears the hidden artefact. At the end of the third battle round, you score 1 victory point if the bearer has not been taken down.	At the end of the third battle round, you score 1 victory point if 1 or more friendly fighters are within 6" horizontally of the centre of the battlefield and no enemy fighters are within 6" horizontally of the centre of the battlefield.
PURGE	**HIGHER GROUND**	**THE ARCHITECT**
Secretly note down one of the quarters of the battlefield: north-east, north-west, south-east or south-west. At the end of the third battle round, you score 1 victory point if 1 or more friendly fighters are wholly within that quarter of the battlefield and no enemy fighters are wholly within that quarter of the battlefield.	At the end of the third battle round, you score 1 victory point if 1 or more friendly fighters are 3" or more vertically above the battlefield floor and all enemy fighters that are on the battlefield are less than 3" vertically above the battlefield floor.	At the end of the third battle round, count the number of fighters taken down in each warband. You score 1 victory point if each enemy warband has had half or more of its fighters taken down, but your warband has had less than half of its fighters taken down.

4. TWIST
Draw a twist card as normal.

PLAYING TRIUMPH & TREACHERY
When fighting a Triumph & Treachery battle, follow the core rules with the following amendments:

HERO PHASE
In the hero phase, an **initiative order** is determined by counting the number of singles each player has. The player with the most singles is first in the initiative order, the player with the second most is second in the initiative order, and so on through to the player with the least singles, who is last in the initiative order. If players are tied, those players roll off to determine who is before the other in the initiative order. Players declare how they will use wild dice in initiative order.

SEIZING THE INITIATIVE
Players can still attempt to seize the initiative (pg 39) from those before them in the initiative order by adding wild dice to the total number of singles they have.

Once all players have declared any wild dice they will use this battle round, count the number of singles each player has once more to redetermine the initiative order. If the number of singles any players have is now tied (and was not previously), those players roll off to determine who is before the other in the initiative order.

RESERVE PHASE
The reserve phase is resolved in initiative order.

COMBAT PHASE
The combat phase is resolved in initiative order.

If a fighter is said to have fallen (pg 42) in a Triumph & Treachery battle, the player who controls the closest enemy fighter to the fighter that has fallen is treated as the 'opposing player' to resolve the rule (if there are multiple enemy fighters that are the closest, the players who control those enemy fighters roll off to determine who is treated as the 'opposing player').

NARRATIVE PLAY

Every warband that sets foot upon the blood-soaked lands of the Eightpoints has their own ambitions and motives. Narrative play looks to explore the stories of each warband and bring them to life on the battlefield.

Although it is fun to play one-off battles of Warcry, for many players the real challenge of the game is to play through a campaign. In a campaign, you chart the progress of your warband across the wastes of the Eightpoints towards the Varanspire, linking each of your battles into an ongoing narrative that tells the story of your warband's rise to glory as you strive to complete your campaign quest. Along the way some of your fighters may die – after all, life is harsh and unforgiving in the Eightpoints – but those who survive will grow in power as they carve out a bloody legend for themselves and your warband. The following section details how to play through a Warcry campaign.

The intrepid Vanguard-Hunters of the Stormcast Eternals range deep into the most hostile enemy lands, risking both life and soul to see the God-King's will done.

The Ironjawz rampage across the realms, and some have found their way into the wilds of the Eightpoints. These hulking Brutes delight in the carnage they have found there.

CAMPAIGNS

Beneath the tormented skies of the Eightpoints, rival warbands clash in battle. Some of these encounters are no more than brutal skirmishes, fought for territory or plunder. Others are calculated steps in a greater plan, a campaign of dominance designed to draw the eye of the Everchosen himself.

EMBARKING UPON A CAMPAIGN

To play through a campaign, you will first need to choose a campaign quest and fill out a warband roster for your warband. Once you have done so, you are ready to challenge any opponent to a campaign battle.

In Warcry, the campaign quest you choose for your warband is unique to you, and charts the progress of your warband only. This means you can challenge any opponent to a campaign battle, so long as they too have chosen a campaign quest and filled out a warband roster.

Some players may be part of a group of players that decide to all embark upon a Warcry campaign at the same time, and to only challenge those within their group to campaign battles. Other players might play a different opponent each week at their local club or games store. There is no right or wrong way to play through your campaign, and the rules presented here are flexible to cater to the needs of the individual player.

CAMPAIGN QUESTS

At the heart of every Warcry campaign is the quest your warband is striving to achieve. This is referred to as a **campaign quest**. You can find a whole array of different campaign quests to choose from in the campaign section of this book (pg 82-127).

Each campaign quest has one or more faction runemarks to denote which warbands can embark upon it. The campaign quests in the campaign section have a single faction runemark, and so choosing a campaign quest often goes hand-in-hand with choosing which warband you wish to play through the campaign with. In addition, each campaign quest contains the following:

1. TERRITORY RULES

Each campaign quest has its own territory rules that enable your warband to dominate areas within the Eightpoints. For the aspiring followers of the Dark Gods, these territory rules allow your warband to raise sinister monoliths and enslave chaotic beasts as thralls. For other warbands, such as the Stormcast Eternals, the territory rules will allow your warband to purge the chaotic taint from the lands and create areas of hallowed ground. The territory rules for each campaign quest are detailed in full upon it.

2. ARTEFACTS OF POWER AND COMMAND TRAITS TABLES

Each campaign quest has 1 table of artefacts of power and 1 table of command traits. As your warband progresses you will be awarded items from these lists at certain points; this is explained in the **aftermath sequence** (pg 66-70).

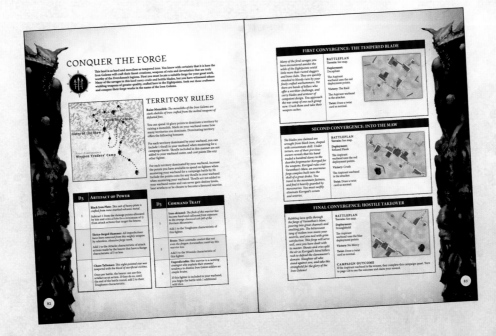

WARBAND ROSTER

After choosing a campaign quest, you will need to fill out a warband roster (pg 160). First, note down the campaign quest you have chosen, then fill in the other areas of player and warband information such as your warband's name (you can draw inspiration from the many warbands mentioned in this book and others).

The warband roster has space for 1 leader/favoured warrior and 10 fighters. For a full 20-strong warband you will need two copies of this page.

ADDING FIGHTERS

The next step in completing your warband roster is to add fighters to it. Your warband roster is the pool of fighters from which you will pick up to 15 when mustering your warband for a campaign battle (see Playing a Campaign Battle, pg 65).

Before your first campaign battle, you can add up to 20 fighters to your warband roster. These fighters can total any number of points, but it should contain at least 1000 points' worth of fighters to allow you to field a full warband during your first campaign battle. You do not have to add the full 20 fighters to begin with – you can instead choose to add additional fighters as the campaign progresses. You'll be able to add and remove fighters from your warband roster after each campaign battle (pg 67). When adding fighters to your warband roster, you must adhere to the following restrictions:

1. Your warband roster must include at least 3 fighters.

2. Your warband roster cannot exceed 20 fighters.

3. All fighters added to your warband roster must share the same faction runemark as the campaign quest you have chosen.

4. There can be only 1 fighter added to your warband roster with the **Leader** runemark.

On pages 134-151 you can find background tables to help you personalise all the fighters in your warband.

CAMPAIGN PROGRESS TRACKER

The warband roster includes a **campaign progress tracker**. This tracks how close your warband is to completing the goal of their quest. There are 12 points on the campaign tracker referred to as **map points**. Your warband begins on the map point labelled 'Start'. You can indicate the progress of your warband by marking the map point they have reached. You can find the rules for advancing map points on page 70.

PREPARING FOR YOUR FIRST CAMPAIGN BATTLE

When first filling out your warband roster, you can ignore the Lesser Artefacts, Artefacts of Power, Command Traits, Destiny Levels, Territories and Glory Points sections, as these only come into play after your first campaign battle.

ARTEFACTS AND COMMAND TRAITS

Each fighter can be the bearer of 1 artefact of power and 1 lesser artefact. In addition, your leader can have 1 command trait. How to gain these is described on page 70.

DESTINY LEVELS

Each fighter can gain up to 3 destiny levels. If a fighter gains a destiny level (pg 67) you can mark one of the icons to indicate so. During a campaign battle, if a fighter spends their destiny level, you can place a counter on it to indicate it is spent.

TERRITORIES

Your warband can dominate up to six pieces of territory at any one time. The campaign quest you have chosen will detail how your warband can dominate territory and what effect territory has on your warband.

GLORY POINTS

After a campaign battle, your warband will gain a number of glory points, which can be spent during the aftermath sequence (pg 66).

PLAYING A CAMPAIGN BATTLE

Once you have chosen your campaign quest and filled out your warband roster, you are ready to start playing campaign battles against opponents. You can challenge any player to a campaign battle if they too have chosen a campaign quest and filled out a warband roster. Both players must agree to playing a campaign battle instead of a normal battle.

To play a campaign battle, players use the core rules for setting up a battle (pg 36-37) with the following amendments:

- When mustering a warband for the battle, all fighters chosen must be taken from your warband roster.

- Players may be able to muster more than 1000 points of fighters if they have dominated territory or have spent glory points on reinforcements (pg 66).

- After playing the battle, both players must complete the **aftermath sequence** (pg 66-70).

CONVERGENCES

Each campaign quest includes three unique campaign battles referred to as **convergences**. On the campaign progress tracker of your warband roster there are three map points marked as the **first convergence**, the **second convergence** and the **final convergence**. Each of these map points is referred to as a **convergence map point**, and corresponds to a convergence on your campaign quest.

When a player's warband is on a convergence map point, that warband must play the corresponding convergence and be victorious to advance further along the campaign progress tracker. The next time the player controlling that warband plays a campaign battle, they can ask their opponent if they would like to play through their convergence.

Each convergence has unique rules to follow when generating the battleplan. If both players' warbands are on convergence map points, the players will have to decide which convergence they will play through. Only 1 player's warband can play through their convergence, even if both warbands are embarked upon the same campaign quest and have reached the same convergence map point.

In a convergence battle, the warband whose convergence the players are playing through is referred to as the **Aspirant warband**. Their opponent's is referred to as the **Adversary warband**. To play through the convergence, use the guidelines for campaign battles to the left but generate the battleplan according to the corresponding convergence on the campaign quest. This means you might know some of the battleplan cards in play before you muster your warband – use this knowledge to your advantage!

DECISIVE BATTLES

If the Aspirant warband loses the convergence, they must play through it again and win the battle before they can advance to the next map point on their campaign progress tracker. The next time the convergence is played through, it can be against the same opponent or a new opponent.

SPOILS OF WAR

The player controlling the Adversary warband gets to make an additional search for lesser artefacts in the aftermath sequence after a convergence (pg 67).

THE NARRATIVE OF CONVERGENCES

For the Aspirant warband, a convergence represents a pivotal moment in their quest. Success or failure balances on the edge of a blade, with only the Adversary warband standing between them and their goal. To build up the drama and tension of the battle to come, it is recommended that the player controlling the Aspirant warband reads aloud the introductory narrative to the convergence, and also tells the tale of the campaign quest their warband is embarked upon and the key events that have happened so far.

For the player controlling the Adversary warband, playing through the convergence offers not only a chance to earn some extra treasure, but also lets you interact with the world of the Eightpoints as the fighters of your warband take on a new role, such as becoming the hired swords to a Chaos warlord or ambushers springing a trap. For some players, they might decide that they do not wish to take the role of the Adversary warband because it does not suit the character of their warband; in such cases, it is fine to ask your opponent to find another player to play through the convergence with, and to play a standard campaign battle instead.

AFTERMATH SEQUENCE

After each campaign battle has ended, both players must complete a series of steps referred to as the **aftermath sequence**. It is best for both players to do this immediately after the battle has finished, as it is required that each player witnesses the aftermath sequence of the other.

There are 7 steps in the aftermath sequence. The steps must be completed in order and are as follows:

1. **Earn and Spend Glory Points**

2. **Make Injury Rolls**

3. **Roll for Destiny Levels**

4. **Add and Remove Fighters**

5. **Search for Lesser Artefacts**

6. **Advance on the Campaign Progress Tracker**

7. **Earn Artefacts of Power or Command Traits**

1. EARN AND SPEND GLORY POINTS

After playing a campaign battle, each player receives a number of glory points as described in the table below (these factors are all cumulative):

Players note down their total glory points on their warband roster. These glory points are kept from battle to battle during the campaign until spent.

There are a few ways players can spend their glory points during the campaign:

DOMINATING TERRITORY
Players can choose to spend glory points straight away to dominate an area of territory. Each campaign quest has its own territory rules which detail how to dominate territory; for example, many warbands aligned to Chaos can raise monoliths with their glory points.

REINFORCEMENTS
Players can choose to spend any of their glory points before picking their warband for a campaign battle if their warband has less dominated territory than their opponent. To do so, they choose to spend either 1 glory point or 3 glory points. If they spend 1 glory point they can increase the number of points they have available to spend on fighters by 50. If they spend 3 glory points, they can increase the number of points they have available to spend on fighters by 100. A player cannot spend more than 3 glory points in this manner before a campaign battle.

ADDITIONAL SEARCH ROLL
Players can choose to spend glory points in the Search for Lesser Artefacts step. To do so, they can choose to spend 3 glory points to make an additional search roll upon the lesser artefacts table (pg 68-69). A player cannot spend more than 3 glory points in this manner during that step.

2. MAKE INJURY ROLLS
If a fighter from your warband was taken down in the battle, there is a chance the wounds received will be fatal and the fighter will die. You must make an injury roll for each fighter that was taken out in the battle. To do so, roll a 2D6 and consult the table below.

If you roll the 'Slain' result for a fighter, you must remove that fighter from your warband roster. If that fighter has lesser artefacts or artefacts of power, these too are lost.

This will free up a space on your warband roster to add a new fighter (see opposite).

2D6	RESULT
2-3	Slain
4-5	Lost Favour
6+	Full Recovery

DESTINED FOR GREATNESS
If you roll the 'Slain' result for a fighter with the **Leader** runemark (☀), that fighter does not die. Instead treat the result as 'Lost Favour'.

LOST FAVOUR
If you roll the 'Lost Favour' result for a fighter that has gained any destiny levels, they lose one of those destiny levels. Otherwise, it has no effect.

FULL RECOVERY
If you roll the 'Full Recovery' result for a fighter, they suffer no effects.

Took part in a campaign battle	**1 glory point**
The leader of your opponent's warband was taken down	**1 glory point**
At least one third of the fighters in your opponent's warband were taken down	**1 glory point**
At least two thirds of the fighters in your opponent's warband were taken down	**1 glory point**
All the fighters in your opponent's warband were taken down	**1 glory point**
Won the battle	**5 glory points**

3. ROLL FOR DESTINY LEVELS

As your warband grows in power, certain fighters will begin to carve their own legends and stand apart as destined by the gods for glory.

After a campaign battle, you can make a destiny roll for each fighter from your warband that was not taken down during the battle. To do so, roll a dice; on the roll of a 6 that fighter gains a destiny level. Mark it on your warband roster by colouring in a destiny level icon.

A fighter can have up to 3 destiny levels at once. Each destiny level gives the following benefit in future campaign battles:

FAVOUR OF THE GODS

During a campaign battle, a player can choose to spend 1 of their fighter's destiny levels to re-roll 1 dice during an attack action made by that fighter. A spent destiny level replenishes at the end of the battle.

---

4. ADD AND REMOVE FIGHTERS

Players can choose to remove any fighters from their warband roster and add new fighters if there is space. This step uses the following rules:

- Any fighter except the leader can be removed from your warband roster. If you do so, any lesser artefacts or artefacts of power that fighter bears are lost.

- New fighters can be added to the warband roster. The limits on page 64 still apply when adding new fighters.

5. SEARCH FOR LESSER ARTEFACTS

There are many items of treasure that warbands may come to acquire. Some are much sought-after treasures found in hidden vaults, locked away since the Age of Myth amidst the ruins circling the Varanspire; others are more common and can be bartered for and obtained in the dark streets of anarchic settlements.

After a campaign battle, each player can make 1 search roll upon the lesser artefacts table (pg 68-69) to see if they obtain any lesser artefacts. To do so, roll 2 dice: the first indicates the tens roll, the second indicates the units roll (this is also referred to as a **D66**). Then, look up the corresponding result on the table.

BEARING LESSER ARTEFACTS

If your warband obtains a lesser artefact, you must decide which one of the fighters in your warband will bear it. A fighter can bear no more than 1 lesser artefact at any time, but can bear both a lesser artefact and an artefact of power (pg 70). Make a note on your warband roster of which fighter bears the lesser artefact.

A lesser artefact can never be swapped from one fighter to another, but if you wish for a fighter who already bears a lesser artefact to bear another, you can discard any lesser artefacts they have to allow you to do so.

USING LESSER ARTEFACTS

Each lesser artefact has a description of how they work on the lesser artefacts table. The rules for a lesser artefact will often refer to the **bearer**. The bearer is the fighter that bears that lesser artefact. Some lesser artefacts are labelled as **[Consumable]**. These give the bearer a one-use action they can make when activated. Once the action has been made, that lesser artefact is then removed from your warband roster.

Other lesser artefacts are labelled as **[Perishable]**. These lesser artefacts have rules which are always in play. This means they do not require an action to trigger their effect. However, at the end of a campaign battle, you must roll a dice for each **[Perishable]** lesser artefact borne by a fighter from your warband that took part in that battle. On a 4+, the lesser artefact retains its power and can remain on your warband roster. On a 1-3, the lesser artefact has lost its power: remove it from your warband roster.

SPINE-CRUSHER MAUL

As befits a warrior culture that favours the use of heavy, plated armour, the Iron Golems wield weapons that can pierce and crumple even the toughest metal. Spine-crusher mauls are crafted with spikes on the striking surface of the weapon. These maximise the lethality of each strike, puncturing armour and flesh and shattering the bones beneath.

'Not so eager with a shattered leg, are we?'

D66	LESSER ARTEFACT	
11-16	**NOTHING BUT DUST** You do not find a lesser artefact.	
21-22	**HEALING POTION** *This glass bottle is filled with a sparkling crimson liquid that heals and refreshes.*	**[Consumable]:** The bearer can use this lesser artefact as an action. If they do so, remove D6 damage points allocated to them.
23-24	**SWIFTWIND DUST** *This silvery powder sparkles like sunlight reflecting on water. When scattered into the air, it summons a magical zephyr that hastens those nearby.*	**[Consumable]:** The bearer can use this lesser artefact as an action. If they do so, add 1 to the Move characteristic of the bearer until the end of the battle.
25-26	**SILKSTRIDER WEBBING** *These lengths of sticky filament are capable of bearing immense weight.*	**[Perishable]:** The bearer does not suffer impact damage.
31-32	**SKIN OF FLAME-ALE** *Brewed in Aqshy, this potent and fiery concoction fills one with mighty strength, if only for a few, brief moments.*	**[Consumable]:** The bearer can use this lesser artefact as an action. If they do so, add 1 to the Strength characteristic of attack actions made by the bearer that have a Range characteristic of 3 or less until the end of the battle.
33-34	**JAR OF CHAMONIC GLOWFLIES** *Native to Chamon, these lambent insects are regarded as symbols of good fortune.*	**[Consumable]:** The bearer can use this lesser artefact as an action. If they do so, add 1 to the value of abilities (to a maximum of 6) used by the bearer until the end of the battle.
35-36	**CARVOLAX-SCALE ANKLET** *This iridescent trinket is shaped from enchanted carvolax scales, and grants the bearer a fraction of these avian hunters' lightning speed.*	**[Perishable]:** Add 1 to the Move characteristic of the bearer.
41-42	**CHRONOMANTIC DIAL** *This strange mechanical device thrums with arcane power. When activated, it quickens the passage of time for the bearer, but its chronomantic magic is soon exhausted.*	**[Consumable]:** The bearer can use this lesser artefact as an action. If they do so, add 1 to the Attacks characteristic of attack actions made by the bearer that have a Range characteristic of 3 or less until the end of the battle.
43-44	**IRONOAK SEED** *This is an enchanted seed of a mighty ironoak tree. When split open it releases a sap that swiftly hardens into an all but impenetrable shell.*	**[Consumable]:** The bearer can use this lesser artefact as an action. If they do so, add 1 to the Toughness characteristic of the bearer until the end of the battle.
45-46	**GREATER HEALING POTION** *This crystal decanter is filled with a life-giving liquid. When imbibed, it stitches flesh back together and mends shattered bone.*	**[Consumable]:** The bearer can use this lesser artefact as an action. If they do so, remove 2D6 damage points allocated to them.

D66	LESSER ARTEFACT	
51-52	**GODBEAST IDOL** *This crudely carved figurine of a long-dead godbeast still pulses with an ancient power.*	**[Perishable]:** Add 1 to the value of abilities (to a maximum of 6) used by the bearer.
53-54	**VIAL OF JABBERSLYTHE BLOOD** *This green-brown mucal substance reeks like stagnant swamp-water and rotten meat. A mere drop is enough to curdle the flesh and blacken the blood of an unfortunate victim.*	**[Consumable]:** The bearer can use this lesser artefact as an action. If they do so, add 1 to the damage points allocated by critical hits from attack actions made by bearer that have a Range characteristic of 3 or less until the end of the battle.
55-56	**UR-GOLD SIGIL** *This heavy pendant bears a single rune fashioned from glowing ur-gold, and grants the bearer formidable reserves of stamina and endurance.*	**[Perishable]:** Add 1 to the Toughness characteristic of the bearer.
61	**BLIGHT SERPENT VENOM** *This acidic fluid is taken from the corpse of a blight serpent. It eats through flesh and armour with terrifying ease.*	**[Perishable]:** Add 1 to the Strength characteristic of attack actions made by the bearer that have a Range characteristic of 3 or less.
62	**BAUBLE OF SHADOWS** *Swirling shadows spin within this glass orb. When shattered, a glamour of smoke engulfs the bearer.*	**[Consumable]:** The bearer can use this lesser artefact as an action. If they do so, that fighter can fly when making move actions until the end of their activation.
63	**FLASK OF AQUA GHYRANIS** *Found only in the springs of Ghyran, the magical properties of this water heal grievous wounds in an instant.*	**[Consumable]:** The bearer can use this lesser artefact as an action. If they do so, remove 3D6 damage points allocated to them.
64	**PENDANT OF BLOODGLASS** *Warm to the touch, the red-veined glass of this pendant emanates power.*	**[Perishable]:** Add 1 to the Attacks characteristic of attack actions made by the bearer that have a Range characteristic of 3 or less.
65	**RAVEN-FEATHER NECKLACE** *Raven feathers and bones criss-cross a strip of leather. What strange power could this crude item hold?*	**[Perishable]:** Add 1 to the damage points allocated by critical hits from attack actions made by bearer that have a Range characteristic of 3 or less.
66	**RUNE-ETCHED VAMBRACES** *The provenance of the strange language that covers these frayed leather bindings is unknown, but they can absorb a fearsome amount of physical damage.*	**[Perishable]:** Subtract 1 from the damage points allocated by hits and critical hits (to a minimum of 1) from attack actions that target the bearer.

Iron Golem
Prefector

The Unmade
Ascended One

6. ADVANCE ON THE CAMPAIGN PROGRESS TRACKER

After each campaign battle, both players can advance their warband on their campaign progress tracker 1 map point closer to the map point labelled 'Campaign Goal'.

The exception to this is if a player's warband is currently on a convergence map point. In this case, the player's warband can only advance if they played the corresponding convergence as the Aspirant warband (pg 65) and won the battle.

7. EARN ARTEFACTS OF POWER AND COMMAND TRAITS

After advancing your warband on the campaign progress tracker, if it has moved onto a map point marked 'Artefact of Power' or 'Command Trait', you will receive one of these as described below:

ARTEFACTS OF POWER

When you receive an artefact of power, pick one from the artefact of power table on your campaign quest. Alternatively, you can roll a D3 to determine which artefact of power you receive. Artefacts of power follow many of the same rules as lesser artefacts (pg 67). First, you must decide which fighter in your warband will bear it. A fighter can bear no more than 1 artefact of power at any time, but can bear both an artefact of power and a lesser artefact. Make a note on your warband roster of which fighter bears the artefact of power.

If the fighter you wish to bear the artefact of power already bears another, you can first give the old artefact of power to a fighter who bears none, and then give the first fighter the new artefact of power. This is the only time an artefact of power can be swapped from one fighter to another.

Each artefact of power has a description of how it works on the artefact of power table on each campaign quest. The rules for artefacts of power will often refer to the **bearer**. The bearer is the fighter that bears that artefact of power. Unlike lesser artefacts, artefacts of power are not labelled as [Consumable] or [Perishable]. An artefact of power instead provides a permanent benefit to the fighter that bears it.

COMMAND TRAITS

When you receive a command trait, pick one from the command trait table on your campaign quest. Alternatively, you can roll a D3 to determine which command trait you receive. A command trait is an additional bonus given to your leader.

Each command trait has a description of how it works on the command trait table on each campaign quest. Each provides a permanent benefit to the fighter.

A leader can only have 1 command trait. If you receive another (for example, if you move on to a new campaign quest after completing your first – see opposite), you can choose 1 of the other fighters in your warband to become a **favoured warrior** (see below).

FAVOURED WARRIORS

As your warband grows in power, some fighters will stand apart from their peers, having earned the favour of their leader through glorious feats in battle.

If your warband receives a command trait but your leader already has one, you can at that point nominate one of the other fighters in your warband to become the **favoured warrior**. This fighter receives the command trait instead of your leader, in the same manner a leader would (see above). A warband can only have 1 favoured warrior, so any further command traits gained are discarded. However, if the favoured warrior has been slain or removed from the warband when a new command trait is gained, you can nominate a new fighter to be the favoured warrior and give them that command trait.

When you nominate a fighter to become the favoured warrior, it can be fun to roll on the leader/ favoured warrior background table in the background tables section (pg 134-151) to see how their character has developed.

COMPLETING A CAMPAIGN QUEST

When your warband advances onto the map point marked as the campaign goal, your warband is said to have completed its quest. On the campaign quest you will find a page reference that will lead you to both the narrative outcome of your quest and your reward (a mighty artefact of power).

A warband that has completed its campaign quest can continue to play campaign battles but will no longer advance a map point during the aftermath sequence.

CHOOSING A NEW CAMPAIGN QUEST

Once they have completed their campaign quest, some warbands choose to remain and exert dominance over the territories they have conquered. For others, the call of their gods, the allure of fresh challenges and the promise of further artefacts of power leads them to leave behind their territories as they embark on a new quest.

If you have completed your campaign quest, you can choose to start a new campaign quest with the same warband roster. To do so, follow these steps:

1. **Choose a new campaign quest with a faction runemark that matches the one on your warband roster. Note down the new campaign quest on your warband roster.**

2. **Remove all dominated territories and glory points from your warband roster.**

3. **Move your warband back to the map point labelled 'Start' on the campaign progress tracker.**

Once a campaign quest has been completed, the same campaign quest cannot be started again by the same warband.

A blank version of this roster can be found on page 160.

WARCRY WARBAND ROSTER

WARBAND NAME		GLORY POINTS	DOMINATED TERRITORY
Chosen of Axranathos		7	

WARBAND ORIGIN	PLAYER NAME
Onyx Guard	Sam P.

CAMPAIGN QUEST
Conquer the Forge

CAMPAIGN PROGRESS TRACKER

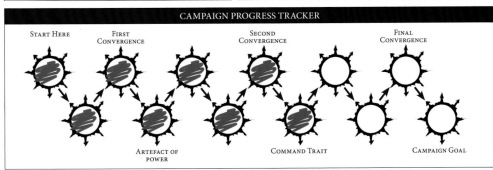

START HERE   FIRST CONVERGENCE   SECOND CONVERGENCE   FINAL CONVERGENCE

ARTEFACT OF POWER   COMMAND TRAIT   CAMPAIGN GOAL

LEADER / FAVOURED WARRIOR

LEADER / FAVOURED WARRIOR NAME	LEADER / FAVOURED WARRIOR BACKGROUND	ARTEFACTS
Sever Greel	Cruel Tyrant	Thrice-forged Hammer
COMMAND TRAIT	**DESTINY LEVELS**	Vial of Jabberslythe Blood
Iron-skinned	◉ ○ ○	

FIGHTERS

FIGHTER NAME	FIGHTER TYPE	ARTEFACTS	DESTINY LEVELS
Vos	Ogor Breacher	Pendant of Bloodglass	◉ ◉ ○
Broch Sorgev	Signifer		◉ ○ ○
Varka	Drillmaster	Ur-gold Sigil	○ ○ ○
Drammer	Iron Legionary		◉ ○ ○
Crola Scorl	Iron Legionary with Bolas	Pendant of Bloodglass	◉ ◉ ◉
Haddun	Armator	Swiftwind Dust	◉ ○ ○
Garn Dredj	Prefector		○ ○ ○
Malek	Ogor Breacher		◉ ○ ○
			○ ○ ○
			○ ○ ○

THE STORY SO FAR...

After nine bitterly fought battles, the Iron Golem warband known as the Chosen of Axranathos are well on their way to completing their campaign quest. With four areas of dominated territory they can now muster an additional 200 points' worth of fighters in each campaign battle, including up to 4 thralls. In their last battle the Iron Golems succeeded in their second convergence (on their second attempt), and now their leader has gained the 'Iron-skinned' command trait.

MATCHED PLAY

Matched play focuses on creating as fair and as level a playing field as possible, giving players the chance to show their tactical acumen. There are many times players may wish to play a matched play battle; for example, you and a friend might want to have a friendly grudge-match to decide who is the better player (well, this time, at least), or you might want to organise a tournament where many warbands battle it out to see who is crowned the victor. At times like this, matched play battles are exactly what you need.

In this section you will find rules for two types of matched play battles. The first are referred to as **Exhibition Battles**, and allow you and an opponent to quickly generate a fair battleplan with limited decks of battleplan cards. The second are referred to as **Pitched Battles**. These make use of 12 preset battleplans that are designed to challenge each player with a variety of tactical situations.

Lastly, this section provides a host of rules and guidelines for organising Warcry tournaments.

EXHIBITION BATTLES

If you want to test your cunning and skill in a one-off battle, an Exhibition Battle is ideal. To set up an Exhibition Battle, follow the rules for setting up a battle in the core rules as normal (pg 36-37), but before drawing the battleplan cards, first go through the deployment and victory decks and remove every card which does not have the **Symmetrical** runemark (⚝).

This will remove the asymmetrical cards from the deployment and victory decks and will enable you and your opponent to quickly set up a battle where both warbands have the same victory condition.

PITCHED BATTLES

Pitched Battles use preset battleplans designed to set a level playing field, and offer a wide range of tactical challenges. There are 12 Pitched Battle battleplans in total, divided into two sets of 6. Each of these sets encourages players to build a well-balanced warband if they are to master all the battleplans contained within, making them a great tool for both tournament organisers and two players looking for a challenging battle.

SETTING UP A PITCHED BATTLE

To set up a Pitched Battle between two players, follow all the core rules for setting up a battle as normal, but do not draw a deployment card or victory card. Instead, first draw a terrain card and twist card, then the players roll off. The winner chooses which battleplan table to roll on (A or B), and then rolls a dice to determine which battleplan is used.

Once the battleplan has been determined, resolve the terrain, deployment, victory and twist rules in the order described in the core rules (pg 36-37).

BATTLEPLAN TABLE A
1 Drawn and Quartered
2 Bloodmarked
3 Sudden Death
4 Raze
5 No Mercy
6 The Comet

BATTLEPLAN TABLE B
1 Hunt for Glory
2 Shock and Awe
3 Burn and Pillage
4 No Quarter
5 Vanquish
6 The Prize

WARCRY TOURNAMENT ROSTER

Player: Sam P   Warband Name: The Jagged Talons

DAGGER

NAME	FIGHTER TYPE	POINTS	DESTINY LEVELS	LESSER ARTEFACT
Ugula	Plains-runner	55		
Shroya the Hungerer	Beastspeaker	125		
Bloodtooth	Rocktusk Prowler	180	▨	Blight Serpent Venom

SHIELD

NAME	FIGHTER TYPE	POINTS	DESTINY LEVELS	LESSER ARTEFACT
Ekuth Spinerender	Heart-eater	180	▨	
Kurgo Bonecrusher	First Fang	140	▨	
Tenyet Truthspeaker	Preytaker with Fanged Axe	105		
Gantul Vorrnslayer	Preytaker with Sawtooth Blade	105		

HAMMER

NAME	FIGHTER TYPE	POINTS	DESTINY LEVELS	LESSER ARTEFACT
Thuka	Plains-runner	55		
Makat	Plains-runner	55		

THE CHAMPION	HIDDEN ARTEFACT	HOLD THE CENTRE	PURGE	HIGHER GROUND	THE ARCHITECT
☀	☀	☀	☀	☀	☀

A blank version of this roster can be found on page 161.

BATTLEPLAN TABLE A

BATTLEPLAN 1: DRAWN AND QUARTERED

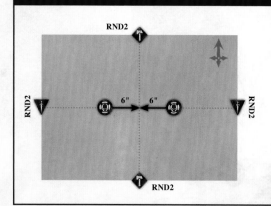

To know victory, we must seize this entire region.

Starting with the player who won the priority roll, players alternate placing objectives until they have placed 2 objectives each. Each objective can be placed anywhere on the battlefield more than 3" horizontally from the centre of the battlefield and more than 4" from the battlefield edge and any other objectives.

At the end of each battle round, each player scores 1 victory point for each objective they control. The battle ends after 3 battle rounds. When the battle ends, the player with the most victory points wins the battle.

BATTLEPLAN 2: BLOODMARKED

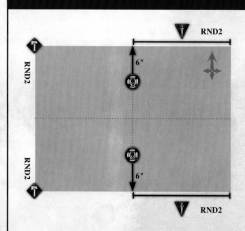

The gods mark those whose doom draws nigh.

At the start of the combat phase of the first battle round, starting with the player who has the initiative, each player picks a fighter in their warband to be **bloodmarked**. The fighter must be on the battlefield.

A player wins the battle as soon as their opponent's bloodmarked fighter is taken down.

At the end of the fourth battle round, and each subsequent battle round, any bloodmarked fighters within 4" of the battlefield edge immediately count as being taken down (if playing a campaign battle, do not make an injury roll for fighters taken down in this manner).

BATTLEPLAN 3: SUDDEN DEATH

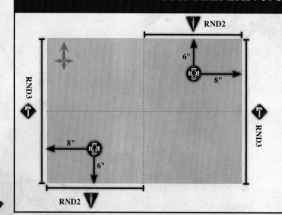

They who hold both idols can unleash the Dark Gods' curse.

Starting with the player who won the priority roll, players place 1 objective each, anywhere on the battlefield more than 8" from any other objectives and more than 6" from the battlefield edge.

If a player controls both objectives at the end of a battle round, that player wins the battle.

BATTLEPLAN 4: RAZE

Drive into their lands like a spear into a foe's gut, and burn all you see.

Starting with the player who won the priority roll, each player picks a different battlefield edge to be their warband's territory. Any fighter that finishes a move action within 1" of an enemy warband's territory can enter it. Remove the fighter from the battlefield but do not count them as being taken down.

The battle ends after 4 battle rounds. When the battle ends, count the number of fighters that entered an enemy warband's territory. The player with the most wins the battle.

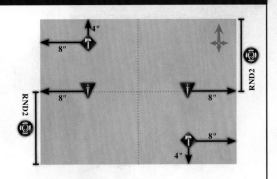

BATTLEPLAN 5: NO MERCY

Reap them like the crops grown by Sigmar's weakling thralls.

A player wins the battle as soon as half or more of their opponent's fighters have been taken down.

At the end of the fourth battle round, and each subsequent battle round, any fighters within 4" of the battlefield edge immediately count as being taken down (if playing a campaign battle, do not make an injury roll for fighters taken down in this manner).

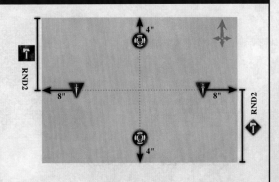

BATTLEPLAN 6: THE COMET

Seize the riches that fall from the skies.

Roll a dice at the start of the second battle round, before the hero phase. On a 1-4, place 1 objective on the battlefield floor at the centre of the corresponding table quarter, as shown on the map below. On a 5-6, place 1 objective on the battlefield floor at the centre of the battlefield. The battle ends after 3 battle rounds. When the battle ends, the player that controls the objective wins the battle.

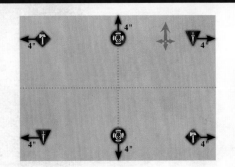

1	2
5-6	
3	4

BATTLEPLAN TABLE B

BATTLEPLAN 1: HUNT FOR GLORY

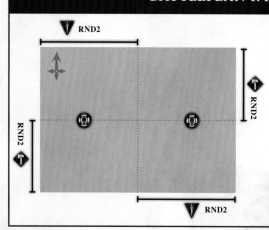

Anoint the ritual sites in honour of the Dark Gods.

Place 1 objective at the centre of the battlefield on the battlefield floor. Then, starting with the player who won the priority roll, each player places 1 objective on the battlefield more than 9" horizontally from any other objectives and more than 4" from the battlefield edge.

At the end of each battle round, each player scores 1 victory point for each objective they control. The battle ends after 3 battle rounds. When the battle ends, the player with the most victory points wins the battle.

BATTLEPLAN 2: SHOCK AND AWE

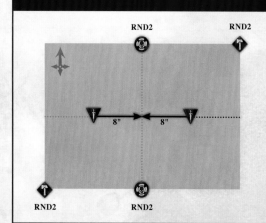

Slaughter sends a stark message.

A player wins the battle as soon as every fighter in their opponent's Dagger is taken down.

At the end of the fourth battle round, and each subsequent battle round, any Dagger fighters within 4" of the battlefield edge immediately count as being taken down (if playing a campaign battle, do not make an injury roll for fighters taken down in this manner).

BATTLEPLAN 3: BURN AND PILLAGE

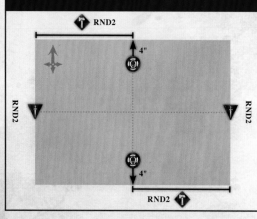

Leave naught but ashes blowing upon the bitter winds of war.

Starting with the player who won the priority roll, players alternate placing objectives until they have placed 3 objectives each. Each objective can be placed anywhere on the battlefield more than 4" from the battlefield edge and any other objectives.

A player can choose to **burn** an objective they control at the end of a battle round. To do so, remove it from play. The first player to burn 4 objectives wins the battle.

BATTLEPLAN 4: NO QUARTER

Purge them from these lands and claim the territory for your own.

The battlefield is divided halfway along its width and length into quarters of equal dimensions.

At the end of each battle round, each player scores 1 victory point for each quarter of the battlefield that has more fighters from their warband wholly within it than it does enemy fighters. Models within more than one quarter do not contribute towards the number of models in any quarter.

The battle ends after 3 battle rounds. When the battle ends, the player with the most victory points wins the battle.

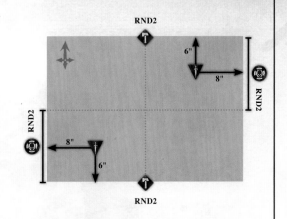

BATTLEPLAN 5: VANQUISH

Disarmed, the foe has no recourse but surrender.

A player wins the battle as soon as every fighter in their opponent's Hammer is taken down.

At the end of the fourth battle round, and each subsequent battle round, any Hammer fighters within 4" of the battlefield edge immediately count as being taken down (if playing a campaign battle, do not make an injury roll for fighters taken down in this manner).

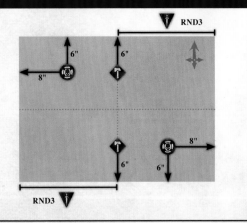

BATTLEPLAN 6: THE PRIZE

Beyond a web of illusion and trickery lies the prize.

The players roll off and the winner places 1 treasure token on the battlefield within 6" horizontally of the centre of the battlefield.

The battle ends after 3 battle rounds. When the battle ends, the player whose fighter is carrying the treasure wins the battle.

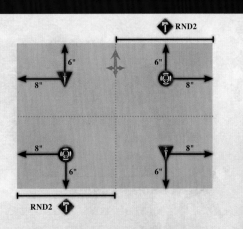

TOURNAMENTS

A Warcry tournament involves a group of players playing a series of tournament rounds before the player with the highest score is crowned the overall champion. Warcry makes an excellent tournament game due to the fast-paced nature of the game and the small footprint it has on the tabletop. Whether they are vying to be the champion, or just looking for a day or weekend of action-packed gaming, players will find Warcry tournaments to be both challenging and rewarding. The following section offers guidelines on how to run a successful Warcry tournament.

WARBANDS

Before attending the tournament, each player prepares a 1000-point warband following the core rules for mustering a warband. They also separate their warband into a Dagger, Shield and Hammer following the core rules, and note down on their **tournament roster** (pg 161) which fighters are in each of these battle groups. This is set for the duration of the tournament, so players cannot alter their warband or groupings from battle to battle.

TOURNAMENT ROUNDS

A tournament is played in a series of tournament rounds. Each round, the tournament organiser will randomly determine the battleplan that all players will play and the twist card that will be in play. The two battleplan tables for Pitched Battles (pg 73) are each designed to be self-enclosed sets of battleplans that encourage players to bring warbands with a good mix of fighters, and to spread their fighters across their Dagger, Shield and Hammer in an even manner.

In the first tournament round, the players are randomly drawn an opponent. In each subsequent tournament round, the players with the two highest tournament points scores play each other, as do the players with the next two highest tournament points scores, and so on.

Players are awarded tournament points after each battle as follows:

Won the battle and less than half of the fighters in your warband were taken down	20 points
Won the battle and half or more of the fighters in your warband were taken down	15 points
Lost the battle and half or more of the fighters in your opponent's warband were taken down	5 points
Lost the battle and less than half of the fighters in your opponent's warband were taken down	0 points
Completed your Hidden Agenda (see opposite)	1 point

HIDDEN AGENDAS

Hidden Agendas are secondary objectives players attempt to achieve during the tournament. There are 6 Hidden Agendas to choose from. Players each choose a Hidden Agenda at the start of the hero phase in the first battle round and reveal them simultaneously (for example, by placing a dice under their hand and revealing them at the same time).

A player cannot choose the same Hidden Agenda twice during a tournament, and any Hidden Agenda they have previously chosen must be clearly marked on their tournament roster.

ESCALATION TOURNAMENTS

Many players are keen to incorporate some aspects of Warcry campaigns into a tournament setting. This allows players to enjoy the narrative elements a campaign brings to a competitive environment. This style of tournament is referred to as an **escalation tournament**. To run an escalation tournament, use the guidelines on running tournaments, opposite, with the following amendments:

1. For each tournament round after the first, each player receives 1 additional wild dice in the hero phase of the first battle round. For example, in the third battle of the tournament, each player would receive 2 additional wild dice in the hero phase of the first battle round.

2. At the start of each battle after the first, the players roll off. Starting with the player who won the roll-off, each player picks 1 fighter to gain a destiny level (pg 67), and then rolls for 1 lesser artefact on the lesser artefact table (pg 68-69). Destiny levels gained are in effect for the rest of the tournament. Lesser artefacts gained before each battle are automatically removed after the end of that battle.

1. THE CHAMPION	2. HIDDEN ARTEFACT	3. HOLD THE CENTRE
At the end of the battle, you complete this quest if the enemy leader has been taken down but your leader has not.	Secretly note down one of your fighters to be the bearer of the hidden artefact. The fighter must be on the battlefield. At the start of the combat phase of the third battle round, reveal which of your fighters bears the hidden artefact. At the end of the battle, you complete this quest if the bearer has not been taken down.	At the end of the battle, you complete this quest if 1 or more friendly fighters are within 6" horizontally of the centre of the battlefield and no enemy fighters are within 6" horizontally of the centre of the battlefield.
4. PURGE	5. HIGHER GROUND	6. THE ARCHITECT
Secretly note down one of the quarters of the battlefield: north-east, north-west, south-east or south-west. At the end of the battle, you complete this quest if 1 or more friendly fighters are wholly within that quarter of the battlefield and no enemy fighters are wholly within that quarter of the battlefield.	At the end of the battle, you complete this quest if 1 or more friendly fighters are vertically 3" above the battlefield floor and no enemy fighters are vertically 3" above the battlefield floor.	At the end of the battle, you complete this quest if your opponent's warband has had half or more of its fighters taken down, but your warband has had less than half of its fighters taken down.

Untamed Beasts Preytaker

CAMPAIGN SECTION

Used alongside the rules in the narrative play section (pg 62-71), this section contains all the resources you need to embark upon your warband's quest for glory and power. On the following pages you will find campaign quests for every faction playable in Warcry. Whatever allegiance you choose, you will brave the deadly wilds of the Eightpoints and make war upon your rivals, gaining unique skills and artefacts as you spread your influence across the land. As you progress upon your individual story path, you will come to several critical junctures, each with an exciting accompanying narrative. Each campaign quest culminates in a thrilling final battle. Should you triumph, you will earn a mighty reward, and perhaps even gain the favour of the Everchosen himself...

'Let the Dark Gods bear witness to our glory, and let our foes tremble at our passing!'

CONQUER THE FORGE

This land is as hard and merciless as tempered iron. You know with certainty that it is here the Iron Golems will craft their finest creations, weapons of ruin and devastation that are truly worthy of the Everchosen's legions. First you must locate a suitable forge for your great work. Many of the savages in this land carry crude and brittle blades, but you have witnessed others wielding weapons of greater quality, crafted here in the Eightpoints. Seek out these craftsmen and conquer their forge-works in the name of the Iron Golems.

FINAL CONVERGENCE
Varanthax's Maw

SECOND CONVERGENCE
Gates of the Maw

FIRST CONVERGENCE
Weapon Traders' Camp

TERRITORY RULES

Raise Monolith: *The monoliths of the Iron Golems are stark obelisks of iron crafted from the melted weapons of defeated foes.*

You can spend 10 glory points to dominate a territory by raising a monolith. Mark on your warband roster how many territories you dominate. Dominating territory offers the following bonuses:

For each territory dominated by your warband, you can include 1 thrall in your warband when mustering for a campaign battle. Thralls included in this manner are not added to your warband roster, and cost points like any other fighter.

For each territory dominated by your warband, increase the points you have available to spend on fighters when mustering your warband for a campaign battle by 50. Include the points costs for any thralls in your warband when mustering your warband. Thralls are not added to your warband roster and can never gain destiny levels, bear artefacts or be chosen to become a favoured warrior.

D3	ARTEFACT OF POWER
1	**Black Iron Plate:** *This suit of heavy plate is crafted from rune-marked volcanic metal.* Subtract 1 from the damage points allocated by hits and critical hits (to a minimum of 1) from attack actions that target the bearer.
2	**Thrice-forged Hammer:** *All imperfections have been removed from this mighty weapon by relentless, obsessive forge-work.* Add 1 to the Attacks characteristic of attack actions made by the bearer that have a Range characteristic of 3 or less.
3	**Chaos Talisman:** *This eight-pointed star was tempered with the blood of sacrificial victims.* Once per battle, the bearer can use this artefact as an action. If they do so, until the end of the battle round, add 2 to their Toughness characteristic.

D3	COMMAND TRAIT
1	**Iron-skinned:** *The flesh of this warrior has become hard and calloused from exposure to the strange chemical ash-fall of the Ferrium Mountains.* Add 1 to the Toughness characteristic of this fighter.
2	**Brute:** *Their comrades contest that not even the dragon Axranathos could lay this warrior low.* Add 5 to the Wounds characteristic of this fighter.
3	**Unpredictable:** *This warrior is a cunning strategist who exploits their enemies' tendency to dismiss Iron Golem soldiers as simple brutes.* If this fighter is included in your warband, you begin the battle with 1 additional wild dice.

FIRST CONVERGENCE: THE TEMPERED BLADE

Many of the feral savages you have encountered amidst the wilds of the Eightpoints wield little more than rusted daggers and bone clubs. They are quickly smashed to bloody ruin by your finely crafted warhammers. Yet there are bands of killers who offer a worthier challenge, and carry blades and armour of competent design. You approach the war camp of one such group now. Crush them and take their weapon caches.

BATTLEPLAN
Terrain: See map.

Deployment:
Decapitate

The Aspirant warband uses the red deployment points.

Victory: The Raid

The Aspirant warband is the attacker.

Twist: Draw a twist card as normal.

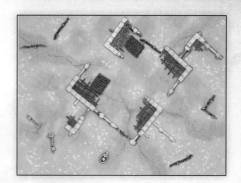

SECOND CONVERGENCE: INTO THE MAW

The blades you claimed are wrought from black iron, shaped with consummate skill. Under torture, one of their previous owners reveals that his band traded a hundred slaves to the duardin forgemaster Korrgad for the weapons. Korrgad rules over Varanthax's Maw, an enormous forge complex built into the skull of a great drake. You travel to the mountain fastness, and find it heavily guarded by mercenaries. You must swiftly eliminate Korrgad's scouts and sentries.

BATTLEPLAN
Terrain: See map.

Deployment:
Refused Flank

The Aspirant warband uses the red deployment points.

Victory: Crush

The Aspirant warband is the attacker.

Twist: Draw a twist card as normal.

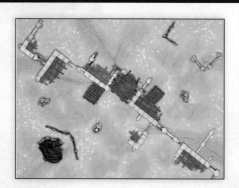

FINAL CONVERGENCE: HOSTILE TAKEOVER

Bubbling lava spills through the fangs of Varanthax's Maw, pouring into great channels and smelting pits. The bittersweet tang of molten iron meets your nostrils, and you nod with grim satisfaction. This forge will serve well, once you have dealt with its master. Shouts and cries split the air as Korrgad's hired killers rush to defend the slavemaster's domain. Slaughter all who stand against you, and take this stronghold for the glory of the Iron Golems!

BATTLEPLAN
Terrain: See map.

Deployment:
Stranglehold

The Aspirant warband uses the blue deployment points.

Victory: No Mercy

Twist: Draw a twist card as normal.

CAMPAIGN OUTCOME
If the Aspirant warband is the winner, they complete this campaign quest. Turn to page 128 to see the outcome and claim your reward.

CURSED METAL

A weapon is only as good as the material from which it is wrought. Those blades you have recovered from slain foes in the Eightpoints are as weak as their erstwhile bearers. Without a source of strong metal, you will never be able to forge weapons worthy of Archaon's armies. Word reaches you of shipments passing through the Kardeb Ashwaste, carrying rare ore and heading for the forges of Carngrad. Perhaps the metals being transported are of fitting quality.

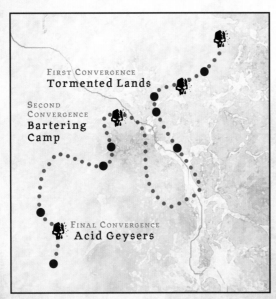

FIRST CONVERGENCE
Tormented Lands

SECOND CONVERGENCE
Bartering Camp

FINAL CONVERGENCE
Acid Geysers

TERRITORY RULES

Raise Monolith: *The monoliths of the Iron Golems are stark obelisks of iron, crafted from the melted weapons of defeated foes.*

You can spend 10 glory points to dominate a territory by raising a monolith. Mark on your warband roster how many territories you dominate. Dominating territory offers the following bonuses:

For each territory dominated by your warband, you can include 1 thrall in your warband when mustering for a campaign battle. Thralls included in this manner are not added to your warband roster, and cost points like any other fighter.

For each territory dominated by your warband, increase the points you have available to spend on fighters when mustering your warband for a campaign battle by 50. Include the points costs for any thralls in your warband when mustering your warband. Thralls are not added to your warband roster and can never gain destiny levels, bear artefacts or be chosen to become a favoured warrior.

D3	ARTEFACT OF POWER
1	**Infernal Helm:** *The daemonic visage of this helmet is enough to strike terror into any foe.* Once per battle, the bearer can use this artefact as an action. If they do so, subtract 1 from the Attacks characteristic (to a minimum of 1) of attack actions made by visible enemy fighters while they are within 6" of the bearer until the end of the battle round.
2	**Gore-slick Hammer:** *Crafted with cursed invictunite, this hammer constantly seeps caustic blood.* Add 1 to the Strength characteristic of attack actions made by the bearer that have a Range characteristic of 3 or less.
3	**Rune-etched Armour:** *This hauberk of black iron is marked with enervating sigils.* Subtract 1 from the Strength characteristic of attack actions (to a minimum of 1) made by enemy fighters while they are within 1" of the bearer.

D3	COMMAND TRAIT
1	**Resourceful:** *This warrior never wastes an opportunity, and ruthlessly exploits their foe's every mistake.* Add 1 to the value of abilities used by this fighter (to a maximum of 6).
2	**Mighty Strength:** *A lifetime of brutal forge-work has granted this warrior formidable strength.* Add 1 to the Strength characteristic of attack actions made by this fighter.
3	**Master Forger:** *The weapons crafted by this warrior are exquisite tools of death.* Add 1 to the damage points allocated to enemy fighters by each hit or critical hit from attack actions made by this fighter that have a Range characteristic of 3 or less.

FIRST CONVERGENCE: CARAVAN AMBUSH

Weapons are the prime currency in the Eightpoints. The barter pits of Carngrad are filled with all manner of killing instruments, and your keen eye soon separates poorly fashioned trash from keen-edged blades. You hear tell that the finest swords are transported across the Tormented Lands by armed caravans guarded by hired killers. You plan to prepare an ambush and take this prize for the Iron Golems.

BATTLEPLAN
Terrain: See map.

Deployment: Ambush

The Aspirant warband uses the red deployment points.

Victory: Steal the Prize

The Aspirant warband is the attacker.

Twist: Draw a twist card as normal.

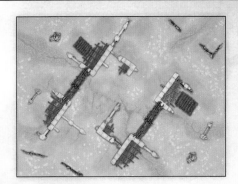

SECOND CONVERGENCE: FOLLOWING THE TRAIL

The caravan you ambushed was transporting tainted invictunite, an incredibly rare and resilient metal suffused with the warping energies of Chaos. It is a fine material to work with, but you require much more. You follow the trail taken by the caravan, and come across a bartering camp filled with slavers, scavengers and merchants dealing in weapons. Burn the camp to ashes and take prisoners; one of these wretches must know where the invictunite is being mined.

BATTLEPLAN
Terrain: See map.

Deployment:
Blood Rush

The Aspirant warband uses the red deployment points.

Victory:
Scorched Earth

The Aspirant warband is the attacker.

Twist: Draw a twist card as normal.

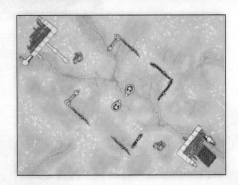

FINAL CONVERGENCE: THE BLAZING COMET

You discover that blazing comets formed from pure invictunite have been raining down across the Bilegush, a rancid stretch of lowland dotted with geysers that spew flesh-melting acid. You see the fiery trail of such a comet now, burning with sickening colour as it passes through the storms of fell magic that scar the sky. You must reach the impact site swiftly, before the comet is claimed by a rival warband.

BATTLEPLAN
Terrain: See map.

Deployment:
Unseen Blade

The Aspirant warband uses the red deployment points.

Victory: The Comet

Twist: Draw a twist card as normal.

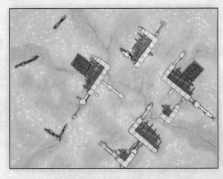

CAMPAIGN OUTCOME
If the Aspirant warband is the winner, they complete this campaign quest. Turn to page 128 to see the outcome and claim your reward.

THE HUNT FOR FIRESCAR

Archaon the Everchosen will never grant the Untamed Beasts a place in his great hunt unless they offer worthy tribute. The tribe must prove its devotion and its power. You will hunt the fiercest of beasts – the legendary ash-drake known as Firescar, a serpentine horror that has preyed upon the Bloodwind Spoil for as long as any can remember. When you travel to the gates of the Varanspire with that fell beast's skull upon your shoulders, its hot blood slathered across your flesh, surely then the Everchosen will know the might of the Untamed Beasts.

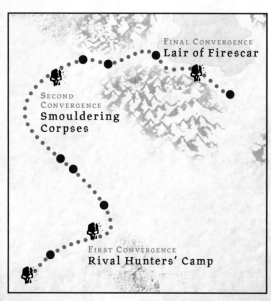

FINAL CONVERGENCE
Lair of Firescar

SECOND CONVERGENCE
Smouldering Corpses

FIRST CONVERGENCE
Rival Hunters' Camp

TERRITORY RULES

Raise Monolith: *The Untamed Beasts pile the skins of slain beasts and the ruined corpses of their foes as an offering to the Devourer of Existence.*

You can spend 10 glory points to dominate a territory by raising a monolith. Mark on your warband roster how many territories you dominate. Dominating territory offers the following bonuses:

For each territory dominated by your warband, you can include 1 thrall in your warband when mustering for a campaign battle. Thralls included in this manner are not added to your warband roster, and cost points like any other fighter.

For each territory dominated by your warband, increase the points you have available to spend on fighters when mustering your warband for a campaign battle by 50. Include the points costs for any thralls in your warband when mustering your warband. Thralls are not added to your warband roster and can never gain destiny levels, bear artefacts or be chosen to become a favoured warrior.

D3	ARTEFACT OF POWER
1	**Skin Wolf Pelt:** *Stripped from a slain lycanthropic horror, this hide grants its wearer bestial power.* Add 1 to the value of abilities used by the bearer (to a maximum of 6).
2	**Fanged Helm:** *This osseous helm was carved from the skull of a voracious predator whose teeth remain razor sharp.* Add 1 to the Attacks characteristic of attack actions made by the bearer that have a Range characteristic of 3 or less.
3	**Hookbeak Gauntlet:** *A hookbeak's serrated bill is a fearsome disembowelling weapon.* Add 1 to the damage points allocated to enemy fighters by each hit or critical hit from attack actions made by this fighter that have a Range characteristic of 3 or less.

D3	COMMAND TRAIT
1	**Bestial Speed:** *This warrior is as swift as a hunting shadowprowler, and just as deadly.* Add 1 to the Move characteristic of this fighter.
2	**Thick Hide:** *This warrior has consumed the armoured hide of thundering behemoths, and gained a portion of their resilience.* Add 1 to the Toughness characteristic of this fighter.
3	**Wild Fighter:** *This warrior fights with pure untamed savagery.* If this fighter is included in your warband, you begin the battle with 1 additional wild dice.

FIRST CONVERGENCE: THE HUNTERS, HUNTED

You race across the jagged, broken plains of the Eightpoints, your pack following close behind. The visions of the shamans guide you onwards, for the glory of the Untamed Beasts. The creature they call Firescar is close. You can smell its acrid reek upon the wind, and your blood simmers with eagerness for the kill. Yet you are not the only warband on The Hunt. Your rivals follow in your wake, no doubt wishing to claim this worthy kill in your stead. Turn the tables on your foes with a night-time assault, and burn their camp to ashes.

BATTLEPLAN
Terrain: See map.

Deployment: Draw a deployment card as normal.

Victory:
Scorched Earth

The Aspirant warband is the attacker.

Twist:
Dead of Night

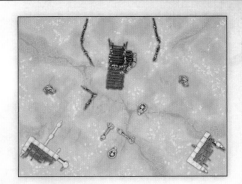

SECOND CONVERGENCE: ASH AND BONE

Firescar leaves nothing but ash and smouldering corpses in its wake as it rampages across the wilderness. This trail of devastation has drawn forth predators and scavengers both. You must read the charred entrails of those beasts slain by the monstrous creature in order to divine the location of its lair. Swiftness is essential, for even now the predators and hunters of the Bloodwind Spoil descend upon the bodies to feast and plunder.

BATTLEPLAN
Terrain: See map.

Deployment: Draw a deployment card as normal.

Victory: No Mercy

Twist:
Rampaging Beasts

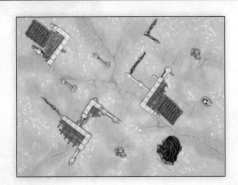

FINAL CONVERGENCE: BUTCHERY AT BLOOD LAKE

The visions lead you to Blood Lake Basin, a valley encircled by jagged cliffs of black rock. A trail of fire and spitting embers leads you through the mountainous passes and into this strange, primordial land. You follow it to the ruined skeleton of an ancient temple. Charred skulls and bones the height of a man litter the ground. You see movement amidst the shimmering heat-haze ahead: rival hunters, come to claim Firescar's head. Kill them swiftly, before they interfere with your prize.

BATTLEPLAN
Terrain: See map.

Deployment:
The Hunt

The Aspirant warband uses the blue deployment points.

Victory: Vanquish

Twist: Draw a twist card as normal.

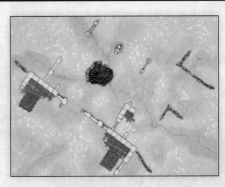

CAMPAIGN OUTCOME
If the Aspirant warband is the winner, they complete this campaign quest. Turn to page 128 to see the outcome and claim your reward.

TOOTH AND CLAW

Even amidst the sacred wilds of the Eightpoints, your rivals cling to the falsehoods of civilisation, cowering behind bladed palisades and high watchtowers. Such cowardice disgusts you. The predatory creatures of the Bloodwind Spoil are many and terrible. You will drive them into a killing frenzy, and stoke their savage fury until they descend upon the slums of Carngrad in a tide of ripping fangs and tearing claws. Then the weak-blooded denizens of this realm will know the true might of the Untamed Beasts.

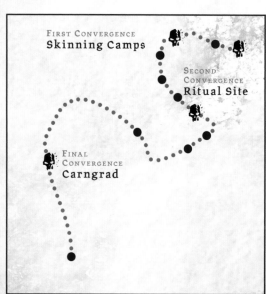

FIRST CONVERGENCE
Skinning Camps

SECOND CONVERGENCE
Ritual Site

FINAL CONVERGENCE
Carngrad

TERRITORY RULES

Raise Monolith: *The Untamed Beasts pile the skins of slain beasts and the ruined corpses of their foes as an offering to the Devourer of Existence.*

You can spend 10 glory points to dominate a territory by raising a monolith. Mark on your warband roster how many territories you dominate. Dominating territory offers the following bonuses:

For each territory dominated by your warband, you can include 1 thrall in your warband when mustering for a campaign battle. Thralls included in this manner are not added to your warband roster, and cost points like any other fighter.

For each territory dominated by your warband, increase the points you have available to spend on fighters when mustering your warband for a campaign battle by 50. Include the points costs for any thralls in your warband when mustering your warband. Thralls are not added to your warband roster and can never gain destiny levels, bear artefacts or be chosen to become a favoured warrior.

D3	ARTEFACT OF POWER
1	**Blood-soaked Furs:** *These thick shamanic furs have been anointed with the gore of a worthy kill.* Subtract 1 from the damage points allocated by hits and critical hits (to a minimum of 1) from attack actions that target the bearer.
2	**Prowler-fang Axe:** *This axe is tipped with the sabre-like canines of a shadowprowler, and punches through armour with ease.* Add 1 to the damage points allocated to enemy fighters by each hit or critical hit from attack actions made by this fighter that have a Range characteristic of 3 or less.
3	**Primordial Fetish:** *This talisman of cured flesh resonates bestial fury.* Once per battle, the bearer can use this artefact as an action. If they do so, until the end of the battle round, add 1 to the Strength characteristic of attack actions made by friendly fighters while they are within 6" of the bearer.

D3	COMMAND TRAIT
1	**Reckless Flurry:** *This warrior leaps upon their foe in a blood-addled frenzy.* Add 1 to the Attacks characteristic of attack actions made by this fighter that have a Range characteristic of 3 or less.
2	**Bestial Vigour:** *This warrior has the endurance of an armoured flathorn.* Add 5 to the Wounds characteristic of this fighter.
3	**Resilient:** *This warrior can fight on even when riddled with grievous wounds.* When this fighter is picked to activate, you can remove 1 damage point allocated to them.

FIRST CONVERGENCE: THE KILLING WILDS

Skinning camps line the bluffs to the north of Carngrad, staining the cracked earth red with seeping blood. Here, huntmasters and findsmen bring the corpses of slain beasts or captured enemies and strip their valuable hides, trading these grisly treasures for weapons, slaves or other goods. Soaked with gore and rife with pain and fear, this ground will serve well as the site for your ritual. Lay waste to the camps and slay the beast-hunters that reside within. None can be allowed to interfere with what is to come.

BATTLEPLAN
Terrain: See map.

Deployment:
Divide and Slaughter

The Aspirant warband uses the red deployment points.

Victory:
Seize Territory

The Aspirant warband is the attacker.

Twist: Draw a twist card as normal.

SECOND CONVERGENCE: THE SCENT OF PREY

From your vantage point overlooking Carngrad, you partake in rituals of The Hunt. Clad in the bloody skins of slain predators, your shamans dance and howl, their flint knives carving the flesh of still-living prisoners. The pooling blood and tormented screams draw forth the beasts of the wastes in great numbers. You must raise the bone-totems, which contain the trapped spirits of raging monsters. Their primal magic will drive the gathering beasts into a blood-frenzy.

BATTLEPLAN
Terrain: See map.

Deployment:
Defiant Stand

The Aspirant warband uses the blue deployment points.

Victory: The Ritual

The Aspirant warband is the defender.

Twist: Draw a twist card as normal.

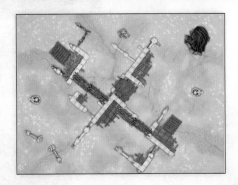

FINAL CONVERGENCE: FEEDING FRENZY

The tide of frenzied beasts sweeps down upon the outskirts of Carngrad. You and your warriors run amidst the throng of bodies, your own battle cries no less animalistic than the creatures you fight beside. You roar in triumph as you hear the screams of prey brought down and devoured alive. This night, all will fear the might of the Untamed Beasts.

BATTLEPLAN
Terrain: See map.

Deployment: Draw a deployment card as normal.

Victory: Purge

The Aspirant warband is the attacker.

Twist: Rampaging Beasts

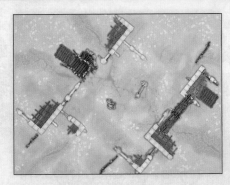

CAMPAIGN OUTCOME
If the Aspirant warband is the winner, they complete this campaign quest. Turn to page 129 to see the outcome and claim your reward.

WAR OF TALONS

The stroke of a knife can bring down a kingdom or end an empire. There is great power in murder, and there are no finer practitioners of the art than the Corvus Cabal – it is why the call of the Everchosen summoned you from afar. It is common knowledge on the streets of Carngrad that two of the Seven Talons who rule over the city – Vesca Mirror-Eye and Brand Headsplitter – are on the verge of bloodshed. Both Talons command many hundreds of hired killers. If the right throats are cut, open conflict will break out between them and the streets would be littered with carrion – a fine offering for the Great Gatherer.

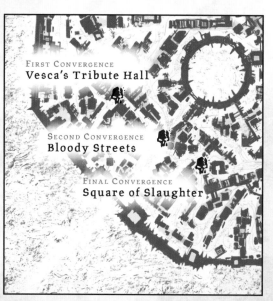

FIRST CONVERGENCE
Vesca's Tribute Hall

SECOND CONVERGENCE
Bloody Streets

FINAL CONVERGENCE
Square of Slaughter

TERRITORY RULES

Raise Monolith: *The Cabal impales the butchered corpses of those it has slain upon the branches of trees and the spires of buildings, along with offerings of loot for the Great Gatherer.*

You can spend 10 glory points to dominate a territory by raising a monolith. Mark on your warband roster how many territories you dominate. Dominating territory offers the following bonuses:

For each territory dominated by your warband, you can include 1 thrall in your warband when mustering for a campaign battle. Thralls included in this manner are not added to your warband roster, and cost points like any other fighter.

For each territory dominated by your warband, increase the points you have available to spend on fighters when mustering your warband for a campaign battle by 50. Include the points costs for any thralls in your warband when mustering your warband. Thralls are not added to your warband roster and can never gain destiny levels, bear artefacts or be chosen to become a favoured warrior.

D3	ARTEFACT OF POWER
1	**Eyeball Pendant:** *This gruesome trophy bestows great accuracy upon its bearer.* When the bearer uses the '**Raven Dart**' ability, roll 2 dice instead of 1 (allocate damage for each result separately).
2	**Shadow-blessed Dagger:** *This lethal blade appears to be formed from a wisp of shadow.* Add 1 to the damage points allocated to enemy fighters by each hit or critical hit from attack actions made by this fighter that have a Range characteristic of 3 or less.
3	**Pinion of the Great Gatherer:** *This sleek, black feather grants worshippers of the Great Gatherer unnatural speed and grace.* Once per battle, the bearer can use this artefact as an action. If they do so, add 1 to the Move characteristic of friendly fighters within 6" of the bearer when the bearer uses this artefact, until the end of the battle round.

D3	COMMAND TRAIT
1	**Prey-bird's Swiftness:** *This warrior is unnaturally swift and agile.* Add 1 to the Move characteristic of this fighter.
2	**Tendrils of Shadow:** *Tendrils of shadow-stuff wreath this warrior, obscuring their every motion.* Add 3 to the Toughness characteristic of this fighter while it is targeted by an attack action made by an enemy fighter more than 3" away.
3	**Sinister Familiar:** *This leader's crow has learnt the dark tongue and whispers vile promises.* If this fighter is included in your warband, you begin the battle with 1 additional wild dice.

FIRST CONVERGENCE: FANNING THE FLAMES

Vesca Mirror-Eye maintains a great tribute hall filled with the loot she has extorted from lesser warlords. Many mercenaries guard the structure, but the guards' watch is slack and their attention wanders – they are complacent, believing that none dare challenge one of the city's dreaded Seven Talons. They know nothing of the Corvus Cabal. Burn the Mirror-Eye's treasures to ashes, and plant the corpses of Headsplitter's men amidst the ruins.

BATTLEPLAN
Terrain: See map.

Deployment:
Relentless Assault

The Aspirant warband uses the red deployment points.

Victory:
Defend the Find

The Aspirant warband is the attacker.

Twist: Draw a twist card as normal.

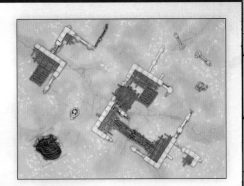

SECOND CONVERGENCE: WAR IN THE STREETS

Mirror-Eye's response to the destruction of her tribute hall was swift and merciless. Several of Brand Headsplitter's named men were hanged from the ramparts of Carngrad, their bellies torn open and their eyes plucked out. The streets now echo to the sounds of open war between the two Talons. You have blood-marked several minor gang bosses in thrall to both warring leaders. Slaying these lieutenants will only spur an escalation in the bloodletting.

BATTLEPLAN
Terrain: See map.

Deployment:
Decapitate

The Aspirant warband uses the red deployment points.

Victory: The Hunted

The Aspirant warband is the attacker.

Twist: Draw a twist card as normal.

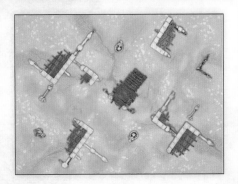

FINAL CONVERGENCE: PICK CLEAN THE DEAD

The streets of Carngrad are littered with bodies. The Great Gatherer unfurls its jet-black wings and shrieks in triumph. Your warriors move amidst the carnage like fleeting shadows, stripping the dead and wounded of valuables. The bodies of Mirror-Eye and Headsplitter lie amidst a mound of butchered dead, each slain at the other's hand. The former's silver-handled rapier and the latter's notched brass axe are mighty weapons indeed. Claim these treasures for the Cabal.

BATTLEPLAN
Terrain: See map.

Deployment:
Bloodbath

The Aspirant warband uses the red deployment points.

Victory: The Prize

Twist: Draw a twist card as normal.

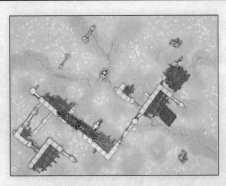

CAMPAIGN OUTCOME
If the Aspirant warband is the winner, they complete this campaign quest. Turn to page 129 to see the outcome and claim your reward.

THE HUNGER OF ISIPHUS

The Slaanesh-worshipping gargant Isiphus the Bloated once roamed the Eightpoints, gorging himself obsessively upon not just the flesh of mortals, but also piles of jewels and treasures that he stole during his many rampages. Eventually, Isiphus grew so obese that he could no longer move or even stand. The gargant's appetite remains insatiable to this day; he gladly vomits up the valuables in his belly to any who offer him new and ever more decadent tastes. A thriving market shanty-town of illicit pleasures has formed around Isiphus' immense bulk. Such a rare bounty might even appease the burning avarice of the Great Gatherer, if only for a moment.

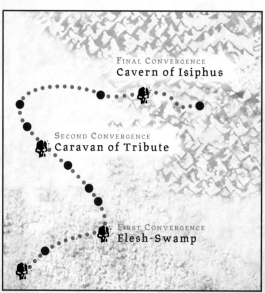

FINAL CONVERGENCE
Cavern of Isiphus

SECOND CONVERGENCE
Caravan of Tribute

FIRST CONVERGENCE
Flesh-Swamp

TERRITORY RULES

Raise Monolith: *The Cabal impales the butchered corpses of those it has slain upon the branches of trees and the spires of buildings, along with offerings of loot for the Great Gatherer.*

You can spend 10 glory points to dominate a territory by raising a monolith. Mark on your warband roster how many territories you dominate. Dominating territory offers the following bonuses:

For each territory dominated by your warband, you can include 1 thrall in your warband when mustering for a campaign battle. Thralls included in this manner are not added to your warband roster, and cost points like any other fighter.

For each territory dominated by your warband, increase the points you have available to spend on fighters when mustering your warband for a campaign battle by 50. Include the points costs for any thralls in your warband when mustering your warband. Thralls are not added to your warband roster and can never gain destiny levels, bear artefacts or be chosen to become a favoured warrior.

D3	ARTEFACT OF POWER
1	**Crowskull Fetish:** *This sacred amulet seems to steal the strength from nearby foes.* Subtract 1 from the Strength characteristic of attack actions (to a minimum of 1) made by enemy fighters while they are within 3" of the bearer.
2	**Cloak of Onyx Feathers:** *The pinions that make up this cloak are as firm as steel.* Add 1 to the Toughness characteristic of the bearer.
3	**Talons of Night:** *These metal claws make not a sound as they carve through the air.* Add 1 to the Attacks characteristic of attack actions made by the bearer that have a Range characteristic of 3 or less.

D3	COMMAND TRAIT
1	**Roof-runner:** *This warrior leaps and tumbles with the poise of a natural acrobat.* This fighter does not suffer impact damage.
2	**Eye-taker:** *This warrior plucks the eyes from their victims, rendering them helpless.* Each time an enemy fighter is taken down by an attack action made by this fighter, add 1 to the damage points allocated by hits and critical hits from attack actions made by this fighter until the end of the battle.
3	**Master of Shadows:** *This warrior is suffused with the shadow magic of Ulgu.* Add 1 to the value of abilities (to a maximum of 6) used by this fighter.

FIRST CONVERGENCE: THE FLESH-SWAMP

The path to the Cavern of Isiphus is a long one, and it takes you through some of the deadliest wilds of the Bloodwind Spoil. As you pass through a swamp of rotten flesh and blubber, you find yourself under attack from a rival warband. Before the killing can begin, the very earth groans beneath you, and tendrils of protean matter reach forth from below to grasp at you with fang-filled maws and lacerating tentacles. Nearby is a cluster of ruins. Fend off your foes and make for the high ground!

BATTLEPLAN
Terrain: See map.

Deployment: Draw a deployment card as normal.

Victory:
Higher Ground

Twist:
Murky Swampland

SECOND CONVERGENCE: THE GARGANT'S DEMAND

The closer you come to Isiphus' domain, the greater the number of armed caravans you see trailing through the wilderness. One such company has made camp amidst the remnants of a fallen statue, and you can see armed guards dotted around the flickering light of a campfire. If you are to get close enough to Isiphus to carve open his belly, you will need a fitting tribute to offer. Slay these fools and take their goods for your own.

BATTLEPLAN
Terrain: See map.

Deployment:
Defiant Stand

The Aspirant warband uses the red deployment points.

Victory: Isolated

The Aspirant warband is the attacker.

Twist: Draw a twist card as normal.

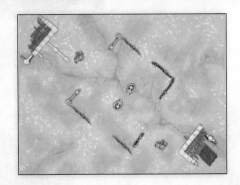

FINAL CONVERGENCE: THE BELLY OF THE BEAST

Your stolen litter sees you past the gold-masked guards who bar the gates to Isiphus' domain. Within you are met with a truly grotesque sight – the gargant slumps, snoring in the midst of the cavern, walkways and market stalls built around his immense, worm-white belly. Above dangles a huge censer in the shape of the Dark Prince's symbol, spewing perfumed mist. Great chains connect this device to the walls, and if they are broken it will fall like a great blade to carve open Isiphus' gut.

BATTLEPLAN
Terrain: See map.

Deployment:
Vengeance

The Aspirant warband uses the red deployment points.

Victory:
Vantage Point

Twist: Draw a twist card as normal.

CAMPAIGN OUTCOME
If the Aspirant warband is the winner, they complete this campaign quest. Turn to page 129 to see the outcome and claim your reward.

A SPY IN THE HOUSE OF TALONS

The Seven Talons – the cabal of warlords that control the reaver city of Carngrad – are but minor threads in the vast spider's web of intrigue and brutality that controls the Eightpoints. Yet they answer to the Varanspire, and rumour has it that some of their number have even stepped within the sheer black walls of that dread fortress. It would behove the Cypher Lords to have an eye amongst their number. The masters of Nochseed can offer no greater proof of their vital talents than to breach the walls of the Everchosen's fortress.

SECOND CONVERGENCE
Northern Run-offs

FIRST CONVERGENCE
Roof-runner Haunts

FINAL CONVERGENCE
Feral Wilderness

TERRITORY RULES

Raise Monolith: *The Eyes of Nochseed are wrought from precious metals and embossed with maddening Chaos sigils. The masters of the Cypher Lords can spy upon their foes through these strange devices.*

You can spend 10 glory points to dominate a territory by raising a monolith. Mark on your warband roster how many territories you dominate. Dominating territory offers the following bonuses:

For each territory dominated by your warband, you can include 1 thrall in your warband when mustering for a campaign battle. Thralls included in this manner are not added to your warband roster, and cost points like any other fighter.

For each territory dominated by your warband, increase the points you have available to spend on fighters when mustering your warband for a campaign battle by 50. Include the points costs for any thralls in your warband when mustering your warband. Thralls are not added to your warband roster and can never gain destiny levels, bear artefacts or be chosen to become a favoured warrior.

D3	ARTEFACT OF POWER
1	**Aetherquartz Anklets:** *These enchanted anklets are crafted from realmstone, and grant their wearer great speed.* Add 1 to the Move characteristic of the bearer.
2	**Formless Blade:** *This weapon flows like water, reaching out to strike distant foes.* Add 1 to the Range characteristic of attack actions made by the bearer. If the attack action has a minimum and maximum range, add 1 to the maximum range only.
3	**Whisper-mirror:** *This cursed looking glass can reflect its bearer across the battlefield.* When the bearer uses the 'Shadowy Recall' ability, the friendly fighter picked can be anywhere on the battlefield.

D3	COMMAND TRAIT
1	**Strange Physiology:** *Strikes that should slay this warrior seem to affect them not at all.* Subtract 1 from the damage points allocated by hits and critical hits (to a minimum of 1) from attack actions that target this fighter.
2	**Martial Dancer:** *This warrior is an expert sword fighter whose mastery of form is unrivalled.* Add 1 to the Attacks characteristic of attack actions made by this fighter that have a Range characteristic of 3 or less.
3	**Weightless Fall:** *This warrior seems to float through the air as lightly as a drifting feather.* This fighter does not suffer impact damage.

FIRST CONVERGENCE: THE EYES OF NOCHSEED

Carngrad is a cesspool of anarchy and murder – the perfect place for the Cypher Lords to operate. If you are to plant an agent within the ranks of the Seven Talons, you must first gather information. Eliminate the roof-runner gangs and other cut-throats that haunt the upper levels of Carngrad, and secrete the Eyes of Nochseed in key locations. These sorcerous sigils will allow you to spy upon the denizens of the Reaver City from afar.

BATTLEPLAN
Terrain: See map.

Deployment:
Show of Strength

The Aspirant warband uses the red deployment points.

Victory:
Higher Ground

Twist: Draw a twist card as normal.

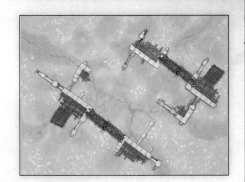

SECOND CONVERGENCE: THE MAJORDOMO

Urdesh Rask is the newest and youngest member of the Seven Talons, having disembowelled his predecessor in an honour duel. Ambitious and cruel, he has assumed control of the slave pits and the flesh districts, consolidating his power and earning great prestige. His majordomo, Illucin, frequents a pleasure house along the Northern Run-offs. Eliminate the lieutenant's sentries as swiftly as possible, and then lie in wait for your target.

BATTLEPLAN
Terrain: See map.

Deployment:
Blindfight

The Aspirant warband uses the blue deployment points.

Victory: Crush

The Aspirant warband is the attacker.

Twist: Draw a twist card as normal.

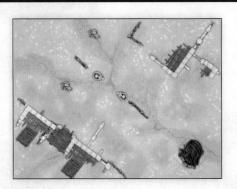

FINAL CONVERGENCE: THE FALL OF URDESH RASK

You take Illucin's face and memories, and grant them to one of your finest agents, who slowly and skilfully infiltrates Rask's inner circle. The false majordomo's whispers guide Rask north, under the pretence of viewing a new batch of slaves. In fact, you guide him to an ambush point of your choosing, amidst the wilderness that lies beyond Carngrad's walls. There, you launch your ambush. Slaughter Urdesh Rask's retinue, and capture the warlord alive so that he in turn may be replaced.

BATTLEPLAN
Terrain: See map.

Deployment: Ambush

The Aspirant warband uses the red deployment points.

Victory: No Mercy

Twist: Draw a twist card as normal.

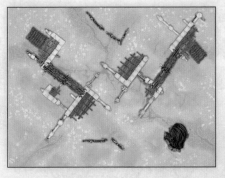

CAMPAIGN OUTCOME
If the Aspirant warband is the winner, they complete this campaign quest. Turn to page 129 to see the outcome and claim your reward.

COLD VENGEANCE

The name Barek Coldiron is spoken with hushed fear throughout the Bloodwind Spoil. The reaver chieftain is a deranged and sadistic killer, responsible for so many torturous deaths that his enemies swear he has the blood of daemons running in his veins. His hounds stalked the Cypher Lords as you made the deadly journey across the wastes of the Eightpoints, for Coldiron sought the fine weapons carried by your battle-thralls. Many valuable warriors were hacked down and torn apart. Yet Coldiron made one critical mistake – he failed to kill you all.

FINAL CONVERGENCE
Coldiron's War Camp

SECOND CONVERGENCE
Scalper's Trail

FIRST CONVERGENCE
Firegrog Shipment

TERRITORY RULES

Raise Monolith: *The Eyes of Nochseed are wrought from precious metals and embossed with maddening Chaos sigils. The masters of the Cypher Lords can spy upon their foes through these strange devices.*

You can spend 10 glory points to dominate a territory by raising a monolith. Mark on your warband roster how many territories you dominate. Dominating territory offers the following bonuses:

For each territory dominated by your warband, you can include 1 thrall in your warband when mustering for a campaign battle. Thralls included in this manner are not added to your warband roster, and cost points like any other fighter.

For each territory dominated by your warband, increase the points you have available to spend on fighters when mustering your warband for a campaign battle by 50. Include the points costs for any thralls in your warband when mustering your warband. Thralls are not added to your warband roster and can never gain destiny levels, bear artefacts or be chosen to become a favoured warrior.

D3	ARTEFACT OF POWER
1	**Blazing Chakram:** *When thrown, this chakram erupts with multi-coloured flames.* When the bearer uses the '**Throwing Stars and Chakrams**' ability, roll 2 dice instead of 1 (and allocate damage for each result separately).
2	**Dazzling Mask:** *This bewitching sun-crystal veil disorients those who look upon it.* Subtract 1 from the Attacks characteristic of attack actions (to a minimum of 1) made by visible enemy fighters while they are within 3" of the bearer.
3	**Orb of Binding:** *This glass sphere contains the raging essence of a daemonic spirit.* Once per battle, the bearer can use this artefact as an action. If they do so, pick a visible enemy fighter within 6" of the bearer and roll a dice. On a 4-5, allocate 5 damage points to that fighter. On a 6, allocate 10 damage points to that fighter.

D3	COMMAND TRAIT
1	**Unknowable:** *Attempting to predict this warrior's actions is utterly futile.* If this fighter is included in your warband, you begin the battle with 1 additional wild dice.
2	**Unerring Aim:** *This warrior never seems to miss their target.* Add 3 to the damage points allocated to enemy fighters by critical hits from attack actions made by this fighter that have a Range characteristic of 3 or less.
3	**Wind Dancer:** *This warrior seems to barely touch the ground when they run.* Add 1 to the Move characteristic of this fighter.

FIRST CONVERGENCE: THE PATIENT BLADE

The way of the Cypher Lords is that of patience, cunning and merciless vengeance. You have observed Barek Coldiron's war camp for many days, noting every opening and every potential weakness. You discover that the reaver chieftain has a taste for Delerian firegrog – shipments are brought in from the barter pits of Carngrad in a regular cycle. Travel to the slum city, and steal a shipment of the rare liquor from Coldiron's supplier.

BATTLEPLAN
Terrain: See map.

Deployment:
Hold Out

The Aspirant warband uses the blue deployment points.

Victory:
Hold Our Gains

The Aspirant warband is the attacker.

Twist: Draw a twist card as normal.

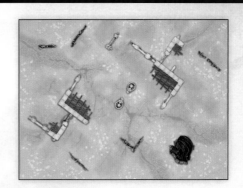

SECOND CONVERGENCE: CAMP ASSAULT

Your stolen casks of firegrog have been liberally dosed with Khemidian nightbane. Anyone who samples the tainted blend will suffer from maddening hallucinations. You take Scalper's Trail north, carrying your goods back to Coldiron's camp in the guise of hired blades, and make shelter in the shadow of a ruined bell tower. In the crimson haze of early morning a cry goes up from your sentries. Raiders, racing through the waist-high grass towards you. Protect your stolen goods!

BATTLEPLAN
Terrain: See map.

Deployment: Draw a deployment card as normal.

Victory:
Steal the Prize

The Aspirant warband is the defender.

Twist: Dawn

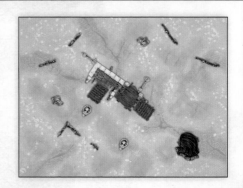

FINAL CONVERGENCE: MADNESS UNLEASHED

The sentries at the gate of Coldiron's war camp admit your caravan, and take the proffered firegrog. You learn that Coldiron is to hold a revelry this night, culminating in the sacrifice of prisoners to the Dark Gods. As night falls you begin to hear the sounds of screams and the clatter of blades – your gift is spreading its deranged madness through the camp. Kill the sentries and bar the gates. This night Barek Coldiron dies, and the Cypher Lords will have their vengeance.

BATTLEPLAN
Terrain: See map.

Deployment: Stranglehold

The Aspirant warband uses the red deployment points.

Victory: Conquer

The Aspirant warband is the attacker.

Twist: Draw a twist card as normal.

CAMPAIGN OUTCOME
If the Aspirant warband is the winner, they complete this campaign quest. Turn to page 130 to see the outcome and claim your reward.

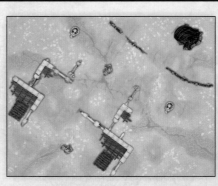

PATH OF THE FLAYED PRINCE

Centuries ago the prophet and progenitor of the Unmade, the figure known as the Flayed Prince, made pilgrimage to the Eightpoints. Guided by visions granted to him upon the flensing rack by the Dark Powers, he disappeared into the wilds of that untamed realm, never to be seen again. It was the call of the Everchosen that brought you to the Bloodwind Spoil, but you feel in its undeniable pull the presence of your beloved master. Somewhere in the wilds of this untamed land the Flayed Prince left behind a grand legacy of torment and darkness for his children to inherit, and you seek it with single-minded purpose.

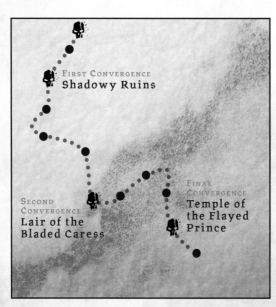

FIRST CONVERGENCE
Shadowy Ruins

SECOND CONVERGENCE
Lair of the Bladed Caress

FINAL CONVERGENCE
Temple of the Flayed Prince

TERRITORY RULES

Raise Monolith: *In order to fill their foes with terror, the Unmade raise nightmarish effigies of metal and tortured flesh, bedecked with the mutilated remains of their victims – not all of whom are dead.*

You can spend 10 glory points to dominate a territory by raising a monolith. Mark on your warband roster how many territories you dominate. Dominating territory offers the following bonuses:

For each territory dominated by your warband, you can include 1 thrall in your warband when mustering for a campaign battle. Thralls included in this manner are not added to your warband roster, and cost points like any other fighter.

For each territory dominated by your warband, increase the points you have available to spend on fighters when mustering your warband for a campaign battle by 50. Include the points costs for any thralls in your warband when mustering your warband. Thralls are not added to your warband roster and can never gain destiny levels, bear artefacts or be chosen to become a favoured warrior.

D3	ARTEFACT OF POWER
1	**Gutting Dagger:** *This disembowelling blade is a favoured tool of Unmade torturers.* When the bearer uses the 'Barbed Strike' ability, subtract 2 from the Toughness characteristic of the target fighter (to a minimum of 1) instead of 1.
2	**Chained Flesh-hooks:** *Attached to a warrior's own flesh, these barbed chains whip and lash madly as the bearer fights.* After the bearer finishes a move action, allocate 1 damage point to visible enemy fighters within 1" of the bearer.
3	**Mask of the Flayed Prince:** *This mask is fashioned in the image of Prince Vourneste.* Once per battle, the bearer can use this artefact as an action. If they do so, until the end of the battle round, add 2 to their Toughness characteristic.

D3	COMMAND TRAIT
1	**Seeping Blood:** *This warrior's self-inflicted agonies constantly seep reeking black blood.* Subtract 1 from the Strength characteristic of attack actions (to a minimum of 1) made by enemy fighters while they are within 3" of this fighter.
2	**Master of Torture:** *This warrior is skilled at inflicting unimaginable agony.* Add 3 to the damage points allocated by critical hits from attack actions made by this fighter that have a Range characteristic of 3 or less.
3	**Flenser:** *This warrior ritualistically flays the skin from his victims, living or dead.* Add 1 to the value of abilities (to a maximum of 6) used by this fighter.

FIRST CONVERGENCE: SCREAMS IN THE DARK

Ever since you followed the path of the Flayed Prince to the Eightpoints, rival hunters have pursued you through the wilds. Likely they think you are fleeing in terror, for you have led them far into the wastes, towards a cluster of broken-down ruins. As soon as your warriors enter the ruins they peel off into the shadows, and your pursuers stumble right into the trap. Skinning blades glimmer in the gloom, and then the screaming starts. Teach your would-be hunters the true meaning of fear.

BATTLEPLAN
Terrain: See map.

Deployment:
Close the Jaws

The Aspirant warband uses the blue deployment points.

Victory: Isolated

The Aspirant warband is the attacker.

Twist: Draw a twist card as normal.

SECOND CONVERGENCE: INSTRUMENTS OF AGONY

Legend tells that the Flayed Prince sought out the daemon-thing known as the Bladed Caress, a master of torture. He bade the creature to work its art upon his flesh, and thus bring him closer to ascension. You seek out the daemon's lair, but only ruins remain. Your own suffering may bring you communion with the Ruinous Powers, and illuminate your path. Recover the implements of the Bladed Caress, so that you might test them upon your unworthy flesh.

BATTLEPLAN
Terrain: See map.

Deployment: Strike from the Shadows

The Aspirant warband uses the red deployment points.

Victory: The Prize

Twist: Draw a twist card as normal.

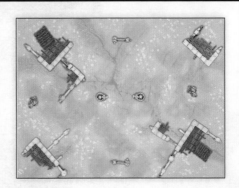

FINAL CONVERGENCE: TEMPLE OF THE FLAYED PRINCE

Your suffering grants you blinding visions that burn their way into your skull. Now you know the path taken by the Flayed Prince. It takes you to the edge of the Murderlands, those damned wastes utterly suffused with the power of Chaos. Here, amidst this nightmarish expanse, he built his temple to the Ruinous Powers from flesh and bone. Within can be found the last teachings of your beloved leader, but unworthy souls contaminate this holy place. They must be cleansed.

BATTLEPLAN
Terrain: See map.

Deployment:
Outflank

The Aspirant warband uses the red deployment points.

Victory:
Seize Territory

The Aspirant warband is the attacker.

Twist: Draw a twist card as normal.

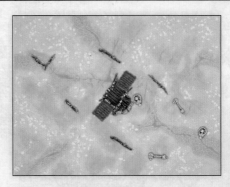

CAMPAIGN OUTCOME
If the Aspirant warband is the winner, they complete this campaign quest. Turn to page 130 to see the outcome and claim your reward.

SONG OF SUFFERING

Pain is a gift. Through the blissful embrace of suffering one can commune with the Dark Gods, escaping the limitations and weaknesses of mortal flesh. You have heard rumours of a device that lies within the Bloodwind Spoil, an ancient, arcane mechanism powered by the anguish of tormented souls. You hear its call across the plains, a haunting and irresistible chorus of agony. You must seek out this structure and claim it in the name of the Unmade, for with it you could unleash a tidal wave of pain across the Spoil, a scream of suffering that will reach all the way to the gates of the Varanspire.

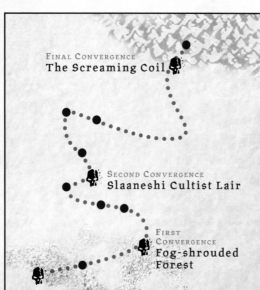

FINAL CONVERGENCE
The Screaming Coil

SECOND CONVERGENCE
Slaaneshi Cultist Lair

FIRST
CONVERGENCE
**Fog-shrouded
Forest**

TERRITORY RULES

Raise Monolith: *In order to fill their foes with terror, the Unmade raise nightmarish effigies of metal and tortured flesh, bedecked with the mutilated remains of their victims – not all of whom are dead.*

You can spend 10 glory points to dominate a territory by raising a monolith. Mark on your warband roster how many territories you dominate. Dominating territory offers the following bonuses:

For each territory dominated by your warband, you can include 1 thrall in your warband when mustering for a campaign battle. Thralls included in this manner are not added to your warband roster, and cost points like any other fighter.

For each territory dominated by your warband, increase the points you have available to spend on fighters when mustering your warband for a campaign battle by 50. Include the points costs for any thralls in your warband when mustering your warband. Thralls are not added to your warband roster and can never gain destiny levels, bear artefacts or be chosen to become a favoured warrior.

D3	ARTEFACT OF POWER
1	**Crown of Agony:** *This circlet is fashioned from tortured flesh, and still radiates a sensation of unbearable pain.* Subtract 1 from the Attacks characteristic of attack actions (to a minimum of 1) made by enemy fighters while they are within 3" of the bearer.
2	**Vourneste's Blade:** *Legend has it that this blade was once wielded by the Flayed Prince.* Add 1 to the Strength characteristic of attack actions made by the bearer that have a Range characteristic of 3 or less.
3	**Grisly Banner:** *This banner is stitched together from still-screaming faces.* Once per battle, the bearer can use this artefact as an action. If they do so, until the end of the battle round, add 1 to the Strength characteristic of attack actions made by friendly fighters while they are within 6" of the bearer.

D3	COMMAND TRAIT
1	**Fuelled by Pain:** *Agony drives this warrior into a rapturous frenzy.* Each time an enemy fighter is taken down by an attack action made by this fighter, add 1 to the damage points allocated by hits and critical hits from attack actions made by this fighter until the end of the battle.
2	**Lurking Killer:** *This warrior lies in wait for their victims before striking from the darkness.* If this fighter is included in your warband, you begin the battle with 1 additional wild dice.
3	**Horrific Mutilation:** *This warrior's face is a nightmare of ruined and tormented flesh that is terrifying to look upon.* When the bearer uses the 'Nightmarish Visage' ability, pick a visible enemy fighter within 9" instead of a number of inches equal to the value of the ability.

FIRST CONVERGENCE: A GIFT OF TORMENT

The forests south of the Skullpikes are littered with fog-shrouded ruins inhabited by deranged cultists and cannibal tribes. Impaled bodies are pinned to black-limbed, trees, and bloody bones crunch beneath your feet with every step. You feel at home for the first time in many moons. The denizens of this place deserve the gift of pain, and you will share it with them should they wish it or not.

BATTLEPLAN
Terrain: See map.

Deployment:
Deadly Gambit

The Aspirant warband uses the red deployment points.

Victory:
Shock and Awe

Twist: Draw a twist card as normal.

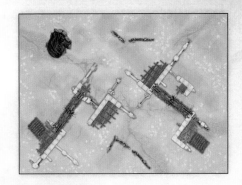

SECOND CONVERGENCE: IN SEARCH OF DARK SECRETS

The locals call the device you seek the Screaming Coil. Who built it and for what purpose remains a mystery, though it is currently in the possession of Slaaneshi cultists, who are using it for their own perverse ends. The sorcerers of the Dark Prince have long studied the workings of the mysterious device, noting their findings in perfumed tomes bound in living flesh. You must seek out some of these illicit books, which have fallen into the possession of rival warbands.

BATTLEPLAN
Terrain: See map.

Deployment:
Fog of War

The Aspirant warband uses the red deployment points.

Victory:
Steal the Prize

The Aspirant warband is the attacker.

Twist: Draw a twist card as normal.

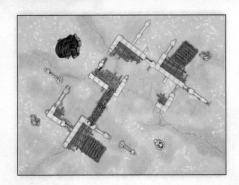

FINAL CONVERGENCE: CHOIR OF PAIN

The Screaming Coil emanates waves of torment so powerful that you can feel them deep in your bones, reaching parts of your soul you had long thought immune to pain. Truly, this is a creation of the gods. You can see trapped spirits within the violet crystal of the structure, disembodied faces locked eternally in horrified howls. Seek out and secure the crystalline workings of the soul-engine that are scattered throughout the ruins surrounding the Coil, and bend the device to your will.

BATTLEPLAN
Terrain: See map.

Deployment:
Relentless Assault

The Aspirant warband uses the red deployment points.

Victory:
Drawn and Quartered

Twist: Draw a twist card as normal.

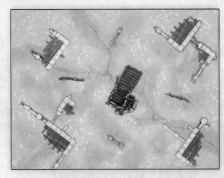

CAMPAIGN OUTCOME
If the Aspirant warband is the winner, they complete this campaign quest. Turn to page 131 to see the outcome and claim your reward.

NAGENDRA'S GULLET

Deep in the Skullpike Mountains there exists an ancient temple of worship to Great Nagendra, Father of Serpents. This ancient godbeast was slain in battle by the Solar Drake Ignax, so the legends say, and his torn flesh fell away and gave rise to the snakes of the realms. It is said that the floor of Nagendra's Gullet writhes with thousands of his serpentine children, each blessed with mutations and unnatural poisons. The shamans of the Splintered Fang wish to claim this place in the name of their daemonic patrons, the Coiling Ones, they who bless your blades with murderous gifts. You will seek out this fabled shrine and claim it in the name of your cult.

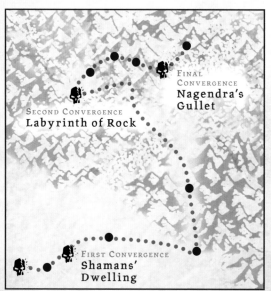

TERRITORY RULES

Raise Monolith: *The Splintered Fang mark the borders of their land with serpentine idols erected in worship of the mysterious Coiling Ones, their daemonic patrons.*

You can spend 10 glory points to dominate a territory by raising a monolith. Mark on your warband roster how many territories you dominate. Dominating territory offers the following bonuses:

For each territory dominated by your warband, you can include 1 thrall in your warband when mustering for a campaign battle. Thralls included in this manner are not added to your warband roster, and cost points like any other fighter.

For each territory dominated by your warband, increase the points you have available to spend on fighters when mustering your warband for a campaign battle by 50. Include the points costs for any thralls in your warband when mustering your warband. Thralls are not added to your warband roster and can never gain destiny levels, bear artefacts or be chosen to become a favoured warrior.

D3	ARTEFACT OF POWER
1	**Nagendra's Kiss:** *This concealable punch-dagger is crafted from the poisoned fang of a lurkviper.* Once per battle, the bearer can use this artefact as an action. If they do so, pick a visible enemy fighter within 1" of the bearer and roll a dice. On a 4+, allocate 10 damage points to that fighter.
2	**Torc of the Serpentfather:** *This enchanted neck-guard is fashioned in the shape of two entwined serpents.* Add 1 to the value of abilities (to a maximum of 6) used by the bearer.
3	**Embrace of Pain:** *This vambrace slowly seeps agonising poison into the blood of its wearer, allowing them to grow accustomed to intense pain.* Add 1 to the Toughness characteristic of the bearer.

D3	COMMAND TRAIT
1	**Swift Reflexes:** *This warrior slips past their foe's attacks with sinuous grace.* Subtract 1 from the damage points allocated by hits and critical hits (to a minimum of 1) from attack actions that target this fighter.
2	**Master of Venoms:** *This warrior is regarded as a master at the brewing of debilitating poisons.* Add 3 to the damage points allocated by critical hits from attack actions made by this fighter that have a Range characteristic of 3 or less.
3	**Hypnotic Gaze:** *This warrior's unblinking gaze can strike their opponents dumb.* Enemy fighters within 1" of this fighter cannot make Disengage actions.

FIRST CONVERGENCE: FROM THE BLOOD

Before you set off on your journey, the shamans of the Coiling Ones work their fell rituals, brewing a blessed concoction from the venom of deadly serpents and drops of tainted blood. A willing supplicant steps forward to imbibe the black liquid. As the unfortunate soul collapses and begins to convulse, you hear the sound of bellowed war cries. An ambush! You must fend off these assailants, buying time for the ritual to finish, and the shamans to draw their potent poison from the clotted veins of the sacrificial victim.

BATTLEPLAN
Terrain: See map.

Deployment:
The Hunt

The Aspirant warband uses the red deployment points.

Victory: The Ritual

The Aspirant warband is the defender.

Twist: Draw a twist card as normal.

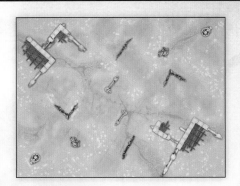

SECOND CONVERGENCE: SKIRMISH IN THE SKULLPIKE MOUNTAINS

The winding passages of the Skullpike Mountains form a maddening labyrinth, haunted by ravenous monsters and bands of marauders. As you enter a clearing dominated by the immense stone head of a toppled monolith, you nearly run straight into a rival warband. As you draw your blades and charge forwards, one of the enemy makes to flee, doubtless in an attempt to warn more of his comrades. Kill the running scout before he escapes!

BATTLEPLAN
Terrain: See map.

Deployment:
Encircle

The Aspirant warband uses the blue deployment points.

Victory:
The Messenger

The Aspirant warband is the attacker.

Twist: Draw a twist card as normal.

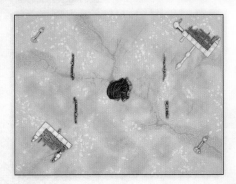

FINAL CONVERGENCE: THE SERPENT'S MAW

Nagendra's Gullet is a sweltering underground cave system. Serpents cover every surface, coiling about one another, gazing at your warband through yellow eyes as you pass. The ruins of an ancient temple are scattered throughout the caverns. Ahead you see a thick pall of smoke. Raiders have reached the heart of the temple and set fires to burn away the carpet of serpents. You are outraged at such blasphemy. Quell the flames and bring death to those who ignited them.

BATTLEPLAN
Terrain: See map.

Deployment:
Knife to the Back

The Aspirant warband uses the red deployment points.

Victory:
Seize Territory

The Aspirant warband is the attacker.

Twist: Draw a twist card as normal.

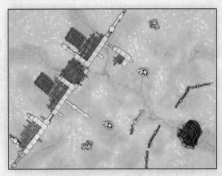

CAMPAIGN OUTCOME
If the Aspirant warband is the winner, they complete this campaign quest. Turn to page 130 to see the outcome and claim your reward.

VENOM OF THE GODS

There are few foes that the Splintered Fang cannot bring low with their holy poisons. Even a single cut, left to fester and suppurate, can spell agony and death. Yet for the mightiest creatures, a venom of singular strength is required. You plan to brew such a concoction, created from the gizzards and toxin glands of the deadliest beasts in the Bloodwind Spoil. Once it is made, you will test this poison upon the flesh of your foes, and thus prove the superiority of the Splintered Fang's way of war.

FINAL CONVERGENCE
Flensing Pits

SECOND CONVERGENCE
Hag's Claw Forest

FIRST CONVERGENCE
Raknid Stalking Grounds

TERRITORY RULES

Raise Monolith: *The Splintered Fang mark the borders of their land with serpentine idols erected in worship of the mysterious Coiling Ones, their daemonic patrons.*

You can spend 10 glory points to dominate a territory by raising a monolith. Mark on your warband roster how many territories you dominate. Dominating territory offers the following bonuses:

For each territory dominated by your warband, you can include 1 thrall in your warband when mustering for a campaign battle. Thralls included in this manner are not added to your warband roster, and cost points like any other fighter.

For each territory dominated by your warband, increase the points you have available to spend on fighters when mustering your warband for a campaign battle by 50. Include the points costs for any thralls in your warband when mustering your warband. Thralls are not added to your warband roster and can never gain destiny levels, bear artefacts or be chosen to become a favoured warrior.

D3	ARTEFACT OF POWER
1	**Sacred Unguent:** *A gift from the Coiling Ones, this scented oil enhances the senses and toughens the constitution.* Add 5 to the Wounds characteristic of the bearer.
2	**Coiling Kris:** *At its wielder's command, this curved dagger can wind around a victim like a razor-sharp vine.* Add 1 to the Strength characteristic of attack actions made by the bearer that have a Range characteristic of 3 or less.
3	**Pendant of Nagendra:** *This symbol of the Serpentfather has been corrupted with daemonic power.* Add 1 to the value of abilities (to a maximum of 6) used by the bearer.

D3	COMMAND TRAIT
1	**Cold-blooded Killer:** *This warrior feels no pity, and does not relent until their enemies are utterly destroyed.* Add 1 to the Attacks characteristic of attack actions made by this fighter that have a Range characteristic of 3 or less.
2	**Scaly Skin:** *The flesh of this warrior is covered in shimmering, iron-hard scales.* Add 1 to the Toughness characteristic of this fighter.
3	**Sibilant Whispers:** *The whispered words of the Coiling Ones guide this warrior in battle.* If this fighter is included in your warband, you begin the battle with 1 additional wild dice.

FIRST CONVERGENCE: A POTENT BLEND

There are many creatures in the Eightpoints that use venoms and poisons to strike their prey down. Indeed, the effects of these attacks are often horrific beyond imagination. Skullweb raknids, for example, inject their victims with a toxin that dissolves their prey into a puddle of gore that they can better consume with their spear-like proboscises. Raknid venom is incredibly rare, but you have heard of a band of mercenaries in the wilds who have several casks of the stuff. Hunt them down and secure this bounty for the Splintered Fang.

BATTLEPLAN
Terrain: See map.

Deployment:
Death Spiral

The Aspirant warband uses the red deployment points.

Victory:
Defend the Find

The Aspirant warband is the attacker.

Twist: Draw a twist card as normal.

SECOND CONVERGENCE: HARROWMASK HARVEST

The raknid venom proves a lethal base for your concoction, but those who possess a sufficiently fearsome constitution can shake its effects off and fight through the pain. In the Hag's Claw Forest there grows a unique flower known as harrowmask, the spores of which are said to inflict such agony that they can bring a gargant to its knees. You travel to the distant forest, but find a rival warband out to claim the deadly flowers for their own. Let your poisons clot the blood in their veins.

BATTLEPLAN
Terrain: See map.

Deployment:
Death Blow

The Aspirant warband uses the red deployment points.

Victory:
Hunt for Glory

Twist: Draw a twist card as normal.

FINAL CONVERGENCE: ARENA OF DEATH

The shamans have perfected their bane. It bubbles and hisses as you apply it to your blade, staining the metal pitch black. You travel to the Flensing Pits, a notorious gladiatorial arena in which some of the most monstrous killers in the land vie for the title of champion. These fools will fall to the poison that stains your weapons, and an audience of witnesses will tell of the deadly skill of the Splintered Fang. Fill the arena with the tortured corpses of your victims!

BATTLEPLAN
Terrain: See map.

Deployment:
Blood Rush

The Aspirant warband uses the red deployment points.

Victory: No Mercy

Twist: Draw a twist card as normal.

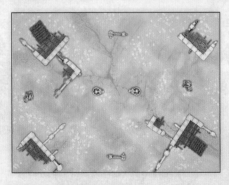

CAMPAIGN OUTCOME
If the Aspirant warband is the winner, they complete this campaign quest. Turn to page 130 to see the outcome and claim your reward.

TIDE OF FIRE

The Ever-Raging Flame guides you. It cleanses your body and soul, burning away your doubt and leaving only the purest strength behind. You look upon the cannibals, cut-throats and savages of this land and feel nothing but contempt. They are wasteful, petty creatures, ignorant of anything beyond their own desires. They must burn. All must burn, and the Scions of the Flame will stoke the fires that consume them. Only the strongest will emerge from the ashes.

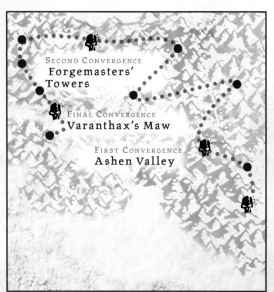

SECOND CONVERGENCE
Forgemasters' Towers

FINAL CONVERGENCE
Varanthax's Maw

FIRST CONVERGENCE
Ashen Valley

TERRITORY RULES

Raise Monolith: *The Scions of the Flame erect burning braziers filled with smouldering brimstone and ragerock fragments that burn eternally.*

You can spend 10 glory points to dominate a territory by raising a monolith. Mark on your warband roster how many territories you dominate. Dominating territory offers the following bonuses:

For each territory dominated by your warband, you can include 1 thrall in your warband when mustering for a campaign battle. Thralls included in this manner are not added to your warband roster, and cost points like any other fighter.

For each territory dominated by your warband, increase the points you have available to spend on fighters when mustering your warband for a campaign battle by 50. Include the points costs for any thralls in your warband when mustering your warband. Thralls are not added to your warband roster and can never gain destiny levels, bear artefacts or be chosen to become a favoured warrior.

D3	ARTEFACT OF POWER
1	**Cursed Emberstones:** *These smouldering coals explode when thrown, unleashing a gout of magical fire.* Add 1 to the Strength characteristic of attack actions made by the bearer that have a Range characteristic of 3 or less.
2	**Salamander Hide Armour:** *Crafted from the cured skins of volcanic salamanders, this armour is formidably resilient.* Subtract 1 from the damage points allocated by hits and critical hits (to a minimum of 1) from attack actions that target the bearer.
3	**Ragerock Pendant:** *Forged from the pure magical essence of Aqshy, this sacred amulet fills its bearer with righteous purpose.* Add 1 to the value of abilities (to a maximum of 6) used by the bearer.

D3	COMMAND TRAIT
1	**Lethal Fighter:** *This leader has mastered the art of despatching enemies with a single strike.* Add 3 to the damage points allocated by critical hits from attack actions made by this fighter that have a Range characteristic of 3 or less.
2	**Flame-seared Skin:** *This warrior's flesh is as tough and impenetrable as volcanic rock.* Add 1 to the Toughness characteristic of this fighter.
3	**Relentless Zeal:** *This warrior strikes with furious purpose and blazing fury.* Add 1 to the Attacks characteristic of attack actions made by this fighter that have a Range characteristic of 3 or less.

FIRST CONVERGENCE: FEED THE FLAME

You have travelled far across the Mortal Realms, guided by the blistering heat of the Ever-Raging Flame. At last you have reached the Eightpoints. It is a harsh, unforgiving realm, not unlike the ashen valleys from which you hail – a fiery crucible in which the mightiest of warriors are forged. Even now you see the shadows of enemy warriors drawing close, blades drawn. Your scorched lips twist into a smile. These fools will serve as fresh fodder for the Ever-Raging Flame.

BATTLEPLAN
Terrain: See map.

Deployment:
Divide and Slaughter

The Aspirant warband uses the blue deployment points.

Victory: Vanquish

Twist: Draw a twist card as normal.

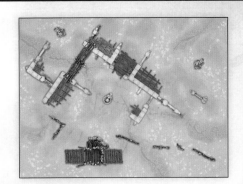

SECOND CONVERGENCE: THE FIRE RISES

Within a mountainous valley choked by swirling clouds of brimstone lies the drake-forge, Varanthax's Maw. You feel the call of its flaming heart, the blazing caldera at the centre of the mountain. Stoked with sacrifice and ritual, the volcano will erupt, drowning the surrounding lands in fire. To prepare the ritual, you first require fragments of ragerock – the crystallised essence of Aqshy – the forgemasters of the Maw use this priceless material in their work. Strip it from their corpses.

BATTLEPLAN
Terrain: See map.

Deployment:
The Duel

The Aspirant warband uses the red deployment points.

Victory:
Realmstone Hunt

Twist: Draw a twist card as normal.

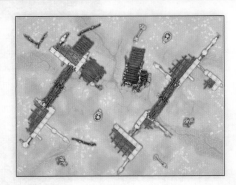

FINAL CONVERGENCE: INFERNO

You travel to the heart of the Maw, the ruins of an ancient city encircling the caldera itself, an immense pit filled with screeching fire-daemons bound to an eternity of servitude. The ritual begins as your acolytes consume the ragerock fragments and hurl themselves into the caldera, burning as they fall. Shouts of alarm reach your ears as the mountain shudders around you. It is time to fight your way free, before the rising lava swallows your warband whole.

BATTLEPLAN
Terrain: See map.

Deployment:
Frontal Assault

The Aspirant warband uses the red deployment points.

Victory: The Gauntlet

The Aspirant warband is the defender.

Twist: Draw a twist card as normal.

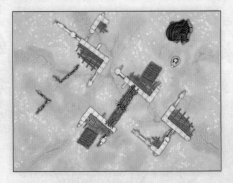

CAMPAIGN OUTCOME
If the Aspirant warband is the winner, they complete this campaign quest. Turn to page 131 to see the outcome and claim your reward.

MAKING YOUR NAME

You have butchered every opponent that has ever faced you in the killing pits of the Eightpoints. The crowd has learned to cheer you on, for they know that when you draw your blade, a spectacle of gory violence ensues. Yet the crushing of a foe's skull no longer sends the same thrill down your spine. You know that you are destined for more than this low slaughter – you seek to fight in the ranks of the Everchosen's armies, alongside the greatest killers in all the realms. Just as you thrived and dominated in the arena, you will ensure that the scum of the Bloodwind Spoil learn to tremble at the mere mention of your name.

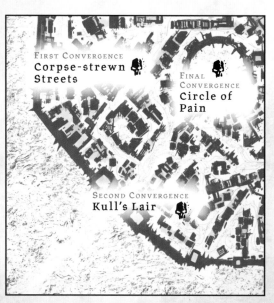

FIRST CONVERGENCE
Corpse-strewn Streets

FINAL CONVERGENCE
Circle of Pain

SECOND CONVERGENCE
Kull's Lair

TERRITORY RULES

Raise Monolith: *The Spire Tyrants leave behind only the piled weapons of those they have slain, and the heads of those unfortunate victims impaled upon spears and swords.*

You can spend 10 glory points to dominate a territory by raising a monolith. Mark on your warband roster how many territories you dominate. Dominating territory offers the following bonuses:

For each territory dominated by your warband, you can include 1 thrall in your warband when mustering for a campaign battle. Thralls included in this manner are not added to your warband roster, and cost points like any other fighter.

For each territory dominated by your warband, increase the points you have available to spend on fighters when mustering your warband for a campaign battle by 50. Include the points costs for any thralls in your warband when mustering your warband. Thralls are not added to your warband roster and can never gain destiny levels, bear artefacts or be chosen to become a favoured warrior.

D3	ARTEFACT OF POWER
1	**Golden Skull:** *This gruesome trophy is the skull of a slaughtered rival, encased in gold and engraved with terrible runes.* Add 1 to the value of abilities (to a maximum of 6) used by the bearer.
2	**Hellforged Gladius:** *This weapon hails from the same daemonic forge-pits that craft the weapons of Archaon's legions.* Add 1 to the Strength characteristic of attack actions made by the bearer that have a Range characteristic of 3 or less.
3	**Armour of Spite:** *This cursed plate compels its bearer to fight on, even as their body is stricken by horrendous wounds.* Add 1 to the Toughness characteristic of the bearer.

D3	COMMAND TRAIT
1	**Dirty Fighter:** *No underhanded tactic is beneath this warrior.* Add 3 to the damage points allocated by critical hits from attack actions made by this fighter that have a Range characteristic of 3 or less.
2	**Veteran Pit-fighter:** *This warrior has fought so many brutal duels that their hide is a tapestry of welts and scars.* Add 5 to the Wounds characteristic of this fighter.
3	**Dark Patron:** *Something terrible and ancient has its eye upon this warrior.* If this fighter is included in your warband, you begin the battle with 1 additional wild dice.

FIRST CONVERGENCE: THE STREETS RUN RED

Your patron lies dead at your own hand. He served his purpose for a while, but in truth he was a minor warlord at best, unworthy of your blade. Killing in his service would never earn you glory enough to ascend to the ranks of the Everchosen's warriors. You must seek a new paymaster, someone with power and influence worthy of your skills. Lay waste to the streets of Carngrad, and teach the cut-throats of this slum why your name is whispered with dread in every fighting pit across the Spoil.

BATTLEPLAN
Terrain: See map.

Deployment:
The Duel

The Aspirant warband uses the red deployment points.

Victory: Purge

The Aspirant warband is the attacker.

Twist: Draw a twist card as normal.

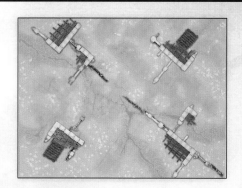

SECOND CONVERGENCE: BUTCHER'S BILL

Your killing spree does not go unnoticed. Many of Carngrad's most vicious warlords now seek the services of your warband. Foremost amongst them is the feared Gyver Kull, Butcher of Diamodia, and one of the most feared gangmasters in Carngrad. The warlord offers a fine bounty of loot and weapons in return for the bloody deaths of those who have angered him. His arrogant demands cause the blood to thunder behind your eyes, but you stay your blade and head off to do his bidding… for now.

BATTLEPLAN
Terrain: See map.

Deployment:
Death Spiral

The Aspirant warband uses the red deployment points.

Victory: Blunt

The Aspirant warband is the attacker.

Twist: Draw a twist card as normal.

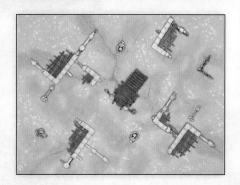

FINAL CONVERGENCE: BETRAYAL AT THE CIRCLE OF PAIN

Gyver Kull is greatly pleased by your bladework, so much so that he honours you – in his own words – with a seat at the blood-games to be held at the Circle of Pain, his personal gladiatorial arena. In attendance are many powerful Chaos Lords, seeking fresh recruits for their personal retinues. Now is the time to truly make your name. At the height of the carnage, as Kull roars delightedly at the butchery occurring below, you turn your blades upon his bodyguards. Gyver Kull must die.

BATTLEPLAN
Terrain: See map.

Deployment:
Refused Flank

The Aspirant warband uses the red deployment points.

Victory: No Mercy

Twist: Draw a twist card as normal.

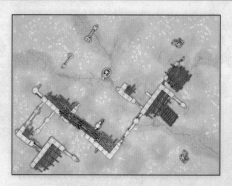

CAMPAIGN OUTCOME
If the Aspirant warband is the winner, they complete this campaign quest. Turn to page 131 to see the outcome and claim your reward.

THE BELLS OF LOST VELORUM

Velorum was once a subterranean metropolis hewn out of the earth by duardin artisans and home to the finest craftsmen in the Allpoints. It fell when Archaon launched his invasion of the island-between-realms, buried in ash and molten rock by a volcanic eruption stoked by the Everchosen's sorcerers. Such was the horror of the city's end that many amongst its populace were condemned to an eternity of grief as tormented spirits. Their mournful processions wind through the ashen streets of the dead city, drawn by the tolling of warning bells, still ringing after so many years. Now Nagash, God of Death, sends you to guide his flock home to Shyish.

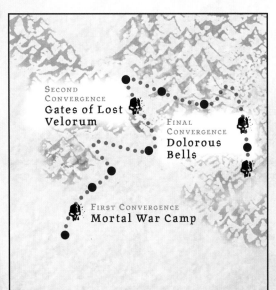

SECOND CONVERGENCE
Gates of Lost Velorum

FINAL CONVERGENCE
Dolorous Bells

FIRST CONVERGENCE
Mortal War Camp

TERRITORY RULES

Forsaken Ground: *Where the cursed agents of the Great Necromancer roam, the earth grows dark and fallow, and the restless dead stir in great numbers.*

You can spend 10 glory points to dominate a territory by creating an area of forsaken ground. Mark on your warband roster how many territories you dominate. Dominating territory offers the following bonuses:

For each territory dominated by your warband, increase the points you have available to spend on fighters when mustering your warband for a campaign battle by 50. Include the points costs for any thralls in your warband when mustering your warband. Thralls are not added to your warband roster and can never gain destiny levels, bear artefacts or be chosen to become a favoured warrior.

D3	ARTEFACT OF POWER
1	**Cloak of the Balemoon:** *This ethereal cape is formed from baleful moonlight, and absorbs both magical and physical force.* Subtract 1 from the damage points allocated by hits and critical hits (to a minimum of 1) from attack actions that target the bearer.
2	**Harrowing Blade:** *Those struck by this weapon are struck by overwhelming grief.* Subtract 1 from the Attacks characteristic (to a minimum of 1) of attack actions made by visible enemy fighters while they are within 3" of the bearer.
3	**Pendant of the Fell Wind:** *This onyx amulet can summon a roaring grave-wind from Shyish.* Add 1 to the Move characteristic of the bearer.

D3	COMMAND TRAIT
1	**Deathless Hate:** *This warrior despises the living with a deranged intensity.* Add 3 to the damage points allocated by critical hits from attack actions made by this fighter that have a Range characteristic of 3 or less.
2	**Vortex Form:** *Like the Shyish Nadir itself, this spirit's form seems to absorb matter.* Add 5 to the Wounds characteristic of this fighter.
3	**Juddering Horror:** *This spirit's unnerving, stop-start movement throws off the enemy's aim.* Add 3 to the Toughness characteristic of this fighter while it is targeted by an attack action made by an enemy fighter more than 3" away.

FIRST CONVERGENCE: DEATH KNELL

The bells of Lost Velorum toll, a sombre death knell audible even above the pandemonium of the Eightpoints. It echoes through your ethereal form like a thunderous proclamation from the Great Necromancer himself. Nagash commands you to reach the ruined city and shepherd the lost spirits within back to the embrace of their one true master. Yet there are bands of mortal savages who would stand in the way of your task. Teach them the true meaning of fear by stealing the life from their leaders.

BATTLEPLAN
Terrain: See map.

Deployment:
Decapitate

The Aspirant warband uses the red deployment points.

Victory: Assassinate

The Aspirant warband is the attacker.

Twist: Draw a twist card as normal.

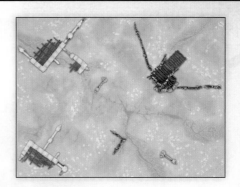

SECOND CONVERGENCE: DISTURBED GRAVES

Passing through solid rock and across fast-flowing channels of molten metal, you come to the ruins of Lost Velorum. To your anger, you find that not only the dead are capable of journeying to this forgotten place. You can sense the presence of mortals amidst the collapsed city, and bitter hatred rises up within you like a gathering storm. Likely they come to loot or defile the resting places of the forlorn dead. Tear the stolen treasures from their hands and return them to the grave.

BATTLEPLAN
Terrain: See map.

Deployment:
Massacre

The Aspirant warband uses the red deployment points.

Victory:
Steal the Prize

The Aspirant warband is the attacker.

Twist: Draw a twist card as normal.

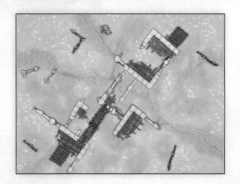

FINAL CONVERGENCE: SILENCE THE BELLS

The bells of Lost Velorum must be silenced. To the spirits of the forgotten city, it is the last memory that anchors them to their mortal lives. They are drawn forth in their multitudes by the incessant clanging, clinging to the solemn sound like a shipwrecked man clings to a shard of driftwood. This lost flock must return to the embrace of all-powerful Nagash; when the city's bells are silenced, your own solemn tocsins will guide them to their rightful fate

BATTLEPLAN
Terrain: See map.

Deployment:
Relentless Assault

The Aspirant warband uses the red deployment points.

Victory: Vantage Point

Twist: Draw a twist card as normal.

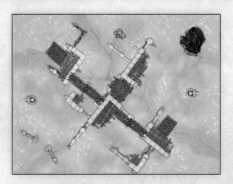

CAMPAIGN OUTCOME
If the Aspirant warband is the winner, they complete this campaign quest. Turn to page 131 to see the outcome and claim your reward.

THE HIDDEN VAULT

The Stormvaults are repositories of arcane treasures and relics of realm-shaking power, established by Sigmar many centuries ago. Scattered far and wide across the realms and hidden by obfuscating magic, they lay undiscovered all through the Age of Chaos. Now, in the wake of the Shyish necroquake, the magic that once concealed them has begun to stutter and fail. You and your fellow Stormcast Eternals are tasked with a mission of the utmost importance and secrecy – to travel to the Eightpoints and recover the Stormvault Sacristy at Forlorn Point. Retrieve its wondrous treasures before the enemy seeks them out and puts them to terrible use.

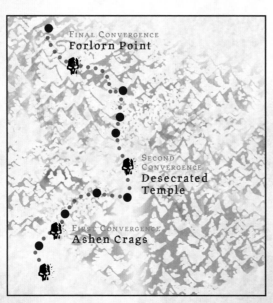

FINAL CONVERGENCE
Forlorn Point

SECOND CONVERGENCE
Desecrated Temple

FIRST CONVERGENCE
Ashen Crags

TERRITORY RULES

Hallowed Ground: *With celestial magic and thrice-blessed Azyrite starwater, the servants of the God-King cleanse the earth of corruption.*

You can spend 10 glory points to dominate a territory by creating an area of hallowed ground. Mark on your warband roster how many territories you dominate. Dominating territory offers the following bonuses:

For each territory dominated by your warband, increase the points you have available to spend on fighters when mustering your warband for a campaign battle by 50. Include the points costs for any thralls in your warband when mustering your warband. Thralls are not added to your warband roster and can never gain destiny levels, bear artefacts or be chosen to become a favoured warrior.

D3	ARTEFACT OF POWER
1	**Armour of Anointed Sigmarite:** *This battle-plate has been tempered with the blood of saints and martyrs.* Subtract 1 from the damage points allocated by hits and critical hits (to a minimum of 1) from attack actions that target the bearer.
2	**Blade of Heroes:** *No task seems insurmountable to the warrior who wields this shining blade.* Add 3 to the damage points allocated by critical hits from attack actions made by the bearer that have a Range characteristic of 3 or less.
3	**Dracothion Talisman:** *This charm, shaped in the image of the Great Drake, bestows its wearer with great resilience.* Add 5 to the Wounds characteristic of this fighter.

D3	COMMAND TRAIT
1	**Shielded by Faith:** *This warrior's blazing fervour has allowed him to fight on through the most terrible of wounds.* Add 1 to the Toughness characteristic of this fighter.
2	**Zealous Crusader:** *This warrior cannot wait to wet his blade with the blood of heretics and monsters.* Add 1 to the Move characteristic of this fighter.
3	**Decisive Leader:** *This warrior was born to command troops in battle.* If this fighter is included in your warband, you begin the battle with 1 additional wild dice.

FIRST CONVERGENCE: PURSUIT AMIDST THE ASHEN CRAGS

Despite your best efforts, your movements within the Eightpoints have been detected. A group of blood-hungry warriors has caught your scent and hounded you for the past few days, thirsty for the glory of killing one of the God-King's champions. But soon The Hunters will become The Hunted as the warriors in your command prepare an ambush. If you can slay the enemy's leader the rest of them will no doubt scatter to the winds.

BATTLEPLAN
Terrain: See map.

Deployment:
Clash of Blades

The Aspirant warband is the red deployment points.

Victory: Assassinate

The Aspirant warband is the attacker.

Twist: Draw a twist card as normal.

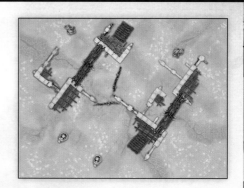

SECOND CONVERGENCE: THE DESECRATED TEMPLE

Hidden amidst the mountainous valleys of the Skullpikes stands a once -proud temple to the God-King. Your thoughts darken as you see the blasphemous mockery it has become. Profane runes and totems of warped flesh bedeck the walls, and you can hear the sounds of screams and deranged chanting echoing from within. This holy place must be purified, every last one of its deviant occupants put to the sword.

BATTLEPLAN
Terrain: See map.

Deployment:
Massacre

The Aspirant warband uses the red deployment points.

Victory: No Mercy

Twist: Draw a twist card as normal.

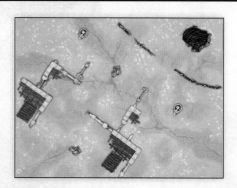

FINAL CONVERGENCE: LAST STAND AT FORLORN POINT

Finally you have reached the bleak mountain known as Forlorn Point. At its summit, capped by drifting snow and as-yet undefiled by the creeping influence of Chaos is the Stormvault Sacristy you were sent here to secure. You feel the strength and surety of the God-King's will as you set foot within its walls. Suddenly you hear the baying of cruel voices, and the sound of steel being drawn. An enemy warband has tracked you here! They must not lay a hand upon the God-King's treasures.

BATTLEPLAN
Terrain: See map.

Deployment:
Hold Out

The Aspirant warband uses the red deployment points.

Victory:
The Hidden Vault

The Aspirant warband is the defender.

Twist: Draw a twist card as normal.

CAMPAIGN OUTCOME
If the Aspirant warband is the winner, they complete this campaign quest. Turn to page 132 to see the outcome and claim your reward.

THE STOLEN TOME

You are one of the Black Disciples, most trusted agents of the Mortarch Arkhan, and a necromancer of formidable power. At the command of your master and the will of Mighty Nagash, you have been tasked with travelling to the Eightpoints to recover the Book of Valagharr, a rare and dreadful tome of necromantic lore. The sorcerer Kakistes, a traitorous former member of the Legion of Sacrament, stole the book from the Sanctus Mortem. It must be returned, and Kakistes subjected to a fittingly gruesome end. Only one as powerful and cunning as yourself could possibly hope to accomplish such a dangerous task.

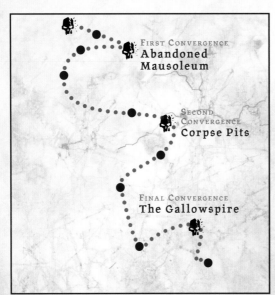

FIRST CONVERGENCE
Abandoned Mausoleum

SECOND CONVERGENCE
Corpse Pits

FINAL CONVERGENCE
The Gallowspire

TERRITORY RULES

Forsaken Ground: *Where the cursed agents of the Great Necromancer roam, the earth grows dark and fallow, and the restless dead stir in great numbers.*

You can spend 10 glory points to dominate a territory by creating an area of forsaken ground. Mark on your warband roster how many territories you dominate. Dominating territory offers the following bonuses:

For each territory dominated by your warband, increase the points you have available to spend on fighters when mustering your warband for a campaign battle by 50. Include the points costs for any thralls in your warband when mustering your warband. Thralls are not added to your warband roster and can never gain destiny levels, bear artefacts or be chosen to become a favoured warrior.

D3	ARTEFACT OF POWER
1	**Skullcap of Black Gold:** *This cap of black metal acts as a negative lodestone.* Subtract 1 from the damage points allocated by hits and critical hits (to a minimum of 1) from attack actions that target the bearer.
2	**Spiritcage:** *This lantern uses captured spirit energy to heal the wounds of undead beasts.* Each time an enemy fighter is taken down by an attack action made by the bearer, add 1 to the damage points allocated by hits and critical hits from attack actions made by the bearer until the end of the battle.
3	**Black Gem:** *This gem contains a storm of deathly magic, ready to be unleashed.* Once per battle, the bearer can use this artefact as an action. If they do so, pick a visible enemy fighter within 6" of the bearer and roll a dice. On a 4-5, allocate 5 damage points to that fighter. On a 6, allocate 10 damage points to that fighter.

D3	COMMAND TRAIT
1	**Reach of the Grave:** *This leader's terrible magic seeks out their foes unerringly.* Add 1 to the Range characteristic of attack actions made by this fighter. If the attack action has a minimum and maximum range, add 1" to the maximum range only.
2	**Suffused With Death:** *This leader's body writhes with the power of amethyst magic.* Add 1 to the value of abilities (to a maximum of 6) used by this fighter.
3	**Favoured of Arkhan:** *The Mortarch of Sacrament himself has marked this leader for greatness.* If this fighter is included in your warband, you begin the battle with 1 additional wild dice.

FIRST CONVERGENCE: AMETHYST BOUNTY

As you press further into the wilds of the Bloodwind Spoil, you come across the ruins of an ancient mausoleum. Driven by curiosity, you search the gloomy halls and discover a filigreed casket of black wood filled to the brim with amethyst crystals – potent foci for your necromantic magic. As you move to secure the treasure, however, you hear footsteps close by. Trespassers, no doubt, come to rob you of your prize. You plan to make them pay for their insolence before making off with the casket.

BATTLEPLAN
Terrain: See map.

Deployment:
Battle Lines

The Aspirant warband is the red deployment points.

Victory: The Prize

Twist: Draw a twist card as normal.

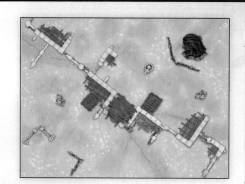

SECOND CONVERGENCE: RITUAL IN THE ASHWASTE

The tower known as the Gallowspire stands at the centre of the Kardeb Ashwaste, several leagues away. The journey is long and dangerous, and more than once you are attacked by scavengers and predatory beasts. You must replenish your undead servants, who are ragged and battered from constant fighting. Fortunately, there is no shortage of corpses buried beneath the black dirt of the Ashwaste. Hold off the enemy long enough to work a necromantic ritual and restore vigour to your thralls.

BATTLEPLAN
Terrain: See map.

Deployment:
The Hunt

The Aspirant warband uses the red deployment points.

Victory: The Ritual

The Aspirant warband is the defender.

Twist: Draw a twist card as normal.

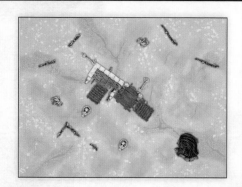

FINAL CONVERGENCE: FALL OF THE GALLOWSPIRE

Arriving before the sheer black walls of the Gallowspire, you discover that Kakistes has surrounded himself with mind-shackled servants, who hurl themselves upon intruders with blank-eyed fury. You can feel the intrusive call of magic in your head, emanating from several orbs of smoky crystal arrayed about the area. Before you can breach the Gallowspire and take back what was stolen from your deathless master, you must unbind this devious sorcery.

BATTLEPLAN
Terrain: See map.

Deployment:
Divide and Slaughter

The Aspirant warband uses the red deployment points.

Victory: The Raid

The Aspirant warband is the attacker.

Twist: Draw a twist card as normal.

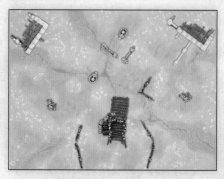

CAMPAIGN OUTCOME
If the Aspirant warband is the winner, they complete this campaign quest. Turn to page 132 to see the outcome and claim your reward.

THE BOTTLE HEIST

To the Gloomspite Gitz, an intact bottle is worth more than a handful of precious gems or a really sharp shiv. Lacking the knowledge to make these rare treasures for themselves, grots are forced to steal them any which way they can, for the shamans of the Gloomspite tribes need an unending supply in which to pour their mind-obliterating potions and sinister poisons. Unfortunately for those trapped in the Eightpoints, good glasswork is incredibly difficult to find. You and your fellow throat-cutters have been tasked with venturing out into the wilds in search of as many shiny bottles as you can lay your hands on.

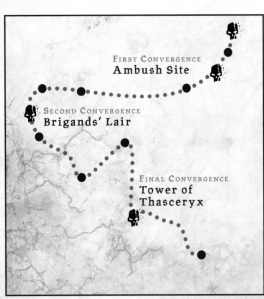

FIRST CONVERGENCE
Ambush Site

SECOND CONVERGENCE
Brigands' Lair

FINAL CONVERGENCE
Tower of Thasceryx

TERRITORY RULES

Summon Loonshrine: *The fanatical grots of the Gloomspite Gitz painstakingly carve the image of the Bad Moon into rock faces, a graven effigy that spreads madness across the land.*

You can spend 10 glory points to dominate a territory by summoning a Loonshrine. Mark on your warband roster how many territories you dominate. Dominating territory offers the following bonuses:

For each territory dominated by your warband, increase the points you have available to spend on fighters when mustering your warband for a campaign battle by 50. Include the points costs for any thralls in your warband when mustering your warband. Thralls are not added to your warband roster and can never gain destiny levels, bear artefacts or be chosen to become a favoured warrior.

D3	ARTEFACT OF POWER
1	**Leering Hood:** *This cursed hood twists the face of its wearer into a hideous, terrifying grimace.* Subtract 1 from the Attacks characteristic (to a minimum of 1) of attack actions that target the bearer.
2	**Glowy Shiv:** *This strange blade seems to glow with the light of the Bad Moon, and sinks through metal and hide with ease.* Add 3 to the damage points allocated by critical hits from attack actions made by the bearer that have a Range characteristic of 3 or less.
3	**Loonstone Talisman:** *This talisman can absorb hostile sorcerous energies.* Subtract 1 from the damage points allocated by hits and critical hits (to a minimum of 1) from attack actions that target the bearer.

D3	COMMAND TRAIT
1	**Stabby Git:** *This grot's wild, frenzied blade thrusts are surprisingly effective.* Add 1 to the Attacks characteristic of attack actions made by this fighter that have a Range characteristic of 3 or less.
2	**Leathery Skin:** *Despite their diminutive size, this warrior's hide is very tough.* Add 5 to the Wounds characteristic of this fighter.
3	**Devious Trickster:** *This unpredictable warrior is full of cruel cunning.* If this fighter is included in your warband, you begin the battle with 1 additional wild dice.

FIRST CONVERGENCE: RUN FER IT!

It has been a long and fruitless hunt, and the morale of your fractious band is running low. You eye your fellow grots suspiciously, trying to work out which of them might be planning to sink a shiv into your back. They stare back through narrowed eyes. Distracted, you almost fail to notice the dark shapes racing towards you from all sides. Ambush! It's every git for himself as your warband scatters and flees, dodging arrows and axe swings.

BATTLEPLAN
Terrain: See map.

Deployment: Defiant Stand

The Aspirant warband uses the blue deployment points.

Victory: No Mercy

Twist: Draw a twist card as normal.

SECOND CONVERGENCE: HONEST WORK

During your flight across the Eightpoints you stumble across a strange, smoke-belching tower surrounded by ruins. A robed figure suddenly appears before you in an explosion of purple flame, accompanied by several burly sell-swords. The human announces himself as Thasceryx of the Ninth Eye, and declares that unless you serve him, he will burn you all to ashes. This seems a fair deal. Thasceryx demands that you return to him several crates of scythyx venom stolen by nearby brigands.

BATTLEPLAN
Terrain: See map.

Deployment: Bait

The Aspirant warband uses the blue deployment points.

Victory:
Defend the Find

The Aspirant warband is the attacker.

Twist: Draw a twist card as normal.

FINAL CONVERGENCE: SMASH AND GRAB

Thasceryx directs you to deposit the returned goods in his alchemical workshop, a chamber filled with a vast collection of gleaming potion bottles containing glowing fluids – your jaw drops as you look upon this magnificent hoard. Unable to curtail your greed, you and your fellow grots run amok, grabbing hold of as many bottles as you possibly can and fleeing, the sorcerer's howls of outrage ringing in your ears. It's not long before you hear Thasceryx and his hired killers in hot pursuit.

BATTLEPLAN
Terrain: See map.

Deployment: No Escape

The Aspirant warband uses the blue deployment points.

Victory: The Gauntlet

The Aspirant warband is the defender.

Twist: Draw a twist card as normal.

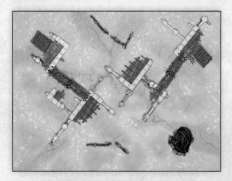

CAMPAIGN OUTCOME
If the Aspirant warband is the winner, they complete this campaign quest. Turn to page 132 to see the outcome and claim your reward.

A BOUNTY OF SOULS

Your Isharann priests heard the siren song resonating from far across the realms: a great gathering of souls, their voices joined as one in a wordless howl of agony. Such a vast bounty cannot be ignored, for war has come to the Idoneth enclaves, and more warriors are needed to replenish your race's dwindling numbers. The risk is deemed too great to send a full phalanx, for to march into Archaon's realm in great number would be foolish beyond imagining. Yet the Everchosen does not know that there is a secret passage to the island-between-realms, one that is fraught with peril but might allow your small, elite force to enter the Eightpoints unnoticed.

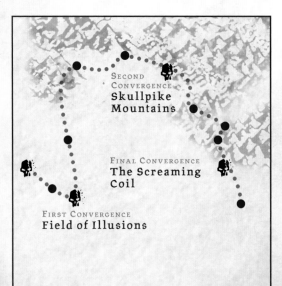

SECOND CONVERGENCE
Skullpike Mountains

FINAL CONVERGENCE
The Screaming Coil

FIRST CONVERGENCE
Field of Illusions

TERRITORY RULES

Harvest Souls: *The Idoneth emerge from the deep places of the realms to prey upon land-dwellers, stealing away their souls and leaving nothing but mournful silence and cold, dripping brine in their wake.*

You can spend 10 glory points to dominate a territory by harvesting its souls. Mark on your warband roster how many territories you dominate. Dominating territory offers the following bonuses:

For each territory dominated by your warband, increase the points you have available to spend on fighters when mustering your warband for a campaign battle by 50. Include the points costs for any thralls in your warband when mustering your warband. Thralls are not added to your warband roster and can never gain destiny levels, bear artefacts or be chosen to become a favoured warrior.

D3	ARTEFACT OF POWER
1	**Razormaw Gambeson:** *This enchanted leather is crafted from the hide of a razormaw, a ferocious predator of the deep.* Subtract 2 from the damage points allocated by critical hits (to a minimum of 1) from attack actions that target the bearer.
2	**Void Trident:** *This weapon strikes with the killing cold of the deepest waters.* Add 1 to the damage points allocated by hits and critical hits from attack actions made by the bearer that have a Range characteristic of 3 or less.
3	**Whirlpool Amulet:** *This talisman can entrap a victim in a swirling cage of icy seawater.* Once per battle, the bearer can use this artefact as an action. If they do so, subtract 1 from the Attacks characteristic (to a minimum of 1) of attack actions made by enemy fighters while they are within 6" of the bearer until the end of the battle round.

D3	COMMAND TRAIT
1	**Flowing Strikes:** *This warrior's attacks are as swift and relentless as a riptide.* Add 1 to the Attacks characteristic of attack actions made by this fighter that have a Range characteristic of 3 or less.
2	**Voidswimmer:** *This warrior has swum the deepest and most treacherous seas, hardening their constitution.* Add 5 to the Wounds characteristic of this fighter.
3	**Aethertide Rush:** *This warrior rides the surging waves of the ethersea.* Add 1 to the Move characteristic of this fighter.

FIRST CONVERGENCE: TIDE OF MADNESS

You have travelled far into the Eightpoints, slipping past packs of roving predators and bands of Chaos-worshipping scavengers. Ahead, the air shimmers strangely, like oil in water. As you advance, laughter echoes from the shadows, and your surroundings seem to shift and reform in a maddening blur. This place is suffused with Chaos. Suddenly, you hear the sound of war cries and the thunder of boots. You are under attack! Stand your ground and fight off these strange illusions.

BATTLEPLAN
Terrain: See map.

Deployment: Escalation

The Aspirant warband is the red deployment points.

Victory: Ebb and Flow

The Aspirant warband is the defender.

Twist: Draw a twist card as normal.

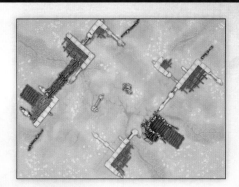

SECOND CONVERGENCE: ENCIRCLED

As you advance into the Skullpike Mountains you feel as though a thousand hungry eyes are locked upon you, and malevolent laughter echoes through the winding passes. As you cautiously move through an eerily silent clearing, there is a thunderous grinding sound. Rocks rain from above, cutting you off from your brethren. You hear the cries of enemy warriors, and figures race towards you through a cloud of choking dust. Hold on until your comrades reach your side.

BATTLEPLAN
Terrain: See map.

Deployment: Close the Jaws

The Aspirant warband uses the red deployment points.

Victory: Isolated

The Aspirant warband is the defender.

Twist: Draw a twist card as normal.

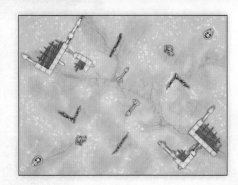

FINAL CONVERGENCE: THE SCREAMING COIL

Finally you reach the Screaming Coil, which rises like a violet serpent from the highest peak of the Skullpike Mountains. Great arcs of rune-marked metal span the length of the structure, sparking with sorcery. Before the Coil lie shattered ruins, within which you can see the remnants of bizarre machinery. The screaming of the trapped souls has reached an intense, ear-bleeding pitch. You must find a way to release the bounty of the Screaming Coil.

BATTLEPLAN
Terrain: See map.

Deployment: Clash of Blades

The Aspirant warband uses the red deployment points.

Victory: The Hidden Vault

The Aspirant warband is the attacker.

Twist: Draw a twist card as normal.

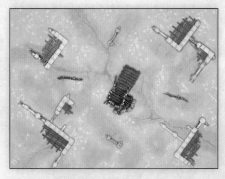

CAMPAIGN OUTCOME
If the Aspirant warband is the winner, they complete this campaign quest. Turn to page 132 to see the outcome and claim your reward.

SEEKERS OF THE CHALICE

Your quest has taken you far indeed, across lands assailed by terrible monsters and kingdoms ruled over by iron-fisted tyrants. In your deluded mind this odyssey was one of chivalrous glory – you do not recall the bloody trail you left in your wake, the terrified mortals you hunted down and devoured. Convinced of the righteousness of your holy task, you seek Ushoran's Chalice – a blessed relic that lavishes great power upon those who imbibe from it. You swear that no servant of evil shall stand in your way, for you have taken a vow to protect the innocent and uphold the honour of your court.

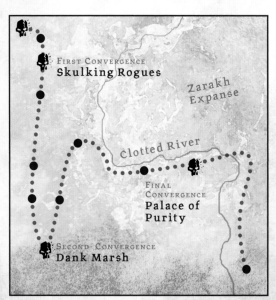

TERRITORY RULES

Raise Flesh Reliquary: *Mordants of the courts believe themselves to be raising soaring cathedrals and shrines of purity – in fact, they pile and shape the gory remains of their victims into grotesque monuments.*

You can spend 10 glory points to dominate a territory by raising a flesh reliquary. Mark on your warband roster how many territories you dominate. Dominating territory offers the following bonuses:

For each territory dominated by your warband, increase the points you have available to spend on fighters when mustering your warband for a campaign battle by 50. Include the points costs for any thralls in your warband when mustering your warband. Thralls are not added to your warband roster and can never gain destiny levels, bear artefacts or be chosen to become a favoured warrior.

D3	ARTEFACT OF POWER
1	**Bone Spear:** *This sharpened thigh bone makes for an effective javelin.* Add 1 to the Attacks characteristic of attack actions made by this fighter that have a Range characteristic of 3 or less.
2	**Winged Ribcage:** *This gruesome bone armour grants the wearer great swiftness.* Add 1 to the Move characteristic of the bearer.
3	**The Bilious Decanter:** *The fluid in this offal flask fills the drinker with unquenchable rage.* Once per battle, the bearer can use this artefact as an action. If they do so, until the end of the battle round, add 3 to the Attacks and Strength characteristics of attack actions made by the bearer that have a Range characteristic of 3 or less.

D3	COMMAND TRAIT
1	**Ravenous:** *Even by the standards of its kind, this mordant's hunger for flesh is terrible.* Add 1 to the Strength characteristic of attack actions made by this fighter that have a Range characteristic of 3 or less.
2	**Jutting Bones:** *The bones that pierce this mordant's flesh deflect blades and arrows.* Add 5 to the Wounds characteristic of this fighter.
3	**Flensing Talons:** *This warrior's unnaturally long claws rake through flesh and bone.* Add 3 to the damage points allocated by critical hits from attack actions made by this fighter.

FIRST CONVERGENCE: FIENDS ON THE ROAD

Visions of glory and wonder brought you to this wretched pit of villainy – visions of sweet wine bubbling from the lip of Ushoran's Chalice. Yet the servants of evil ever seek this grand prize for themselves. You see a band of such rogues before you now, skulking in the shadows. They must be driven before you like rats from a sinking ship. In the depths of your delusion you do not notice the trails of bloody saliva that drool from your fanged mouth, nor the eager rumbling of your stomach.

BATTLEPLAN
Terrain: See map.

Deployment: Escalation

The Aspirant warband is the red deployment points.

Victory: No Mercy

Twist: Draw a twist card as normal.

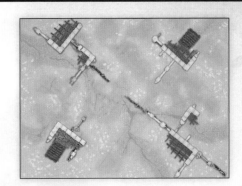

SECOND CONVERGENCE: THE MAIDEN'S REQUEST

Your quest takes you through a dank and shadowy marsh. After several hours you come across a pool of pure, crystal water. Rising from the azure lake is a beautiful woman clad in silver robes. The lady of the lake tells you that she knows where the Chalice can be found, but first you must bring her the head of a monstrous fiend that has stolen a rare treasure from her. As you leave to fulfil her request, the mire-hag sinks back into her pool of blood and filth, chuckling in bemusement.

BATTLEPLAN
Terrain: See map.

Deployment: Draw a deployment card as normal.

Victory: The Prize

Twist: Apex Predator

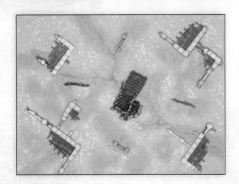

FINAL CONVERGENCE: CLEANSE THE PALACE

True to her word, the maiden of the lake guides you to the Palace of Purity. It fills you with wonder to walk upon the same gilded tiles that the noble Ushoran trod so many centuries ago. Ahead, raised upon a plinth of gleaming gold, lies a goblet of precious metal. Its surface is studded with jewels, and overflowing with rich, scarlet wine. You hear the sounds of growls and slavering mouths – this holy place is befouled by monsters! Reclaim the chalice and put these evil beasts to the sword.

BATTLEPLAN
Terrain: See map.

Deployment: Dance of Death

The Aspirant warband uses the red deployment points.

Victory: Hold Our Gains

The Aspirant warband is the attacker.

Twist: Draw a twist card as normal.

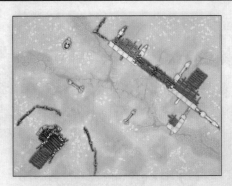

CAMPAIGN OUTCOME
If the Aspirant warband is the winner, they complete this campaign quest. Turn to page 133 to see the outcome and claim your reward.

A PROPER SCRAP

Your warband is the last remnant of an Ironjawz brawl that smashed its way into the Eightpoints many seasons past, before being surrounded and destroyed by the Everchosen's legions. You have come to enjoy life in the Eightpoints well enough; it is a brutal place, filled with deadly monsters to hunt and an endless supply of painted humans to crush beneath your hobnailed boots. Despite this constant, unrelenting violence, you are becoming dangerously bored. So few of the opponents you have hacked and torn apart recently have provided decent entertainment before the end. If you do not find a proper scrap soon, you and your fellow orruks will surely turn on one another.

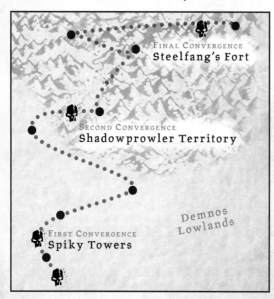

TERRITORY RULES

Raise Idol of Gork (or Mork): *The Ironjawz erect massive pig-iron monuments in honour of the Great Green God, and pile the broken weapons of those they have defeated beneath these idols.*

You can spend 10 glory points to dominate a territory by raising an Idol of Gork (or Mork). Mark on your warband roster how many territories you dominate. Dominating territory offers the following bonuses:

For each territory dominated by your warband, increase the points you have available to spend on fighters when mustering your warband for a campaign battle by 50. Include the points costs for any thralls in your warband when mustering your warband. Thralls are not added to your warband roster and can never gain destiny levels, bear artefacts or be chosen to become a favoured warrior.

D3	ARTEFACT OF POWER
1	**Iron Skull Helm:** *This immense helm encases the already thick skull of its wearer in impenetrable metal.* Add 1 to the Toughness characteristic of the bearer.
2	**Grotsquisha:** *This weapon pulps flesh and bone to paste with every blow.* Add 1 to the damage points allocated by hits and critical hits from attack actions made by the bearer.
3	**Necklace of Teef:** *The teeth of battered foes dangle from this hide strap.* Once per battle, the bearer can use this artefact as an action. If they do so, until the end of the battle round, add 1 to the Toughness characteristic of friendly fighters while they are within 6" of the bearer.

D3	COMMAND TRAIT
1	**Wall of Muscle:** *This orruk is a muscle-bound monster who can snap a foe in half with their bare hands.* Add 1 to the Strength characteristic of attack actions made by this fighter that have a Range characteristic of 3 or less.
2	**Thick-headed Brute:** *It takes an army to put this warrior down for good.* Add 5 to the Wounds characteristic of this fighter.
3	**Blessing of Mork:** *This warrior's devious kunnin' often takes their foes by surprise.* If this fighter is included in your warband, you begin the battle with 1 additional wild dice.

FIRST CONVERGENCE: SMASH AND TRASH

You and your fellow orruks have enjoyed rampaging about the wilds of the Eightpoints, smashing and carving apart anything unfortunate enough to fall in your path. Still, the local packs of scrawny scavengers scarcely offer much challenge. You're the meanest bunch of lads around, and you need a proper scrap. It's time to stir up the bloodwasp nest. Start by tearing down and burning all those spiky towers and piles of gubbinz that are littered across the Eightpoints.

BATTLEPLAN

Terrain: See map.

Deployment:
Battle Lines

The Aspirant warband is the red deployment points.

Victory: The Raid

The Aspirant warband is the attacker.

Twist: Draw a twist card as normal.

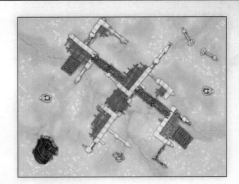

SECOND CONVERGENCE: SEARCH FOR STEELFANG

Trakor Steelfang. That's all these humans shout about as you smash them into pieces. The Chaos Lord's sigil can be seen all across this wasteland – the skull of a shadowprowler, encased in molten metal. Maybe this Steelfang can put up a better fight? You follow the trail of these totems far into the Skullpike Mountains, and there find Steelfang's mountaintop hold. Seek out the toughest of the warlord's champions, and bash their skulls in. Surely that will draw Steelfang into the open.

BATTLEPLAN

Terrain: See map.

Deployment:
Show of Strength

The Aspirant warband uses the red deployment points.

Victory: Conquer

The Aspirant warband is the attacker.

Twist: Draw a twist card as normal.

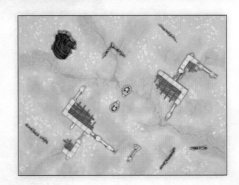

FINAL CONVERGENCE: PIT TRAP

You smash your way into Steelfang's encampment, leaving a trail of broken bones in your wake. There is the warlord himself, a sadistic grin plastered across his ugly face. You charge forward, but the ground suddenly gives way beneath you. The trapdoor deposits your warband in a circular pit filled with wreckage and rotting bodies. A gate opposite you creaks open, revealing another band of prisoners, blades in hand. Dispose of them and haul yourselves out of the pit.

BATTLEPLAN

Terrain: See map.

Deployment:
Frontal Assault

The Aspirant warband uses the red deployment points.

Victory: No Mercy

Twist: Draw a twist card as normal.

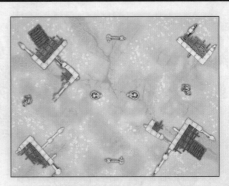

CAMPAIGN OUTCOME
If the Aspirant warband is the winner, they complete this campaign quest. Turn to page 133 to see the outcome and claim your reward.

TRAITOR'S FATE

A traitor to the Bloody-Handed God cowers within the Eightpoints, a deceiver and thief named Malekandra. Once a trusted handmaiden of High Oracle Morathi, the Hag Queen seized several relics of the Bloody-Handed Court and fled Hagg Nar, murdering several of her sisters in the process. The Lady Morathi personally commanded you to see Malekandra slain, and her stolen bounty recovered. You know not what caused the Hag Queen's madness, but it does not matter. There can be no forgiveness for betrayers of the Bloody-Handed God, only a gruesome and drawn-out death.

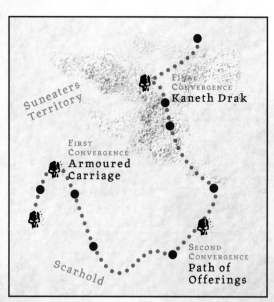

TERRITORY RULES

Enact Ritual of Blood: *The dreadful rites of Khaine are festivals of bloodletting and ritual slaughter, and culminate in the removal of a sacrifice's still-beating heart.*

You can spend 10 glory points to dominate a territory by enacting a ritual of blood. Mark on your warband roster how many territories you dominate. Dominating territory offers the following bonuses:

For each territory dominated by your warband, increase the points you have available to spend on fighters when mustering your warband for a campaign battle by 50. Include the points costs for any thralls in your warband when mustering your warband. Thralls are not added to your warband roster and can never gain destiny levels, bear artefacts or be chosen to become a favoured warrior.

D3	ARTEFACT OF POWER
1	**Bloodsiphon Blade:** *This fell weapon drains the vitality of those it strikes, granting their life essence to the wielder.* Each time an enemy fighter is taken down by an attack action made by the bearer, you can remove up to 3 damage points allocated to the bearer.
2	**Khainite War-mask:** *This nightmarish mask steals the will to fight from those who look upon it.* Once per battle, the bearer can use this artefact as an action. If they do so, until the end of the battle round, subtract 1 from the Toughness characteristic (to a minimum of 1) of visible enemy fighters while they are within 6" of the bearer.
3	**Darkfire Pendant:** *The unnatural flames that emanate from this amulet protect the wearer.* Subtract 1 from the damage points allocated by hits and critical hits (to a minimum of 1) from attack actions that target the bearer.

D3	COMMAND TRAIT
1	**Heart-taker:** *This warrior tears the heart from each of their victims, whether they are alive or dead.* Each time an enemy fighter is taken down by an attack action made by this fighter, add 1 to the damage points allocated by hits and critical hits from attack actions made by this fighter until the end of the battle.
2	**Bewitching Grace:** *To watch this warrior in battle is to become mesmerised by their supernatural grace.* Subtract 1 from the Attacks characteristic (to a minimum of 1) of attack actions that target this fighter.
3	**Mistress of Poisons:** *This warrior specialises in the brewing of lethal poisons.* Add 3 to the damage points allocated by critical hits from attack actions made by this fighter.

FIRST CONVERGENCE: BLOODY WELCOME

After many hours of travel, the armoured carriage grinds to a halt. Your warriors slip from the hold and open the throats of the guards, slinking away under cover of night before the rest of the convoy is alerted. You have arrived in the Eightpoints. The High Oracle's traitorous former handmaiden Malekandra cowers somewhere within these wretched lands. You will find her, and take her heart in the name of Khaine. First, you need information. That means securing prisoners for excruciation and interrogation.

BATTLEPLAN

Terrain: See map.

Deployment:
Vengeance

The Aspirant warband is the red deployment points.

Victory: Crush

The Aspirant warband is the attacker.

Twist: Draw a twist card as normal.

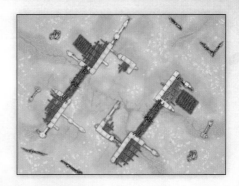

SECOND CONVERGENCE: A WORTHY OFFERING

After hours of torture, your captives finally talk. They speak of a white-haired aelf who passed through the settlement of Carngrad not long ago, hiring bands of mercenaries to accompany her into the wilds. She has taken refuge in an ancient Khainite fortress, hidden deep beneath the earth. To enter this refuge, one must present an offering of worthy hearts before a statue of the Bloody-Handed God. You must seek worthy kills in order to gain entrance to the hidden fortress.

BATTLEPLAN

Terrain: See map.

Deployment:
The Hunt

The Aspirant warband uses the blue deployment points.

Victory: Assassinate

The Aspirant warband is the attacker.

Twist: Draw a twist card as normal.

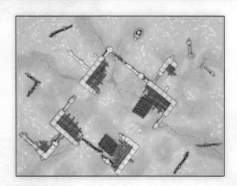

FINAL CONVERGENCE: TREASURES OF KANETH DRAK

You present your offering, and the ground beneath your feet opens up into a spiral stairway, lit by gleaming, violet crystals. This stronghold – Kaneth Drak – was once a refuge for the worshippers of Khaine. Hidden within is a veritable treasure trove of artefacts and tomes of ancient lore regarding the Bloody-Handed God, gathered by the traitor Malekandra. End the life of the treacherous aelf and recover that which belongs to the High Oracle Morathi.

BATTLEPLAN

Terrain: See map.

Deployment:
Defiant Stand

The Aspirant warband uses the red deployment points.

Victory:
Defend the Find

The Aspirant warband is the attacker.

Twist: Draw a twist card as normal.

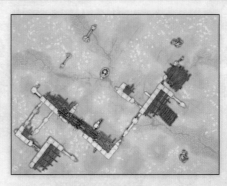

CAMPAIGN OUTCOME
If the Aspirant warband is the winner, they complete this campaign quest. Turn to page 133 to see the outcome and claim your reward.

THE STOLEN TOTEM

You were hunting razorhorns across the Shifting Plains when the humans struck at your warclan's camp, slaughtering scores of orruks and making off with your tribe's sacred totem, the Jaw of Mork. The Wurrgog Prophets foretold bad ju-ju for the warclan if the totem was not returned, and so you and your warriors raced off in pursuit of the thieving band and their leader, the warlord Korak Halfblade. Having travelled incredible distance and having lost scores of your warriors along the way – you find yourself in a strange land indeed. Yet you can feel the Waaagh! energy of the Jaw of Mork calling to you like a distant drum-beat.

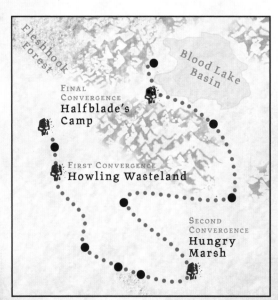

TERRITORY RULES

Raise Idol of Gork (or Mork): *Bonesplitterz raise great totems to mark out their territory, immense monuments formed from skulls, bones and stone and fashioned in the image of the Great Green God.*

You can spend 10 glory points to dominate a territory by raising an Idol of Gork (or Mork). Mark on your warband roster how many territories you dominate. Dominating territory offers the following bonuses:

For each territory dominated by your warband, increase the points you have available to spend on fighters when mustering your warband for a campaign battle by 50. Include the points costs for any thralls in your warband when mustering your warband. Thralls are not added to your warband roster and can never gain destiny levels, bear artefacts or be chosen to become a favoured warrior.

D3	ARTEFACT OF POWER
1	**Shiny Tattooz:** *This orruk has been honoured by the Wurrgog Prophets by being daubed with sacred markings.* Add 1 to the Toughness characteristic of the bearer.
2	**Lucky Bone:** *Some bones are just lucky.* If the bearer is included in your warband, you begin the battle with 1 additional wild dice.
3	**Shrunken Head:** *It is common for Bonesplitterz to lug around trophies from particularly memorable hunts.* Once per battle, the bearer can use this artefact as an action. If they do so, until the end of the battle round, add 1 to the Strength characteristic of attack actions made by visible friendly fighters that have a Range characteristic of 3 or less while they are within 6" of the bearer.

D3	COMMAND TRAIT
1	**Thick Skull:** *This warrior has taken so many blows to the head that such injuries no longer register.* Subtract 1 from the damage points allocated by hits and critical hits (to a minimum of 1) from attack actions that target this fighter.
2	**Killa Instinkt:** *Somehow, this orruk's strikes always seem to find the enemy's weak spot.* Add 3 to the damage points allocated by critical hits from attack actions made by this fighter that have a Range characteristic of 3 or less.
3	**Prophet of da Waaagh!:** *This warrior resonates Waaagh! energy, and attacks with the fury of Gork.* Add 1 to the value of abilities (to a maximum of 6) used by this fighter.

FIRST CONVERGENCE: BONE-BREAKING BREACH

You have tracked Korak Halfblade and your stolen totem to the wastelands of this strange place, but now you find yourself hunted in turn. A band of rival killers is looking for a fight. While normally you would like nothing more than to cave their heads in, you remember the visions of the Wurrgog Prophets – if your heirloom is not returned soon, the Great Green God's fury will be terrible indeed. Smash through the enemy's line with bone-breaking force, then resume your hunt.

BATTLEPLAN
Terrain: See map.

Deployment:
Blood Rush

The Aspirant warband uses the red deployment points.

Victory: The Gauntlet

The Aspirant warband is the defender.

Twist: Draw a twist card as normal.

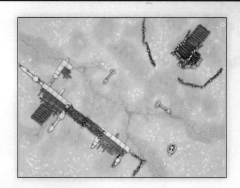

SECOND CONVERGENCE: AMBUSH IN THE HUNGRY MARSH

Korak Halfblade's trail leads through the Hungry Marsh, where fanged maws grow from the earth itself, devouring anything that strays too close. Soon you are lost in this horrific place, which seems to stretch on forever. Fortunately you spot a patch of high ground nearby that would make a good vantage point as you search for an escape route. Even better, it is currently occupied by a band of armed warriors upon whom you can take out your growing frustration.

BATTLEPLAN
Terrain: See map.

Deployment: Draw a deployment card as normal.

Victory:
Vantage Point

Twist:
Murky Swampland

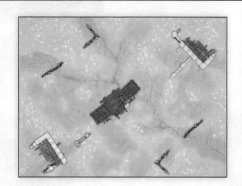

FINAL CONVERGENCE: BLOOD LAKE MASSACRE

As you crest the mountain ridge you see the earth fall away before you, descending towards an immense lake the colour of blood. Korak Halfblade's war camp is situated on a shelf of rock overlooking this great body of water. There, placed atop the largest structure, is your stolen totem. Blood thunders in your veins like the stomping feet of Gork and Mork. Time to reclaim what was taken from you, and add the Halfblade's skull to the top of your tribe's prized artefact.

BATTLEPLAN
Terrain: See map.

Deployment:
Refused Flank

The Aspirant warband uses the blue deployment points.

Victory: The Prize

Twist: Draw a twist card as normal.

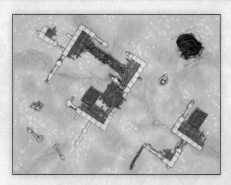

CAMPAIGN OUTCOME
If the Aspirant warband is the winner, they complete this campaign quest. Turn to page 133 to see the outcome and claim your reward.

SPOILS OF VICTORY

Through cunning, fearlessness and strength of arms you have triumphed over your rivals and left your mark on the Bloodwind Spoil. Under your leadership your warband has grown into a truly deadly force, feared by all who have heard the legends of their exploits. Your tale is not yet over, but for now you can relish the rewards of your victory.

On the following pages you will find conclusions for each of the narrative campaigns provided in this book, concluding your warband's epic journey. You will also receive a unique reward for completing each campaign: an item or blessing which

you can grant to your favoured champion to wield in any future battles. Although you have earned a great victory, your warband's odyssey is not over. You can continue to take on all rivals with the new and powerful tools at your disposal,

or embark upon a fresh campaign – either one of those detailed in this book or one provided in another Games Workshop publication. In time, your foes will learn to dread the very mention of your name!

IRON GOLEMS – CONQUER THE FORGE

Korrgad the slavemaster is still spitting hatred and bile at you even as your boot descends to crush his skull. The duardin's maul slips from his grasp and clatters upon the stone floor. You retrieve the weapon, nodding with satisfaction as you look upon its fine craftsmanship and the intricate runes of flame and fury etched across its smooth, black surface. It is a reward befitting the new and undisputed master of Varanthax's Maw. Soon this place will echo to the clangour of striking hammers and the bellows of the Iron Golems' expert forgemasters.

ARTEFACT OF POWER

Korrgad's Infernal Hammer: *In life Korrgad wielded a formidable weapon, a smouldering warhammer infused with daemonic energies. Its power is now your own.*

Add 2 to the damage points allocated by hits or critical hits from attack actions made by the bearer that have a Range characteristic of 3 or less.

IRON GOLEMS – CURSED METAL

The tainted invictunite proves lethal to work with, and several warriors are overcome by sickening mutations as they shape the cursed metal. Yet the strongest amongst you do not succumb, and craft items of tremendous power: heavy-bladed axes, throwing hammers and close-faced helms. You work day and night on a suit of spiked metal, hammering panels of invictunite into shape and etching runes of dark power into the material. When you are done, you are struck with the power of what you have created. Truly, the Dark Gods have guided your arm – you know you will never forge a greater work.

ARTEFACT OF POWER

Plate of the Golem: *This immense suit of corrupted invictunite armour can only be worn by the largest and strongest mortals. It is marked with potent runes of warding, and can turn aside the blow of an enraged gargant without even a scratch to show for it.*

Subtract 2 from the damage points allocated by hits and critical hits (to a minimum of 1) from attack actions that target the bearer.

UNTAMED BEASTS – THE HUNT FOR FIRESCAR

Firescar rises from its slumber, so enraged by your trespass that lashing flames erupt from its huge maw. It is a mighty and deadly creature, but the Devourer of Existence guides your spear arm this day. Barbed javelins and throwing axes cut into the beast's scales, unleashing a tide of scalding blood. The kill is not swift, and Firescar does not die easily, but eventually the ancient monster succumbs to scores of wounds. With triumphant howls, the Untamed Beasts descend upon its corpse, feasting upon the creature's flesh and blood.

ARTEFACT OF POWER

The Teeth of Firescar: *You tear Firescar's fangs from the beast's ruptured corpse. Even in death they retain their terrible heat. When mounted upon a spear or axe, they prove a most devastating weapon.*

Add 2 to the Strength characteristic of attack actions made by the bearer that have a Range characteristic of 3 or less.

UNTAMED BEASTS – TOOTH AND CLAW

The tide of beasts that you summon rampages through Carngrad for a night and a day, devouring scores of inhabitants and turning the filthy streets red with blood. You join in with the butchery, all emotion drowned out by the primal need to kill and feed. You taste the flesh of mortals, and though it is of weak stock, you smile as bloody gobbets fill your mouth. When finally you and your warriors awaken, you find yourselves in the wilds of the Bloodwind Spoil, covered in gore. In your hand is an amulet of carved bone. Where it came from you cannot say, but it resonates a terrible, bestial hunger.

ARTEFACT OF POWER
Devourer's Blessing: This simple, carved hook of bone radiates an aura of savagery. When blood is spilled, it unleashes waves of primordial hunger.

Once per battle, the bearer can use this artefact as an action. If they do so, until the end of the battle round, add 2 to the damage points allocated by each hit or critical hit from attack actions made by friendly fighters that have a Range characteristic of 3 or less while they are within 6" of the bearer.

CORVUS CABAL – WAR OF TALONS

The stench of rotting corpses does not leave Carngrad's streets for many months. Each body hauled out of the gutters by thralls and hurled upon the burning pyres is found to have its eyes plucked out and every item of value taken. Icons of the Great Gatherer are found on rooftops and spires throughout the city, and cut-throats and gangmasters alike whisper of the dreaded Corvus Cabal. From your perch you drink in this pall of fear with cold satisfaction. For once, the piercing cries of the Gatherer have quietened, its murderous greed satisfied by your carrion offering.

ARTEFACT OF POWER
The Blade of Vesca: Vesca Mirror-Eye's ornate, perfectly balanced rapier favours your fighting style. You take it for your own, leaving the axe of Headsplitter as an offering to the Great Gatherer.

Add 1 to the Attacks and Strength characteristics of attack actions made by the bearer that have a Range characteristic of 3 or less.

CORVUS CABAL – THE HUNGER OF ISIPHUS

As the scythe-like censer drops, it cuts open Isiphus' great belly with surgical precision. Rancid, sickly-sweet gore gushes forth, along with trickles of glittering gems and gold. The gargant screeches in pain and rage, but your warriors are already leaping gracefully atop the stricken creature, digging into its flesh and hauling free great handfuls of treasure. Most of this bounty will be offered to the Great Gatherer along with the corpse of Isiphus the Bloated, but amidst the gleaming mass your sharp eyes pick out an intriguing item you will claim as your own.

ARTEFACT OF POWER
Windrunner Greaves: These lightweight leg coverings of enchanted metal allow the wearer to summon a magical zephyr to hasten their movements.

Add 2 to the Move characteristic of the bearer.

CYPHER LORDS – A SPY IN THE HOUSE OF TALONS

Rask tries to scrabble away across the blood-slick stones, but the time for running is long past. Your thralls grasp the defeated warlord and drag him before you, and you begin to work the art of Nochseed upon your priceless captive. His screams carry far across the wilderness, though there are none but the carrion-beasts to bear witness to his end. Days later, Urdesh Rask returns to his seat of power in Carngrad. Hidden beneath his filthy chain hauberk is the Eye of Nochseed, seared into his chest. You are satisfied that your latest agent will prove most useful.

ARTEFACT OF POWER
Nochseed Thrall Stone: The bearer of this magical gem can peer into the minds of all who bear its brand. Such power and information is not wasted by the Cypher Lords.

If the bearer is included in your warband, you begin the battle with 2 additional wild dice.

CYPHER LORDS – COLD VENGEANCE

You slay every last resident of Barek Coldiron's warcamp, leaving only a single survivor to shed light upon what happened here – Coldiron himself, rendered insensible by ceaseless, nightmarish visions. He stumbles into Carngrad alone, screaming and ranting of a great, blazing eye in the darkness, spilling insanity into the realms. That same eye is branded upon his forehead – the symbol of the Cypher Lords. The ravings of this formerly feared warlord attract a large crowd, and last until an opportunistic thug sinks his dagger into Coldiron's back. With that, your vengeance is complete.

ARTEFACT OF POWER

Veil of Illusions: This diaphanous cloak of iridescent fabric fills the minds of those who look upon it with maddening illusions.

Subtract 2 from the damage points allocated by hits and critical hits (to a minimum of 1) from attack actions that target the bearer.

SPLINTERED FANG – NAGENDRA'S GULLET

You put out the fires started by the temple raiders, and dispose of the survivors. One by one they are devoured by the mass of crawling serpents. As you examine the ancient structure which the trespassers sought to breach, you come across an obsidian plinth carved in the image of Great Nagendra. Upon the plinth rests a spear of wondrous craftsmanship, threads of glowing liquid running through its metal head like veins, gleaming even in the darkness. You take up the spear, admiring its sublime balance. Nagendra's Gullet will serve well as a stronghold for the Splintered Fang in this hostile land.

ARTEFACT OF POWER

The Fang of Nagendra: This ancient weapon was crafted in honour of the Serpentfather, and the bite of its fluted blade is fearsome indeed. A single cut, and these pulsing grooves spew poison into the flesh of the victim.

Add 1 to the Attacks and Strength characteristics of attack actions made by the bearer that have a Range characteristic of 3 or less.

SPLINTERED FANG – VENOM OF THE GODS

The bodies of arena champions litter the Flensing Pits, bloated and reeking, clotted blood oozing from their open wounds. Some have entirely come apart in an eruption of gore, their flesh unmade by the daemonic brew smeared across your weapons. Others lie twisted and misshapen, faces contorted in indescribable agony. Even the crowd has fallen quiet. This is an audience not unused to brutal violence, but the sheer nature of the death you have unleashed is something even they have not witnessed before. None will forget the name of the Splintered Fang in a hurry.

ARTEFACT OF POWER

Godslayer Bane: This daemonic concoction is brewed from the most terrible venoms found within the Eightpoints. A single drop causes a most agonising, horrifying death.

Add 5 to the damage points allocated by critical hits from attack actions made by the bearer that have a Range characteristic of 3 or less.

THE UNMADE – PATH OF THE FLAYED PRINCE

With trembling hands you approach the altar of lacquered bone and take up the tome of your ancestor. The holy text of the Flayed Prince is bound in human skin and written with a delicate hand in dried blood. The book speaks of the wonders that the progenitor of your people witnessed beyond the veil, and the blissful ascension that awaits the Unmade when they finally join him in the embrace of agony. Before that day can come there is much work to be done. This book will guide your people onwards to their great destiny.

ARTEFACT OF POWER

Tome of the Flayed Prince: The blessed words of the legendary Prince Vourneste chronicle his enlightenment and his growing devotion to Chaos. They fill his faithful flock with rapturous devotion.

If the bearer is included in your warband, you begin the battle with 2 additional wild dice.

THE UNMADE – SONG OF SUFFERING

The Screaming Coil glows with blinding light, and the tortured wailing of countless tormented souls splits the air. Comrades and foes collapse to the ground, the former writhing in the throes of ecstatic revelation, the latter clawing madly at their faces as the terrible sound overwhelms them. Their screams are joined by those of distant creatures, and for a blissful moment all around are joined as one by the agony of pure sensation. Then there is a deafening crash, and splinters wind their way along the length of the Coil. The intensity of the torturous sound slowly fades to silence.

ARTEFACT OF POWER
Fragment of the Coil: *This amulet is fashioned from a loose crystal taken from the Screaming Coil. It echoes with the agonised screams of tormented souls.*

Subtract 1 from the Attacks and Strength characteristics of attack actions (to a minimum of 1) made by enemy fighters while they are within 3" of the bearer.

SCIONS OF THE FLAME – TIDE OF FIRE

The eruption of Varanthax's Maw drowns a vast swathe of land in molten rock. The fires can be seen for leagues across the Bloodwind Spoil, even as far as the gates of the Varanspire itself. Ash chokes the skies for days. The blessings of the Ever-Raging Flame ensure that the strongest amongst you pass through the rising fires unharmed. From a nearby peak you observe the destruction caused by your handiwork. This is merely the beginning. This inferno will one day grow to swallow the realms themselves.

ARTEFACT OF POWER
Armour of Ashes: *Recovered from the wreckage of the Maw's violent eruption, this chainmail hauberk surrounds the wearer with a swirling ash cloud that intercepts enemy blades and arrows.*

Add 10 to the Wounds characteristic of the bearer.

SPIRE TYRANTS – MAKING YOUR NAME

Gyver Kull spends his last moments cursing your name, a display of boldness which earns him a swift, if bloody, end. His remaining warriors take one look at your gore-splattered blades and the ruptured corpses you have left strewn across the fighting pits and lower their own weapons. You grasp a handful of Kull's lank hair and lift his severed head high for all to see, bellowing the name of the Spire Tyrants as you do so. No one who witnessed how brutally you ended the powerful warlord's reign will ever doubt your might, nor question your rightful place at the Everchosen's side. Not to your face, at least.

ARTEFACT OF POWER
Gyver's Belt: *You claim this magical strap from the corpse of Gyver Kull. Crafted from the leathery hide of a Greater Manticore, it invests the bearer with a portion of the beast's terrible rage.*

Add 1 to the Move characteristic of the bearer. In addition, add 1 to the Attacks characteristic of attack actions made by the bearer that have a Range characteristic of 3 or less.

NIGHTHAUNT – THE BELLS OF LOST VELORUM

The spirits of Lost Velorum still flock to the sound of tolling bells, but now it is the funereal clangour of your own tocsins that shepherds them onwards, away from the ruins of the cavern-city. A baleful night sky looks down upon your eerie procession, and in its bloody, storm-wracked depths you think you catch the briefest glimpse of a skeletal visage – Nagash, your lord and master. Viridian lightning crashes down and strikes the bell you hold in ethereal hands. When it rings again, it does so with a thunderous peal that shakes the earth.

ARTEFACT OF POWER
The Toll of Shyish: *This balefully glowing bell rings out with the dreadful finality of Shyish.*

The bearer can use the following ability:

[Double] Toll of Doom: Pick a visible enemy fighter within 8" of this fighter and roll 2 dice. For each roll of 3-4, allocate 3 damage points to that fighter. For each roll of 5-6, allocate 5 damage points to that fighter.

STORMCAST ETERNALS – THE HIDDEN VAULT

The trespassers slain, you enter the depths of the Stormvault Sacristy at Forlorn Point. Silence fills the halls, but there is no fear or dread, only a sense of serenity. Even in the hateful wilds of the Eightpoints, this monument to the God-King's strength and wisdom remains uncorrupted. You are filled with a sense of purpose and clarity, and you enter the grandest chamber of the structure. Within, secured in floating crystal prisms and chests of burnished gold, are treasures beyond description. You will see these relics returned to Sigmaron, safe once more in Sigmar's hands.

ARTEFACT OF POWER

The Ring of Tempests: *This band of gold and electronite is the ancestral ring of a storm tyrant, and resonates with those legendary titans' thunderous power.*

Add 2 to the value of abilities (to a maximum of 6) used by the bearer.

LEGIONS OF NAGASH – THE STOLEN TOME

With Kakistes' wards and mindstone sentries shattered, you drive your undead thralls onwards into the Gallowspire. You find the traitorous necromancer in his chambers at the summit of the great tower, and though his sorcery is formidable, it cannot match your mastery of amethyst magic. You pluck the Book of Valagharr from Kakistes' lifeless hands, but you are not finished with the betrayer just yet. When you depart the Gallowspire with your prize, Kakistes shambles at your side – his risen corpse will make a fine gift for your master Arkhan.

ARTEFACT OF POWER

The Book of Valagharr: *This tome was penned by the infamous necromancer Valagharr, betrayer of the God-King. It is filled with his musings upon the nature and power of death magic.*

For the bearer, the '**Summon Undead**' ability does not require a [triple], instead it requires a [double].

GLOOMSPITE GITZ – THE BOTTLE HEIST

You evade Thasceryx' clutches and slip away into the wilds of the Bloodwind Spoil, clutching your ill-gotten gains. When you finally arrive back at your tribe's hidden lair, your shamans are delighted with the haul of precious bottles. They waste no time in brewing up all manner of foul-smelling concoctions and unpleasant poisons, filling each recovered container to the brim. For your success, you are honoured with a particularly foul broth that allows you to belch forth a stream of viscous, black bile to blind and sicken your enemies. A mighty gift indeed!

ARTEFACT OF POWER

Bilebreath Brew: *This black liquid smells as foul as a troggoth's underarm, and causes the imbiber to vomit a stream of sticky bile.*

The bearer can use the following ability:

[Triple] Toxic Belch: Roll a dice for each visible enemy fighter within a number of inches of this fighter equal to the value of this ability. On a 3+, until the end of the battle round, the fighter being rolled for cannot make move actions or disengage actions.

IDONETH DEEPKIN – A BOUNTY OF SOULS

You drain the Screaming Coil of many souls, and none resist as they are drawn from the corrupted mechanisms of the strange engine. They are damaged, broken things, but they will serve just as well in the hands of your Isharann priests – all that they have suffered will be forgotten when they are reshaped and reborn to serve the will of the Idoneth. You recover several intriguing fragments of the Coil itself. A cursed thing it might be, but the ability to draw and capture souls in such quantities is potentially of great value to your people.

ARTEFACT OF POWER

Whispering Lurelight: *When you hold this lurelight close, the souls recovered from the Screaming Coil whisper secrets of the Eightpoints into your ear.*

If this fighter is included in your warband, you begin the battle with 2 additional wild dice.

FLESH-EATER COURTS – SEEKERS OF THE CHALICE

You lift Ushoran's Chalice to your lips and pour its sweet-smelling wine into your mouth. As the crimson liquid washes down your throat you feel your muscles swell and your aches and pains disappear. A great sense of serenity overcomes you. Your quest is complete, and your oath fulfilled. You look upon the bodies of the foul creatures which guarded this place, strewn about the hall. You will hold a feast here, you declare to your companions, to honour mighty Ushoran. All will drink from the chalice, and upon the morrow you will seek out a new evil to smite. Their cheers bring a wide smile to your face.

ARTEFACT OF POWER
Ushoran's Chalice: As far as you are concerned, you have located the legendary chalice of Ushoran, progenitor of the Grand Courts. In fact, it is a corrupted relic, a fanged-skull goblet that seeps boiling blood.

Add 2 to the value of abilities (to a maximum of 6) used by the bearer.

IRONJAWZ – A PROPER SCRAP

Steelfang's laughter dies upon his scarred lips as you claw your way out of his pit trap. Too late, his warriors react, rushing forward to strike you down. You bellow with laughter as you smash their puny weapons aside, crushing ribcages and skulls with heavy punches in return. Steelfang waits, greataxe in hand. What follows is a memorable bout of violence. The Chaos warlord strikes blow after blow on your pig-iron armour, even gouging deep cuts in your face and neck, but in the end it is not enough. A vicious headbutt crushes his face, and with one mighty blow you cut Trakor Steelfang in two.

ARTEFACT OF POWER
Steelfang's Greataxe: Steelfang's weapon is an enormous headsman's axe, far too large for the average human to wield. It fits in an orruk's meaty fist rather well, and its edge is sharp enough to carve through stone.

Add 2 to the damage points allocated by hits and critical hits from attack actions made by the bearer that have a Range characteristic of 3 or less.

DAUGHTERS OF KHAINE – TRAITOR'S FATE

Malekandra's death is not a pleasant one. In her final throes she shrieks blasphemous nonsense regarding the High Oracle, some gibberish about Khaine's foremost servant being a deceiver and traitor. Uninterested in the ravings of a mad aelf, you cut out the traitor's beating heart and finally end her wretched existence. The abandoned temple to the Bloody-Handed God is filled with items that Morathi will find most intriguing. You take as much as you can carry, including some exquisitely crafted sciansá.

ARTEFACT OF POWER
The Screaming Daggers of Khaine: These wondrously enchanted blades unleash a deafening scream as they whip through the air, carving through armour as if it were parchment.

Add 1 to the Attacks and Strength characteristics of attack actions made by the bearer that have a Range characteristic of 3 or less.

BONESPLITTERZ – THE STOLEN TOTEM

A new trophy adorns the Jaw of Mork – Korak Halfblade's skull. Perhaps the rage of the Great Green God can be abated, once you have returned the Jaw to your tribe's Wurrgog Prophet. You have absolutely no idea how to get back to the plains you call home, but that fact hardly worries you at this moment, for simply holding the Jaw of Mork makes you feel invincible. Raising the totem high, you let out a furious bellow, and your fellow orruks join in as one. If the humans of this place try to stand in your way they will meet the same grisly fate as the Halfblade.

ARTEFACT OF POWER
Jaw of Mork: The Jaw of Mork is back in the hands of your tribe, bedecked with new trophies and skulls. Its mere presence stirs your fellow orruks into a fighting fury.

Once per battle, the bearer can use this artefact as an action. If they do so, until the end of the battle round, add 1 to the Toughness characteristic of all friendly fighters.

BACKGROUND TABLES

One of the great joys of any narrative campaign is in naming and personalising your warriors, and building a unique story as you lead them into battle against all manner of lethal enemies. Not all will survive, for the Eightpoints is a wild and deadly land, but those that do will become legends amongst their people.

The warbands battling for control of the Bloodwind Spoil do not consist of faceless bands of minions, but hardened killers forged in a crucible of battle and constant danger. These warriors hail from across the Mortal Realms, and though they share a common goal – to gain the favour of the Everchosen and thus be honoured with a place amongst his multitudinous legions – their drives and motivations vary greatly.

Some hail from brutal kingdoms devoted to the Dark Gods, with their own infrastructure and unique warrior culture. Others are from scattered cults or nomadic tribes. Then, of course, there are those who deny the primacy of Chaos, and seek to wreak havoc across the domain of the Everchosen.

Every time you take your chosen warband to the field of battle, they enter a whirlwind of carnage from which some may not return alive. Those who survive these encounters will grow in power and renown, word of their infamous deeds spreading across the Eightpoints.

Perhaps your leader will prove to be an undefeatable duellist capable of matching blades against whatever your opponents throw at them. Or maybe a lowly cut-throat will earn a name and a legend by felling a monstrous beast against the odds, and then rise to become one of your most trusted and deadly lieutenants. These stories are at the heart of any narrative experience, and it's incredibly fun and rewarding seeing them come to life upon the tabletop.

On the following pages you will find inspirational names and background traits for every Warcry faction presented in this book, specific to their unique cultures. It's important to note that these are merely suggestions; if you would rather come up with your own detailed history or unique names, then all the better!

Sorgev stopped and raised his fist. The clatter of iron boots halted.

'What is it, legionary?' came Dominar Golbren's voice, muffled beneath his cage helm.

Ahead, the trail they were following passed underneath a great stone archway hung with gibbets, at the highest point of which stood a crow-like gargoyle with wings spread. Beyond the arch rose a spine of shattered walls, smeared with bloody sigils. The heavy wind set the skeletal occupants of the strung cages to dancing, their yellowed bones rattling against iron. Sorgev frowned. He caught no movement, but he could not shake the sensation of being watched.

'Forward, then,' growled Golbren. 'We've no time for delay.'

Sorgev muttered a curse under his breath. Caution was an alien concept to Golbren, even in this deadly land. As far as the dominar was concerned, there was no problem that could not be solved with his immense spine-crusher maul.

The Iron Golems trudged on, passing beneath the archway. The strange gargoyle gazed impassively into the distance from its vantage point.

And then its beaked head turned and stared directly at Sorgev.

Before the legionary could even shout a warning, the gargoyle spread its wings and leapt down from on high. It landed agilely upon Golbren's back, and there was a flash of bright steel. The Iron Golem stumbled, gasping, hot blood arcing from a slashed neck. The bird-thing fell free and rolled, coming to its feet facing Sorgev, its razor-claw wings spread wide. More ragged, cloaked shapes were dropping all around the Iron Golems, who formed up in a circle, presenting a wall of spiked iron.

'What's yours is now ours,' hissed the gargoyle.

'For the forge!' Sorgev screamed, raising his warhammer high and charging forward to meet it.

IRON GOLEM

Hailing from the Ferrium Mountains in Chamon, the Iron Golems are a hardy and ruthless people who rule over their domain with an iron fist.

The Iron Golems are a stubborn people, preferring to face any threat with direct and overwhelming force. They have carved out an impressive kingdom from the unforgiving rock of their mountain home, erecting enormous forge-complexes powered by the flames of the captive Sun Dragon Axranathos. These forges pump out weapons and armour in huge quantities. A slave class of prisoners and serfs provides the vast amounts of back-breaking labour required for this scale of production, directed by the unforgiving lashes and brands of Iron Golem overseers. Many Chaos-worshipping nations trade with the Golems, for the quality of their work is renowned.

IRON GOLEM FIRST NAMES	
D10	**FIRST NAME**
1	Sever
2	Garn
3	Broch
4	Malek
5	Vos
6	Drann
7	Borscha
8	Varka
9	Crola
10	Brujde

IRON GOLEM LAST NAMES	
D10	**LAST NAME**
1	Drammer
2	Greel
3	Varsk
4	Bannor
5	Sorgev
6	Dredj
7	Scorl
8	Haddun
9	Kolsk
10	Stalis

ORIGIN	
1	**Overseers** – Your warband oversaw the labouring of the Iron Golems' thralls with ruthless cruelty.
2	**Weaponsmiths** – The blades and hammers crafted by your warband are of masterful quality.
3	**Onyx Guard** – Your warband were elite guardians of the Onyx Fist, the Golems' Dreadhold.
4	**Breaching Party** – Your warriors are experts at smashing a path through enemy fortifications.
5	**Voice of the Golem** – It was your duty to enforce the collection of tribute from the Golems' vassal states.
6	**Veterans of the Ash War** – Your warband took part in the battle to recapture the dragon Axranathos, when the creature broke free.

LEADER/FAVOURED WARRIOR BACKGROUND	
1	**Blood of Mithraxes** – This warrior is a proud relation of High Overlord Mithraxes, ruler of the Iron Golems.
2	**Drillmaster** – This warrior is responsible for maintaining cohesion and discipline in the ranks of the Golems.
3	**Dragon-marked** – This warrior was burned by the fires of Axranathos, and wears these marks proudly.
4	**Cruel Tyrant** – This warrior commands through sheer brutality.
5	**Vengeful** – This warrior never forgives a slight, and seeks vengeance with single-minded ferocity.
6	**Unstoppable Force** – This warrior eschews tactical cunning, preferring to face every threat head-on.

UNTAMED BEASTS

The Untamed Beasts hail from the Jagged Savannah, a stretch of grassland dominated by stampeding herd-beasts and hunting packs of predatory monsters.

Such is the primal ferocity of this place that the savannah itself is locked in a battle for survival – razor-sharp maws of living rock periodically burst from beneath the earth, swallowing tracts of land. The strength granted by their worship of Chaos has allowed these nomadic tribespeople not only to survive the feeding frenzy of their homeland, but to thrive. The weakest become meat for the Devourer of Existence to feast upon, while the strongest live long enough to earn a name. This epithet is chosen to honour a notable deed they have performed – the slaying of a deadly beast, perhaps, or a propensity for uncanny foresight.

UNTAMED BEASTS FIRST NAMES	
D10	**FIRST NAME**
1	Syugah
2	Ekuth
3	Gantul
4	Kurgo
5	Makat
6	Ugula
7	Tenyet
8	Mayim
9	Shroya
10	Thuka

UNTAMED BEASTS LAST NAMES	
D10	**LAST NAME**
1	Truthspeaker
2	Cleftskull
3	the Hungerer
4	Heart-eater
5	Vorrnslayer
6	Bloodtooth
7	the Maw
8	Plainsrunner
9	Bonecrusher
10	Spinerender

ORIGIN	
1	**Skinners** – This warband strips and wears the hides of slain beasts, believing it grants them bestial power.
2	**Raiders** – Your warband infiltrates enemy territory to pillage and burn.
3	**Tireless Pursuers** – The warriors at your command never tire and never abandon a hunt.
4	**Beast-marked** – Having consumed the flesh of Chaos-tainted beasts, your warband are frenzied, blood-hungry barbarians.
5	**Iconoclasts** – Your warriors delight in tearing down the falsehoods of civilisation.
6	**Prowlers** – These warriors move unseen and unheard, silently tracking their prey.

LEADER/FAVOURED WARRIOR BACKGROUND	
1	**Wild Tongue** – This warrior has a primal connection with chaotic beasts, and is able to commune with them.
2	**Gruesome Trophy** – This warrior always carries a trophy of flesh cut from a memorable foe.
3	**Child of the Devourer** – This warrior was born with the mark of the Devourer, a sign of holy favour.
4	**Scarred Warrior** – This warrior's hide is covered with hideous scars, gifts from the beasts they have slain.
5	**Sharp-eyed** – This warrior has consumed the flesh of hunting birds, and gained their keen sight.
6	**Destroyer** – This warrior hates city-dwellers, and seeks to burn down all signs of civilisation.

CORVUS CABAL

Masters of ambush and assassination, warriors of the Cabal tend to possess an unnerving focus, talking little and communicating with a combination of complex hand-signals and sharp cries that sound like those of hunting prey-birds.

Though their stronghold, the Shrouded Eyrie, lies in a secluded region of Ulgu, the Corvus Cabal have buried their talons into many mortal cities of the realms. From their perches high above the heave and rush, they observe all. Spates of murders have plagued many of Sigmar's cities – key citizens brutally slain, their eyes removed and trophies stripped from their corpses. Many Chaos Lords have sought to hire the Cabal's services as assassins. The Great Gatherer's flock accept no payment beyond that which they take from the bodies of their victims.

CORVUS CABAL FIRST NAMES	
D10	FIRST NAME
1	Veig
2	Siv
3	Crin
4	Irik
5	Rusa
6	Dis
7	Shen
8	Ao
9	Kiri
10	Tyen

CORVUS CABAL LAST NAMES	
D10	LAST NAME
1	Cohl
2	Drehst
3	Veel
4	Nas
5	Sarak
6	Ranis
7	Kris
8	Shrak
9	Braka
10	Crul

ORIGIN	
1	**Trophy-takers** – Your warband carves trophies from the flesh of those they have slain.
2	**Roof-runners** – Your warband stalks the roofs and spires of ruined cities.
3	**Gargoyles** – You and your warriors are used to spending hours, even days, in the same vantage spot.
4	**Shades of the Eyrie** – Your warband was once tasked with defending the Cabal's mountaintop stronghold.
5	**Infiltrators** – There is no locked door or secured stronghold that your warband cannot breach.
6	**Zealous Killers** – Your warriors seek out and kill those marked for death by the Great Gatherer.

LEADER/FAVOURED WARRIOR BACKGROUND	
1	**Eyetaker** – This warrior plucks out the eyes of their victims as keepsakes.
2	**Patient Cunning** – This warrior always waits for the perfect moment to strike.
3	**Death From Above** – This warrior prefers to end their foe's life with a single, brutal strike from on high.
4	**Realistic** – This warrior is perfectly willing to retreat in order to win another day.
5	**Avaricious** – This warrior will risk everything for a glittering prize.
6	**Ear-splitting Shriek** – This warrior unleashes a piercing cry as they leap in to attack.

CYPHER LORDS

Rulers of the city-state of Nochseed, the Cypher Lords are masters of illusion and deception. They have gazed into the dark heart of Chaos, and embraced its infinite madness.

The Lords of Nochseed are a secretive band, maintaining an image of serene nobility even as their spies embed themselves within the social strata of neighbouring cities and settlements. Theirs is not the way of savage destruction. Instead they seek to spread the taint of madness in a more subtle fashion, turning their enemies upon one another with sadistic cunning, instigating uprisings, coups and assassinations to encourage a constant state of anarchic flux. The lesser ranks of the Cypher Lords' battle thralls are leashed to the will of their masters, bound by mind-altering sorcery and directed into battle like puppets.

CYPHER LORDS FIRST NAMES	
D10	**FIRST NAME**
1	Sentilia
2	Vigus
3	Carastes
4	Benalo
5	Talmen
6	Arelius
7	Vorsima
8	Palania
9	Semili
10	Truscala

CYPHER LORDS LAST NAMES	
D10	**LAST NAME**
1	Baneggio
2	Tatravellan
3	Calcis
4	Fabridian
5	Morenigo
6	Calmarand
7	Halpurnis
8	Ventamilio
9	Pullos
10	Daneggia

ORIGIN	
1	**Alchemists** – Your warriors specialise in the brewing of mind-altering potions and hallucinogenic bombs.
2	**Agents of Nochseed** – Your warriors take the guise of diplomats and traders, infiltrating rival cities.
3	**Deceptive Duellists** – You are students of the College of Mirrors, Nochseed's premier martial academy.
4	**Thrallmasters** – Your warband was charged with recruiting worthy battle-thralls for the Cypher Lords.
5	**Secret Keepers** – Your warband has stared into the depths of madness, and gleaned prophetic secrets.
6	**King-killers** – You and your warriors are experts in the art of instigating coups and violent revolts.

LEADER/FAVOURED WARRIOR BACKGROUND	
1	**Keen Wit** – This warrior is an urbane and charismatic presence, always ready with a cutting quip.
2	**Dark Obsession** – This warrior offers a facade of civility, but indulges in an appalling secret vice.
3	**Master of the Eight Forms** – This warrior is a peerless swordfighter, and takes every chance to prove it.
4	**Unsettling Gaze** – One gaze into this warrior's eyes reveals an inner well of madness.
5	**Connoisseur** – This warrior seeks only the finest things – whether thralls, food or opponents.
6	**Voice-thrower** – This warrior can project their voice, frightening and unsettling their foes.

THE UNMADE

The story of the Unmade is a tragic one, a great kingdom's descent into barbarism. Once, the philosopher-kings of Tzlid were renowned across Shyish for their nobility and wisdom.

Yet the kingdom was plagued by the depredations of undead creatures. Mighty Prince Vourneste swore to find a way to protect his people. In desperation he turned to the powers of Chaos, and his prayers were answered in the most horrific fashion. Twisted and remade by his daemonic patrons, he became the monster known as the Flayed Prince. He led his people in rituals of mutilation in which pain was worshipped as a benediction. His people became the Unmade. They have since abandoned dynastic names, instead taking simple titles that mark them as nothing more than weapons of the Dark Gods.

THE UNMADE FIRST NAMES (1)	
D10	**FIRST NAME**
1	Shadowhaunter
2	Flenser
3	Corpseblade
4	Gouge
5	Throatcutter
6	Scythe
7	Eyepeeler
8	Split-Tongue
9	Leer
10	Smile-in-Darkness

THE UNMADE FIRST NAMES (2)	
D10	**FIRST NAME**
1	Eyebite
2	Ragged
3	Whisper
4	Pale Spider
5	Ghoster
6	Bloodshot
7	Nighteye
8	Catcher
9	Fingerbones
10	Sineater

ORIGIN	
1	**Ragged Clergy** – Your warriors are particularly zealous adherents to the Flayed Prince's teachings.
2	**Hunters of the Dead** – Your warriors are notably adept at tracking and destroying undead foes.
3	**Paincrafters** – Your warband is skilled in the crafting of inventive weapons of torment.
4	**Torturers** – Even amongst the Unmade, your warband is unusually skilled at inflicting pain.
5	**Stalkers** – Your warband once prowled the deep forests of Tzlid, and its warriors are skilled hunters.
6	**Flesh-takers** – Your warband once sailed the seas of Shyish, raiding coastal settlements.

LEADER/FAVOURED WARRIOR BACKGROUND	
1	**Silent One** – Having removed their tongue, this warrior communicates in a series of clicks and hisses.
2	**Jaded Masochist** – This warrior seeks out new and terrible agonies to restore their spiritual harmony.
3	**Descendent of Vourneste** – This warrior claims a blood connection to the legendary Flayed Prince.
4	**Bleeding Sores** – This warrior's many lesions and sores constantly seep blood.
5	**Unnerving Laughter** – This warrior's laughter sounds like the tinkling of broken glass.
6	**Strange Twitching** – This warrior's movements are eerily jerky and unnatural.

SPLINTERED FANG

The warriors of the Splintered Fang descend from the nomadic tribes of the great jungles of Invidia, and once worshipped the godbeast Nagendra as part of a pantheon of animalistic deities.

Over the centuries this primal totemism was corrupted by the influence of Chaos. The shamans of the Splintered Fang came to worship the Coiling Ones, daemonic entities that claimed to be the offspring of Nagendra, and demanded a constant offering of souls in order to awaken their slumbering progenitor. One by one the Splintered Fang destroyed the other tribes of the Invidian Pantheon, hurling the survivors into serpent-filled pits. Those not slain by the searing toxins that seeped into their blood were granted the honour of joining the Splintered Fang, a custom that the warrior cult observes to this day.

SPLINTERED FANG FIRST NAMES	
D10	**FIRST NAME**
1	Sitha
2	Ve'thoss
3	C'lissa
4	Ma'suth
5	Ilthis
6	Lash'ya
7	Ossyuth
8	Sorenis
9	Ethiss
10	Silren

SPLINTERED FANG LAST NAMES	
D10	**LAST NAME**
1	Ullinash
2	Agareth
3	Sorigath
4	Varashma
5	Kushma
6	Odoleth
7	Sinneth
8	Ashmos
9	Annasis
10	Katilash

ORIGIN	
1	**Converts** – Your warband once belonged to a rival tribe that was subsumed into the Splintered Fang.
2	**Pit Vipers** – Your warband was responsible for the brutal training of Splintered Fang warriors.
3	**Ophidian Guard** – Your warband once guarded a temple of the Coiling Ones.
4	**Venom-blooded** – Your warriors have tested the most powerful venoms upon their own flesh.
5	**Faithful of Nagendra** – Your warband secretly worships Nagendra, and not his devious offspring.
6	**Mercenaries** – Your warriors have fought for several Chaos Lords as mercenary troops.

LEADER/FAVOURED WARRIOR BACKGROUND	
1	**Unblinking** – This warrior does not blink, giving them an unnerving intensity.
2	**Scaleskin** – This warrior's skin is smooth-scaled, like that of a serpent.
3	**Forked Tongue** – This warrior has carved their tongue in two, in honour of the Coiling Ones.
4	**Cold-blooded Practicality** – This warrior gladly sacrifices as many lives as are required to see the task done.
5	**Black Blood** – The very blood that runs through this warrior's veins is caustic and deadly.
6	**Unsettling Calm** – This warrior rarely displays any emotion.

SCIONS OF THE FLAME

The Scions of the Flame hail from the Bright Mountains in northern Aspiria, an ash-choked stretch of volcanic peaks under which run sulphurous subterranean caverns and magma flows.

Their temples are littered across these lands, fortresses of bronze and flame that guard deposits of Aqshian realmstone – the deadly substance known as aqthracite or ragerock by scholars of such matters. This realmstone is the living essence of the Ever-Raging Flame. The Scions seek it with single-minded fanaticism, for they use it in dark rituals in order to unleash volcanic eruptions and infernos across the land. To fuel this apocalyptic quest, they require vast quantities of ragerock, which is not easily found. By joining Archaon's wars of conquest, they hope to gather enough to set the realms ablaze.

SCIONS OF THE FLAME FIRST NAMES	
D10	FIRST NAME
1	Helax
2	Vaktrian
3	Krastos
4	Narmastos
5	Travakos
6	Raxos
7	Vatra
8	Ottraya
9	Sephemos
10	Kalexes

SCIONS OF THE FLAME LAST NAMES	
D10	LAST NAME
1	Xetrask
2	Hastanax
3	Xorthanox
4	Khorvax
5	Vortros
6	Grannox
7	Xertes
8	Callanax
9	Tyrannos
10	Carvas

ORIGIN	
1	**Proselytisers** – Your warband has travelled far across Aqshy, preaching its brutal creed.
2	**Ragerock Hunters** – Your warband was responsible for seeking out deposits of precious ragerock.
3	**Ashen Ones** – Your warband reveres the Ashen King, a legendary servant of the Ever-Raging Flame.
4	**Inquisitors** – Your warband roots out any souls who doubt the primacy of the Flame.
5	**Tunnel Fighters** – Veterans of many underground battles, your warriors are experts in close-quarters combat.
6	**True Fanatics** – Utterly devoted to the worship of the Flame, death means nothing to your warriors.

LEADER/FAVOURED WARRIOR BACKGROUND	
1	**Booming Voice** – This warrior's voice rings out thunderously across the field of battle.
2	**Reborn in the Flames** – This warrior has survived immolation, and emerged all the stronger.
3	**Hatred of Duardin** – This warrior despises the covetous duardin, who lay claim to vast stocks of ragerock.
4	**Quick to Anger** – This warrior is hot-blooded and aggressive, a living embodiment of Aqshy.
5	**Holy Warrior** – This warrior seeks out rival preachers to purge with cleansing flame.
6	**Orator** – In battle, this warrior recites the creed of the Ever-Raging Flame.

SPIRE TYRANTS

In the fighting pits of the Varanspire there are no such concepts as honour or valour, and none have mastered the art of sadistic slaughter as completely as the Spire Tyrants.

Even the blood and thunder of the arena ceases to hold any allure for such warriors. Instead, they seek greater tests, venturing out into the lethal wilds of the Eightpoints. There they look for worthy foes and challenges, hoping to earn infamy enough to gain the favour of the Everchosen. These champions retain the names and epithets they earned in the arena. They also maintain the arrogance and showmanship that defines the greatest gladiators, favouring bloody eviscerations and decapitations over a simpler, more efficient kill. The sight of such a gruesome death can steal the nerve from even a veteran fighter.

SPIRE TYRANTS FIRST NAMES	
D10	**FIRST NAME**
1	Norsc
2	Ghraddus
3	Kalenya
4	Banusk
5	Traskor
6	Kroll
7	Sharrak
8	Talya
9	Orresk
10	Nemetta

SPIRE TYRANTS LAST NAMES	
D10	**LAST NAME**
1	of the Bloody Shield
2	Skullsplitter
3	the Black
4	Bane of Cowards
5	the Titan
6	Heart-eater
7	the Spider
8	the Undefeated
9	Spinebreaker
10	Splithelm

ORIGIN	
1	**Errant Gladiators** – Your warriors butchered their guards and broke free of the arena.
2	**Bodyguards** – Your warband has earned coin and prestige as hired spears for several warlords.
3	**Crowd Favourites** – Your warband's reputation for savagery and showmanship precedes them.
4	**Hunted** – Your warband has earned the ire of powerful foes who seek their destruction.
5	**Monster Hunters** – Mere mortals no longer offer a challenge. Your warriors seek greater prey.
6	**Freed Ones** – You put on such a spectacle in the arena that an influential Chaos Lord secured your release.

LEADER/FAVOURED WARRIOR BACKGROUND	
1	**Breathtaking Arrogance** – As far as this warrior is concerned, no enemy is their equal in battle.
2	**Death Tally** – This warrior marks every kill they have ever made upon their flesh or armour.
3	**Disfigured** – This warrior has suffered a horrendous wound that renders them a most fearful sight.
4	**Vaunting Ambition** – This warrior seeks power with a furious intensity.
5	**Signature Kill** – This warrior has a favoured method of despatching their foes.
6	**Oppressor** – This warrior likes nothing more than brutalising those weaker than they.

NIGHTHAUNT

The Nighthaunts are malevolent spirits cursed to an eternity of suffering and enslaved to the will of Nagash, Supreme Lord of the Undead.

Driven by an all-consuming hatred of living things, these spectral horrors sweep across the realms in great hosts, killing everything in their path. They remember only dim echoes of their past, fragments of the person they were, and half-faded memories of the events that led to their current predicament. This is enough to keep them in a state of perpetual torment, which pleases cruel Nagash. On occasion the Great Necromancer will assemble smaller groups of Nighthaunts in order to achieve a particularly delicate task. Their incorporeal nature and resistance to most physical damage makes the gheists particularly suited to such missions.

NIGHTHAUNT FIRST NAMES	
D10	**FIRST NAME**
1	Old
2	Dreidrich
3	Choker
4	Varclav
5	Dravoch
6	Scarabeg
7	Pater
8	Wilhem
9	Lady
10	Agneth

NIGHTHAUNT LAST NAMES	
D10	**LAST NAME**
1	Rattlebones
2	Blacksoul
3	Turncoat
4	Scratchfinger
5	Whispergheist
6	Fraycloak
7	Gallows
8	Chillbreath
9	Gravetouch
10	Merciful

ORIGIN	
1	**Wrongfully Executed** – Your warband consists of executed innocents, consumed by bitterness.
2	**Lady Olynder's Flock** – Your warband hails from Dolorum, domain of the Mortarch of Grief.
3	**Traitors All** – Your warband consists of those spirits who committed a great treason in life.
4	**Deluded Spirits** – Your warriors believe they will find atonement in service to Nagash.
5	**Lost Company** – Your warriors fought together in life, and do so eternally in death.
6	**Kinslayers** – Your warband is comprised of those who slew their own kin, damning their souls forever.

LEADER/FAVOURED WARRIOR BACKGROUND	
1	**Lambent Glow** – This warrior is surrounded by swirling witch-lights.
2	**Grim Recitation** – This warrior is condemned to endlessly recite the crimes they committed in life.
3	**Hatred of Azyr** – This warrior despises above all those who serve the will of the Heavens.
4	**Face of Terror** – This warrior delights in crippling their foes with sheer terror before striking a killing blow.
5	**Unending Sorrow** – This warrior weeps and wails even as they slaughter the living.
6	**Worshipper of Nagash** – This warrior is convinced that if they please Nagash, he will end their torment.

STORMCAST ETERNALS

Forged by Sigmar from the souls of heroes, the Stormcast Eternals are the foremost champions of Order and some of the deadliest fighters in the realms.

Even death cannot conquer these warriors – when their physical form is cut down they are summoned back to Blessed Azyr upon the celestial storm, there to be reforged and sent into battle once again. When there is a task of the utmost importance that requires a deadly venture behind enemy lines, the God-King turns to his Vanguard Chambers. These warriors are trained in the arts of infiltration and guerrilla warfare. When on campaign their home is the wilderness, and they roam deep into enemy territory to wreak ruin upon the enemies of Azyr. Guided by astral devices, the members of the Vanguard Chambers strike with precise and devastating force.

STORMCAST ETERNALS FIRST NAMES	
D10	**FIRST NAME**
1	Haldus
2	Patreus
3	Sannus
4	Balian
5	Zadion
6	Kallean
7	Namestes
8	Lestia
9	Pollatia
10	Verness

STORMCAST ETERNALS LAST NAMES	
D10	**LAST NAME**
1	Lightningfist
2	Arventura
3	Stormsight
4	Swiftsteel
5	Sunhelm
6	Honouris
7	Thunderheart
8	Virtus
9	Shadowstep
10	Brightheart

ORIGIN	
1	**Troubled Souls** – Your warriors have suffered the agony of reforging one too many times.
2	**Hand-picked Champions** – Each member of your warband was specifically chosen for this mission.
3	**Last Survivors** – Your warband is the sole surviving remnant of a much larger force.
4	**Merciless Justice-seekers** – Your warband is ruthless in its pursuit of justice and order.
5	**Agents of Vengeance** – This warband seek to avenge a great wrong committed against their Stormhost.
6	**Friendly Rivalry** – Your warriors compete amongst themselves to slay the greatest number of foes.

LEADER/FAVOURED WARRIOR BACKGROUND	
1	**True Hero** – Tales are told and songs are sung throughout Azyrheim of this warrior's exploits.
2	**Beloved Leader** – This warrior will risk everything to safeguard those under his command.
3	**Sombre** – This warrior is a reserved and melancholy soul, not given to zealous oratory.
4	**Ferocious Combatant** – This warrior battles the enemies of Azyr with a savage ferocity.
5	**Strange Affliction** – Many reforgings have left this warrior with an unsettling physical condition.
6	**Wise Veteran** – This warrior dispenses sage advice to his warriors even in the heat of battle.

LEGIONS OF NAGASH

Nagash commands numberless hordes of undead. Yet even the Great Necromancer cannot be everywhere at once, and so he relies upon generals and agents to enforce his will.

Necromancers are mortal beings that have devoted themselves utterly to studying the deathly magic of Shyish, losing whatever humanity they might once have possessed in the process. Despite their damnation, they remain creatures of cunning and intellect. Thus it is they who are commonly tasked with sensitive missions on behalf of their master Nagash – those duties deemed beneath the attentions of the great lords of undeath. These Deathmages are able to summon hordes of skeletal soldiers and mindless zombies, a near-infinite resource which they can expend in order to achieve their goals.

LEGIONS OF NAGASH FIRST NAMES

D10	FIRST NAME
1	Keinrich
2	Grallem
3	Lhusim
4	Rhedgar
5	Ghorben
6	Ornest
7	Malvolen
8	Rhaglan
9	Tollich
10	Ghurkan

LEGIONS OF NAGASH LAST NAMES

D10	LAST NAME
1	Vollmer
2	Hake
3	Sancren
4	Groust
5	Vallkren
6	Nerenech
7	Krossler
8	Creel
9	Wydren
10	Stohl

ORIGIN

1	**Friends and Family** – Your warband consists of the risen corpses of those once closest to your leader.
2	**The Defeated** – Your warband is comprised of those foes your leader has slain in battle.
3	**Mouldering Experiments** – Your leader has often tested spells and alchemical solutions upon their warband.
4	**Jumble of Parts** – Your leader has stitched together this warband from mismatched corpse-parts.
5	**Faithful Servants** – Your leader has remade and repaired the flesh of this warband many times.
6	**Deathly Ranks** – Your warband hail from the same regiment or army, and still wear their colours in death.

LEADER/FAVOURED WARRIOR BACKGROUND

1	**Silent Companions** – This warrior often converses with his warband as if they were old friends.
2	**Morbid Collection** – This warrior takes great pride in their collection, ensuring they do not rot away.
3	**Student of the Sanctus Mortem** – This warrior studied beneath mighty Arkhan himself.
4	**Corpse-like Visage** – This warrior is horribly withered and worn, looking much like the corpses they command.
5	**Insane Laughter** – This warrior cackles and mutters to themselves incessantly.
6	**Eye for Quality** – This warrior is always looking out for fine specimens to add to their warband.

GLOOMSPITE GITZ

Cruel, cunning and treacherous, the Gloomspite Gitz infest the dank places of the Mortal Realms like a mouldering fungus. Though anarchic creatures by their very nature, when they unite under a common cause they are capable of wholescale destruction.

There are few regions of the realms untroubled by grots. Despite their diminutive size and natural cowardice, these greenskins are remarkably adaptable, somehow managing to thrive in the most hostile conditions. Those scattered tribes that dwell within the Eightpoints are particularly resilient. Chaos warlords irritated by the creatures' scavenging and pillaging often launch purges in an attempt to wipe them out, but should even a few grots manage to flee from the slaughter, their numbers soon begin to swell once more.

GLOOMSPITE GITZ FIRST NAMES	
D10	**FIRST NAME**
1	Skitrag
2	Gripe
3	Snikka
4	Zotbag
5	Norg
6	Shiv
7	Flug
8	Kribba
9	Grark
10	Gitgrik

GLOOMSPITE GITZ LAST NAMES	
D10	**LAST NAME**
1	Neckstabba
2	Eyepoka
3	Pincha
4	Curdletongue
5	Nosebita
6	Skuttlestab
7	Toerag
8	Longears
9	Mooneye
10	Sourtongue

ORIGIN	
1	**Bottle Thieves** – Your warband specialises in pilfering glasswork from the bigger races.
2	**Shroomheads** – Your warband seeks out particularly noxious clusters of mushrooms to sample.
3	**Loon's Luck** – Your warband has survived many disasters, and its members believe themselves invulnerable.
4	**Exiles** – Your warriors have been judged unbearable even by their fellow grots, and exiled into the wilds.
5	**Sneaky Backstabbers** – Your warriors are particularly good at moving about unseen.
6	**Eyepokers** – Your warriors are experts at the old grot tactic of aiming for the foe's most vulnerable areas.

LEADER/FAVOURED WARRIOR BACKGROUND	
1	**Babbling Loon** – Too many looncap shrooms have robbed this warrior of the ability to speak coherently.
2	**Touched by the Clammy Hand** – This warrior is convinced they are destined for great things.
3	**Wicked Tongue** – This warrior enjoys taunting his foes with jibes and unpleasant songs.
4	**Cowardly Git** – This warrior will only risk taking on his opponents when they are fully distracted.
5	**Foul Temper** – This warrior is particularly venomous and cruel, even for a grot.
6	**Strange Growth** – A bizarre fungal growth plagues this warrior, who insists it is a gift from the Bad Moon.

IDONETH DEEPKIN

The mysterious aelves of the deeps emerge from the waves only to raid the lands of surface-dwellers. They seek not treasure nor coin, but the very souls of the living.

Sworn foes of Chaos, the Idoneth Deepkin do not lightly venture into lands as deeply in thrall to the Dark Gods as the Eightpoints. Yet their emergence into the great struggle for the realms has not been without cost; never a numerous people, the Idoneth enclaves have seen a great many of their warriors slain in battle. For all its horrors, the lands of the Varanspire are rich in powerful souls – though many Isharann priests fear that this bounty is irrevocably tainted. Nevertheless, there is little choice but to raid if the Deepkin are to replenish their grievous losses. Thus they slip into Archaon's domain through hidden, dangerous paths, to hunt and raid.

IDONETH DEEPKIN FIRST NAMES	
D10	**FIRST NAME**
1	Alturnis
2	Chlorian
3	Marrathul
4	Nemetha
5	Orphas
6	Matreth
7	Akhmmonis
8	Setha
9	Oriphus
10	Taranth

IDONETH DEEPKIN LAST NAMES	
D10	**LAST NAME**
1	Barionic
2	Kamorthis
3	Carcessean
4	Volthunis
5	Hamaros
6	Sulethos
7	Yuleth
8	Phalendos
9	Balessian
10	Janethess

ORIGIN	
1	**Outriders** – Your warriors are the first swell of the gathering tide, scouts ahead of the Idoneth advance.
2	**Throne Guard** – Your warband was formerly part of an Akhelian King's royal retinue.
3	**Beast Riders** – Your warriors were responsible for training the Idoneth's deadly, aquatic war-beasts.
4	**Enclave Envoys** – Your warband was tasked with securing military alliances with the surface races.
5	**Disgraced** – Your warriors failed in their duties to their enclave, and now seek redemption.
6	**Assassins from the Deep** – Your warband was responsible for eliminating threats in order to preserve the Idoneth's secrets.

LEADER/FAVOURED WARRIOR BACKGROUND	
1	**Ancient Soul** – This warrior was created countless centuries ago, and has a vast breadth of experience.
2	**Elite of the Asydrazor** – This warrior was marked for greatness from their first days in the martial academy.
3	**Contemptuous of Surface-dwellers** – As far as this warrior is concerned, the surface races are worthless.
4	**Merciless** – To this warrior, only the capture of souls matters, and they pursue this task with ruthless zeal.
5	**Haunted by Visions** – This warrior is plagued by strange, half-remembered visions from another life.
6	**Cunning Tactician** – To this warrior, war is art, and they wage it with delicate finesse.

FLESH-EATER COURTS

Victims of an ancient and terrible curse, the mordants of the Flesh-eater Courts believe themselves to be noble knights engaged in a battle against evil, when in fact they are cannibalistic monsters who prey upon the mortal races to satiate their ravenous hunger.

Mordants of the Flesh-eater Courts typically congregate in great numbers, bound tightly together by their shared delusion. Yet this same madness can inspire in others a more ambitious vision. Some mordants, visited by dreams of glory and honour, embark upon great quests across the realms, accompanied by a band of companions. The exact nature of these quests can differ greatly – one mordant might believe it is his destiny to save a fair maiden, while another might seek the legendary Chalice of Ushoran, progenitor-king of the courts.

FLESH-EATER COURTS FIRST NAMES	
D10	**FIRST NAME**
1	Glorich
2	Maldoros
3	Vushor
4	Glabios
5	Ubricht
6	Pergrin
7	Nathran
8	Regulus
9	Bromm
10	Edren

FLESH-EATER COURTS LAST NAMES	
D10	**LAST NAME**
1	the Pious
2	Sunlord
3	the Noble
4	Drakeslayer
5	Oathtaker
6	of the White Order
7	Seeker of the Chalice
8	the Honourable
9	the Fasting Lord
10	the Merry

ORIGIN	
1	**Questing Knights** – Your warband has travelled far across the realms, leaving blood and death in its wake.
2	**Inheritors of Ushoran** – Your warriors believe that they are true inheritors of the Carrion King's power.
3	**Oathtakers** – To prove their honour, each of your warriors has sworn to uphold a sacred vow.
4	**Chevaliers** – In their delusion, your warriors believe they are riding mighty battle steeds.
5	**Feasting Champions** – Each night your warband holds a mighty feast of raw and dripping flesh.
6	**Dragonslayers** – Your warriors seek out the largest monsters to slay – and to subsequently devour.

LEADER/FAVOURED WARRIOR BACKGROUND	
1	**Commanding Crown** – This warrior has stitched together a crown from hide and splintered bone.
2	**Gory Heraldry** – This warrior smears their skin with gore, believing they are displaying noble heraldry.
3	**Flashes of Clarity** – This warrior experiences terrible moments of clarity when feasting upon raw flesh.
4	**Honourable Duellist** – Even as they tear at their foe, this warrior believes they observe proper martial decorum.
5	**Anointed One** – This warrior believes they have been chosen by Ushoran himself for greatness.
6	**Appalling Reek** – This warrior's odour of rotting flesh and unwashed skin is truly abominable.

IRONJAWZ

The Ironjawz are the biggest and hardest orruks of all. Clad in pig-iron armour and swinging enormous, bone-breaking weapons, they wreak untold devastation across the realms.

It is rare to see a small group of orruks alone in enemy lands, for these creatures more usually gather into vast, rampaging hordes. Such bands are typically the remnant of a far larger host that has by some miracle been defeated. Still driven by a boisterous and uncontrollable love of violence, these orruk warbands seek to cause as much destruction as possible, seeking out foes to battle and enemy outposts to crush into rubble. Despite their small numbers, these warbands can wreak a huge amount of damage. Several have been spotted amidst the wilds of the Eightpoints, and thus far have crushed all those sent to slay them.

IRONJAWZ FIRST NAMES

D10	FIRST NAME
1	Drakka
2	Grukk
3	Skrug
4	Urgok
5	Rezgut
6	Grokk
7	Tranka
8	Drog
9	Zagga
10	Krakkfist

IRONJAWZ LAST NAMES

D10	LAST NAME
1	Deffskull
2	Headstompa
3	Nekksnappa
4	Bigtoof
5	Rokknut
6	Fireklaw
7	Blakfist
8	da Biggest
9	Bonekruncha
10	Meaneye

ORIGIN

1	**Siege Smashers** – Your warriors delight in smashing their way through fortifications and defences.
2	**Da Megaboss' Boyz** – Your warband once fought at the side of an Ironjawz Megaboss.
3	**Grotkickers** – Your warriors delight in bullying and brutalising those weaker than they.
4	**Only the 'Ardest** – Your warriors are the toughest and meanest survivors of a shattered Ironjawz brawl.
5	**Uneasy Alliance** – Each of your warriors are vying for command, through methods both brutal and kunnin'.
6	**Filled With Waaagh!** – Your warriors resonate with furious Waaagh! energy.

LEADER/FAVOURED WARRIOR BACKGROUND

1	**Shiny Trophy** – This warrior's prized possession was stripped from the corpse of a defeated foe.
2	**Unstoppable** – This warrior just keeps going, even when stricken by grievous wounds.
3	**Boisterous Laughter** – This warrior loves the crash of combat so much they boom with laughter when in battle.
4	**Brutal but Kunnin'** – Despite their innate savagery, this warrior can be surprisingly devious.
5	**Berserk Lunatic** – This warrior does not stop hacking at his foes until they are piles of splattered meat.
6	**Stubborn Brute** – When this warrior encounters a problem, they simply batter their way through it.

DAUGHTERS OF KHAINE

The Daughters of Khaine seek power through bloodshed. With every butchered foe they worship their murderous deity Khaine, and as gore splatters across their flesh they are driven into a rapturous killing frenzy.

The Lady Morathi, High Oracle of Khaine, commands his warlike Daughters, claiming to be the sole medium through which the deity speaks to his mortal followers. In fact, this is a cruel deception. Khaine is dead, and Morathi's every intrigue favours only herself and her desire to ascend to godhood. Oblivious to the truth, the Daughters of Khaine carry out her commands with ruthless precision, whether they are called upon to engage in full-scale battle or more subtle endeavours, such as infiltrating enemy lands in order to carry out assassinations and other covert actions.

DAUGHTERS OF KHAINE FIRST NAMES	
D10	**FIRST NAME**
1	Cala
2	Vethoir
3	Narenka
4	Scathia
5	Yhuneska
6	Hallenda
7	Scoris
8	Dhula
9	Fheltoir
10	Porthia

DAUGHTERS OF KHAINE LAST NAMES	
D10	**LAST NAME**
1	Khial
2	Rathir
3	Drukhesk
4	Yaemath
5	Khordia
6	Santhiask
7	Ghanith
8	Lhusik
9	Rheska
10	Vatraya

ORIGIN	
1	**Gladiatrixes** – Your warband fought in the bloody fighting pits of Khainite citadels.
2	**Blades of the High Oracle** – When Morathi desired the subtle elimination of a foe, she sent for your warband.
3	**Relic Seekers** – Your warband has travelled the realms in search of lost Khainite relics.
4	**Shadow Stalkers** – Your warband slip through the night like shadows, ambushing their foes.
5	**Zealots** – Your warriors are particularly zealous adherents of Khaine's murderous creed.
6	**Masters of Illusion** – Your warband utilise deception and trickery to outwit their foes.

LEADER/FAVOURED WARRIOR BACKGROUND	
1	**Trusted Hand** – This warrior claims to have the ear of Lady Morathi herself.
2	**Sadistic Killer** – This warrior aims to slay her foes in the most agonising manner possible.
3	**Murderous Voices** – This warrior cannot quieten the whispers in her head that urge her to kill and maim.
4	**Taunting Duellist** – This warrior uses insults and taunts to lure her opponent into a mistake.
5	**Ambitious** – This warrior seeks to rise ever higher in the Khainite faith.
6	**Bewitching** – This warrior is possessed of a haunting, hypnotising grace.

BONESPLITTERZ

Even other orruks regard Bonesplitterz with a certain degree of caution, for these savage greenskins have fully embraced the feral spirit of Gorkamorka.

It is the visions of the Wurrgog Prophets that guide the Bonesplitterz to war. These thoroughly deranged shamans interpret portents and signs from the Great Green God. They then direct their tribe to battle, channelling the immense power of Waaagh! energy to drive the Bonesplitterz into a frenzy of destruction. Not all of Gorkamorka's commands are so straightforward however. The Bonesplitterz are utterly unpredictable, and attempting to divine their intentions is a fool's game. It is not unheard of for a Wurrgog Prophet to send several of his warriors rampaging across the realms in pursuit of some strange and distant goal.

BONESPLITTERZ FIRST NAMES	
D10	**FIRST NAME**
1	Grozgak
2	Korgakk
3	Badbrukk
4	Krakkzog
5	Kragg
6	Worgutz
7	Orgakk
8	Rogga
9	Murgg
10	Ugdrak

BONESPLITTERZ LAST NAMES	
D10	**LAST NAME**
1	Rokkskull
2	Gutklaw
3	Wildtompa
4	Snagtoof
5	Weirdskull
6	Snakechompa
7	Stonejawz
8	Krookfang
9	Eadkrakka
10	Madskull

	ORIGIN
1	**Howling Mad** – Your warband consists of the most battle-crazed lunatics of its tribe.
2	**Glory Hunters** – Your warriors seek to prove themselves by committing the most reckless acts of violence.
3	**Heralds of the Waaagh!** – Your warriors believe that where they roam, the power of the Waaagh! swells.
4	**Painted Ones** – Your warriors have been marked with sacred runes by their tribe's Wurrgog Prophet.
5	**Lost** – You took a wrong turn somewhere, but your warriors are happy enough with where they ended up.
6	**Bone Hunters** – Your warband relentlessly hunts the largest predators, hoping to take their bones.

	LEADER/FAVOURED WARRIOR BACKGROUND
1	**Unpredictable Maniak** – Attempting to predict this warrior's actions is utterly pointless.
2	**Old Rival** – This warrior keeps the mouldering head of a hated rival, which they often argue with.
3	**Relentless** – This warrior never pauses for a moment, and instead simply barrels forward relentlessly.
4	**Head Wound** – Having taken a nasty blow to the head, this warrior babbles a stream of nonsense.
5	**Great Hunter** – This warrior has hunted and killed some of the most ferocious beasts of Ghur.
6	**Unaccountably Lucky** – This warrior is blessed by Gorkamorka, somehow surviving every disaster.

BATTLEPLAN GENERATOR

If you do not have access to the battleplan cards, you can use the tables in this section to determine the battleplan instead. There are 2 tables for each type of battleplan card: Terrain, Deployment, Victory and Twist. Each table is comprised of 6 cards.

The player who won the priority roll picks a table of terrain cards and rolls a dice to determine the card in play this battle.

The player who lost the priority roll then does the same to determine the deployment card.

The players continue alternating in this manner until each card that is to be in play is determined.

GENERATING CONVERGENCES

If you are playing through a campaign (pg 63) and do not have access to the battleplan cards, you can instead generate a convergence using the tables in this section. To do so, before mustering warbands, the player controlling the Adversary warband picks a terrain card, deployment card and victory card that they think best suits the narrative of the convergence. Then, the player controlling the Aspirant warband picks a table of twist cards and rolls a dice to determine the card in play for the convergence.

EXHIBITION BATTLES

You can use these tables to generate a quick Exhibition Battle (pg 72). Table A for the terrain, deployment and victory battleplan cards only includes cards with the **Symmetrical** runemark (※). To generate an Exhibition Battle, the player who won the priority roll rolls a dice on each of these tables to determine the battleplan card in play. The player who lost the priority roll then chooses which table to roll on to determine the twist card in play.

BATTLEPLAN CARDS

Adding the full set of battleplan cards to your collection will really expand your games of Warcry. In the full set there are 36 cards of each type, for a total of 144 cards. With over 30 million combinations, no two games of Warcry ever need to be the same. Having the full set also allows you to make the most of narrative play, as you'll have all the cards you need to play every convergence presented in this book.

⚜ TERRAIN CARD TABLE A

1
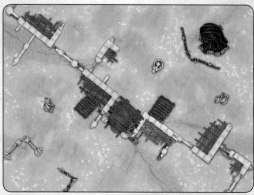

2
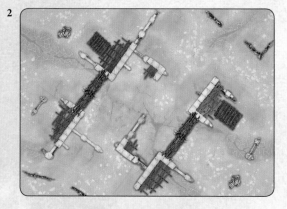

3

4
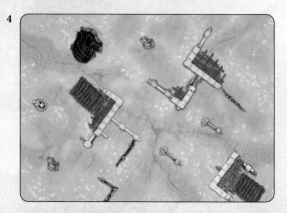

⚔ TERRAIN CARD TABLE A (CONTINUED)

5

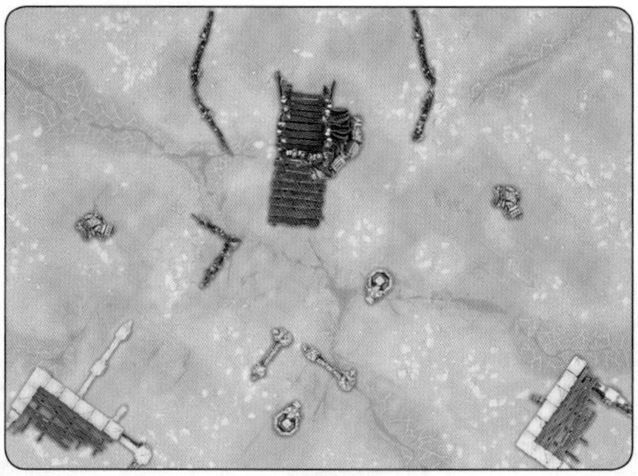

6

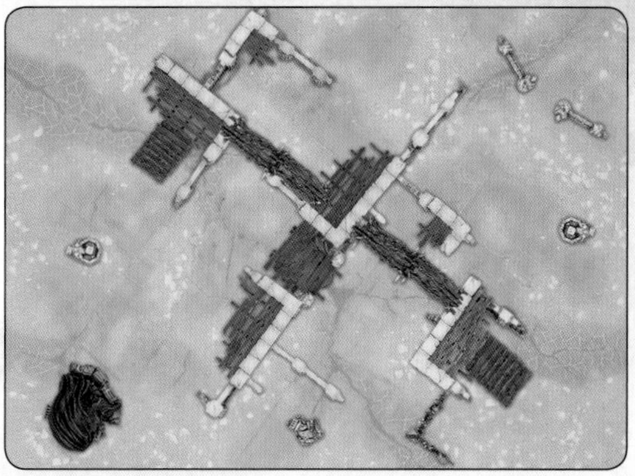

⚔ TERRAIN CARD TABLE B

1

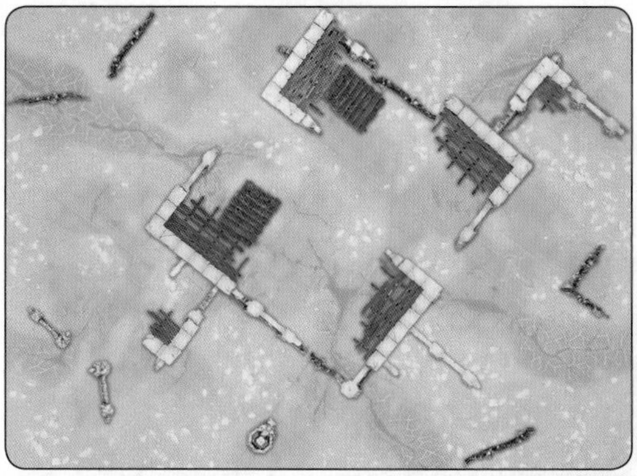

2

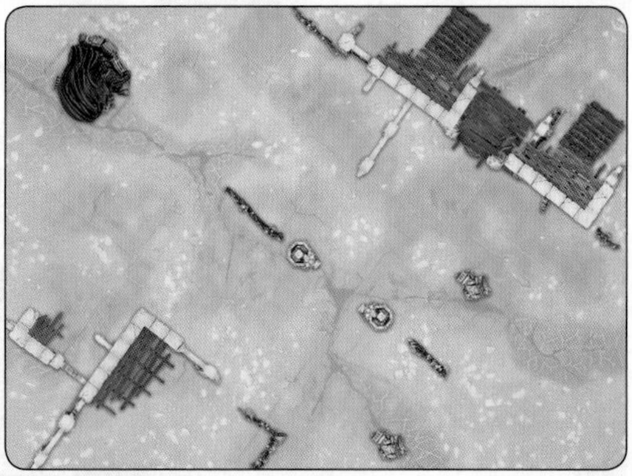

3

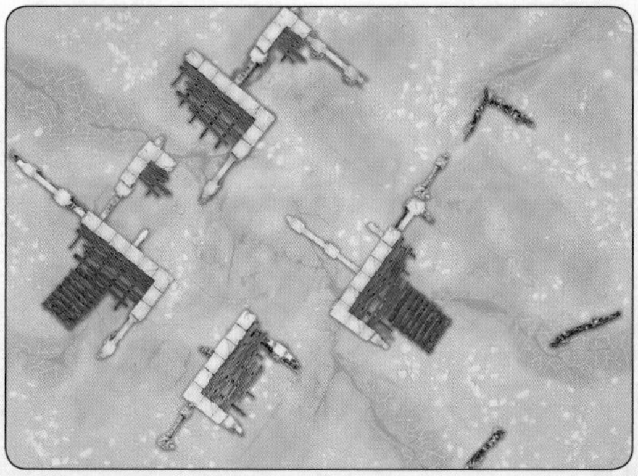

4

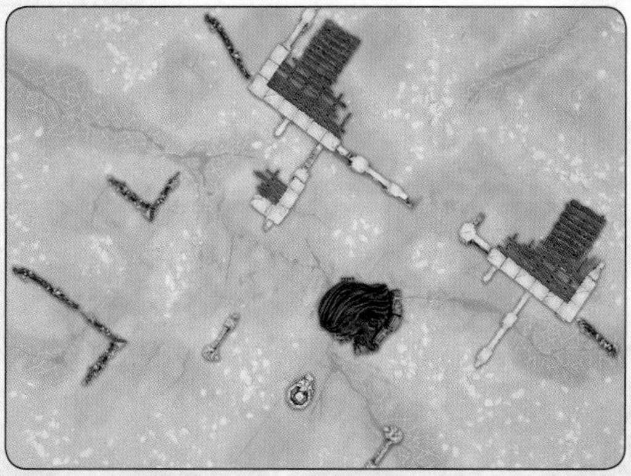

5

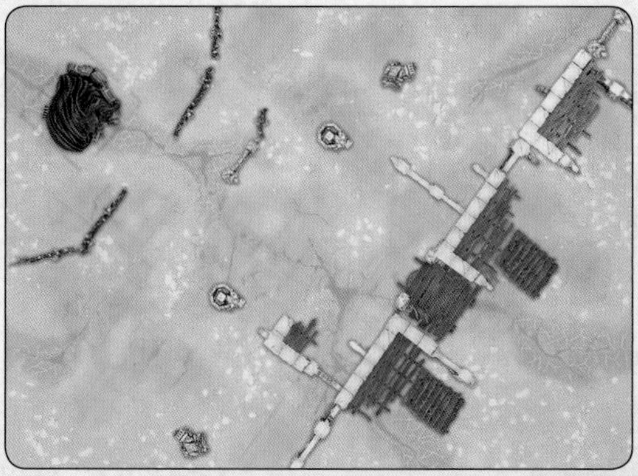

6

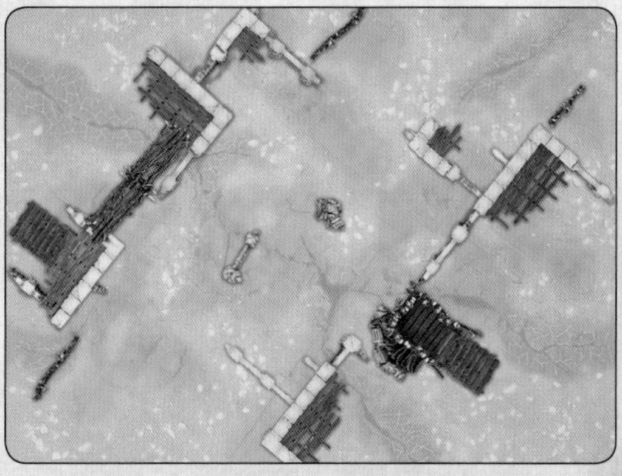

⚔ DEPLOYMENT CARD TABLE A

1
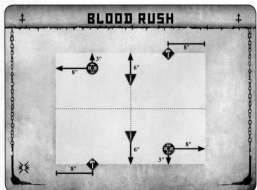
BLOOD RUSH

2
UNSEEN BLADE

3
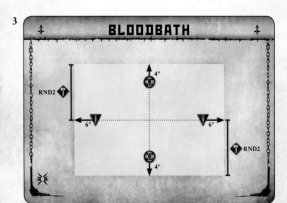
BLOODBATH

4
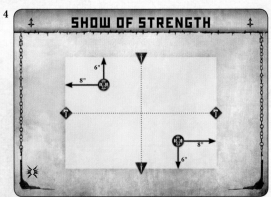
SHOW OF STRENGTH

5
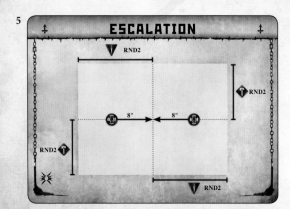
ESCALATION

6
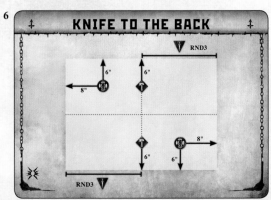
KNIFE TO THE BACK

⚜ DEPLOYMENT CARD TABLE B

1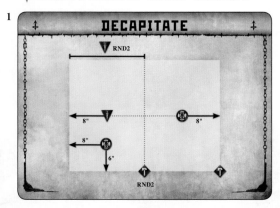

DECAPITATE

2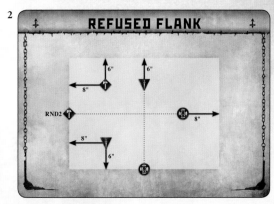

REFUSED FLANK

3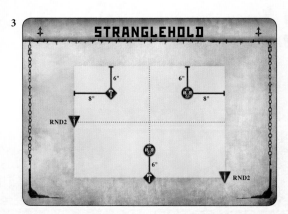

STRANGLEHOLD

4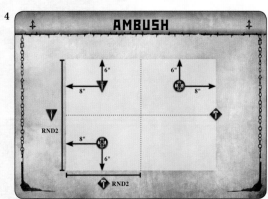

AMBUSH

5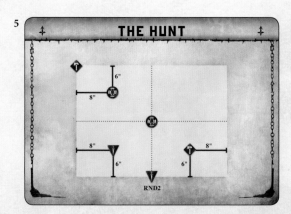

THE HUNT

6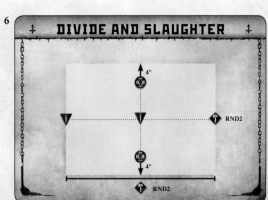

DIVIDE AND SLAUGHTER

VICTORY CARD TABLE A

1

VICTORY
NO MERCY

Reap them like the crops grown by Sigmar's weakling thralls.

A player wins the battle as soon as half or more of their opponent's fighters have been taken down.

At the end of the fourth battle round, and each subsequent battle round, any fighters within 4" of the battlefield edge immediately count as being taken down (if playing a campaign battle, do not make an injury roll for fighters taken down in this manner).

2

VICTORY
VANQUISH

Disarmed, the foe has no recourse but surrender.

A player wins the battle as soon as every fighter in their opponent's Hammer is taken down.

At the end of the fourth battle round, and each subsequent battle round, any Hammer fighters within 4" of the battlefield edge immediately count as being taken down (if playing a campaign battle, do not make an injury roll for fighters taken down in this manner).

3

VICTORY
THE COMET

Seize the riches that fall from the skies.

Roll a dice at the start of the second battle round, before the hero phase. On a 1-4, place 1 objective on the battlefield floor at the centre of the corresponding table quarter, as shown on the map below. On a 5-6, place 1 objective on the battlefield floor at the centre of the battlefield. The battle ends after 3 battle rounds. When the battle ends, the player that controls the objective wins the battle.

4

VICTORY
VANTAGE POINT

Seize the high ground that we might then seize victory.

The players roll off and the winner places 1 objective on a platform at least 6" vertically above the battlefield floor. If there are no platforms that high, the player instead places 1 objective on a platform that is at least 3" vertically above the battlefield floor, and within 12" horizontally of the centre of the battlefield.

The battle ends after 3 battle rounds. When the battle ends, the player that controls the objective wins the battle.

5

VICTORY
THE PRIZE

Seize the Dark Gods' gift no matter the cost.

The players roll off and the winner places 1 treasure token on the battlefield within 6" horizontally of the centre of the battlefield.

The battle ends after 3 battle rounds. When the battle ends, the player whose fighter is carrying the treasure wins the battle.

6

VICTORY
RAZE

Drive into their lands like a spear into a foe's gut, and burn all you see.

Starting with the player who won the priority roll, each player picks a different battlefield edge to be their warband's territory. Any fighter that finishes a move action within 1" of an enemy warband's territory can enter it. Remove the fighter from the battlefield but do not count them as being taken down.

The battle ends after 4 battle rounds. When the battle ends, count the number of fighters that entered an enemy warband's territory. The player with the most wins the battle.

VICTORY CARD TABLE B

1

VICTORY
THE RAID

Move swift, and let the fires of the gods engulf your foes.

The players roll off and the winner chooses who is the attacker and who is the defender.

The defender places 6 objectives on the battlefield, each more than 4" from any other objectives and the battlefield edge.

The attacker can choose to **burn** an objective they control at the end of a battle round. To do so, remove it from play. If the attacker burns 3 objectives, they win the battle. Otherwise, after the end of the third battle round, the defender wins the battle.

2

VICTORY
CRUSH

Send a message by annihilating our foes' advance guard.

The players roll off and the winner chooses who is the attacker and who is the defender.

If every fighter in the defender's Dagger is taken down, the attacker wins the battle. Otherwise, after the end of the fourth battle round, the defender wins the battle.

Any fighters from the defender's Dagger that are within 4" of the battlefield edge at the end of a battle round immediately count as being taken down (if playing a campaign battle, do not make an injury roll for fighters taken down in this manner).

3

VICTORY
SCORCHED EARTH

Stage a fighting retreat, and leave only ash in your wake.

The players roll off and the winner chooses who is the attacker and who is the defender.

The defender places 3 objectives on the battlefield, each more than 6" from any other objectives and the battlefield edge.

At the end of each battle round, the attacker scores 3 victory points for each objective they control. The defender scores 1 victory point for each objective they control. In addition, at the end of each battle round after victory points have been awarded, the defender can remove 1 objective they control from play.

The battle ends after 3 battle rounds. When the battle ends, the player with the most victory points wins the battle.

4

VICTORY
ASSASSINATE

This fool's death has been ordained. Let their end be an example to all who would defy you.

The players roll off and the winner chooses who is the attacker and who is the defender.

If the defender's leader is taken down, or if at the end of a battle round the defender's leader is within 4" of the battlefield edge, the attacker wins the battle. Otherwise, after the end of the fourth battle round, the defender wins the battle.

5

VICTORY
PURGE

Cleanse the enemy's taint from our sacred sites.

The players roll off and the winner chooses who is the attacker and who is the defender.

The attacker secretly picks and notes down one of the quarters of the battlefield: north-east, north-west, south-east or south-west (using the arrow on the terrain card to represent north).

At the end of the third battle round, the attacker reveals the quarter of the battlefield they picked. If any of the defender's fighters are wholly within that quarter, the defender wins the battle. Otherwise, the attacker wins the battle.

6

VICTORY
STEAL THE PRIZE

The foe are transporting their greatest treasure. Seize it now, while it is in the open.

The players roll off and the winner chooses who is the attacker and who is the defender. At the start of the combat phase of the second battle round, the defender picks a fighter in their warband to be carrying treasure. The fighter must be on the battlefield.

The player whose fighter is carrying the treasure at the end of the third battle round wins the battle. If the treasure is instead on the battlefield, the attacker wins the battle.

TWIST CARD TABLE A

1

TWIST
BLOODWIND

Hot winds bring with them the acrid tang of brimstone and blood. Khorne's presence is felt upon this battlefield.

Add 1 to the Attacks and Strength characteristics of all fighters this battle with 1 or more damage points allocated to them.

2

TWIST
DEAD OF NIGHT

Your rivals close in under the shadow of darkness – this night shall taste blood.

No ability or attack action can be used to target an enemy fighter more than 3" away this battle.

3

TWIST
SINISTER BARGAIN

In garbled Dark Tongue, a creature makes a pact with one of the warband leaders before the battle.

The players roll off. The winner can choose 1 chaotic beast with the **Sentience** runemark (✹) to be added to their warband as a thrall for this battle.

Set up the chaotic beast on the battlefield within 3" of a friendly fighter.

4

TWIST
GRUDGE MATCH

These rival warbands have met in battle before. This time there is a score to settle.

Add 1 to the Strength characteristic of attack actions made by fighters this battle that have a Range characteristic of 3 or less.

5

TWIST
MURKY SWAMPLAND

Weeks of endless rain has turned these lands into a thick and squelching quagmire.

If a fighter begins a move action on the battlefield floor, subtract 1 from the Move characteristic of that fighter until the end of that move action. This does not affect fighters with the **Fly** runemark (✦).

6

TWIST
EERIE SILENCE

Not a single cry or rustle of grass can be heard amidst these ruins. The discomforting silence is broken only by the sudden clash of weapons.

This twist card has no effect.

TWIST CARD TABLE B

1
TWIST
RAINSTORM OF GHYRAN

Humid winds have carried rainclouds from deep within Ghyran. Jade droplets can heal wounds and invigorate the spirit.

All fighters can use the following ability:

[Double] Healing Rains: Remove a number of damage points allocated to this fighter equal to the value of this ability.

2
TWIST
DAWN

In the early hours of the morning, battle is met between rival warbands. As blood is shed, Hysh stirs on the horizon.

No ability or attack action can be used to target an enemy fighter more than 3" away in the first battle round, 6" away in the second battle round, 9" away in the third battle round, and 12" away in any subsequent battle rounds.

3
TWIST
RAMPAGING BEASTS

Monstrous creatures come forth, drawn by the din of battle and the promise of flesh.

At the start of each battle round, before the hero phase, the players roll off. The winner can place any number of chaotic beasts on the battlefield with a combined points value of 200 or less. Chaotic beasts set up in the same battle round must all share the same combination of runemarks and each must be placed within 1" of a terrain feature, within 3" of another chaotic beast in the group and more than 5" away from any other fighters.

4
TWIST
NO RESPITE

These two warbands have stalked one another for many long days. Now they finally meet in open battle, and no quarter will be expected nor given.

Fighters cannot use the 'Respite' ability this battle.

5
TWIST
FOREBODING LOCATION

Stark monoliths thrust towards the horizon, marked by sickening runes. This is a fell place, and all who approach feel its dark aura.

Subtract 1 from the value of abilities (to a minimum of 1) used by fighters this battle.

6
TWIST
NO HOLDING BACK

The threat of violence hangs heavy in the air as rival warbands bellow challenges and foul oaths at those who oppose them.

Add 2 to the value of abilities (to a maximum of 6) used by fighters in the first battle round.

WARCRY WARBAND ROSTER

WARBAND NAME

WARBAND ORIGIN | PLAYER NAME

CAMPAIGN QUEST

GLORY POINTS

DOMINATED TERRITORY

CAMPAIGN PROGRESS TRACKER

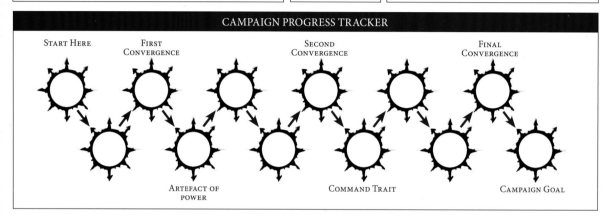

START HERE — FIRST CONVERGENCE — SECOND CONVERGENCE — FINAL CONVERGENCE

ARTEFACT OF POWER — COMMAND TRAIT — CAMPAIGN GOAL

LEADER / FAVOURED WARRIOR

LEADER / FAVOURED WARRIOR NAME	LEADER / FAVOURED WARRIOR BACKGROUND	ARTEFACTS
COMMAND TRAIT	**DESTINY LEVELS**	
	☼ ☼ ☼	

FIGHTERS

FIGHTER NAME	FIGHTER TYPE	ARTEFACTS	DESTINY LEVELS
			☼ ☼ ☼
			☼ ☼ ☼
			☼ ☼ ☼
			☼ ☼ ☼
			☼ ☼ ☼
			☼ ☼ ☼
			☼ ☼ ☼
			☼ ☼ ☼
			☼ ☼ ☼
			☼ ☼ ☼